Cyber Diplomacy

Cyber Diplomacy

Folake Akinyemi
Asha Ali

Kruger Brentt
Publishers
2026

Kruger Brentt Publishers UK. LTD.
Company Number 9728962

Regd. Office: 68 St Margarets Road, Edgware, Middlesex HA8 9UU

ISBN: 978-1-78715-659-3

For information on all our publications visit our website at http://krugerbrentt.com/

Preface

In an era defined by digital connectivity, cybersecurity challenges, and rapid technological transformation, diplomacy has expanded beyond traditional statecraft to include the complex dynamics of cyberspace. Nations now engage not only through political, economic, and military channels, but also through digital platforms, cyber norms, and global technical governance. Cyber diplomacy has emerged as a vital field that bridges international relations, cybersecurity policy, digital rights, and global cooperation.

This book, Cyber Diplomacy, offers a comprehensive introduction to the evolving landscape of diplomatic engagement in the digital age. It is crafted for students, policymakers, diplomats, cybersecurity professionals, and researchers seeking to understand how nations negotiate, collaborate, and sometimes confront each other in cyberspace.

The early chapters lay the foundation by exploring the conceptual development of cyber diplomacy, the historical evolution of internet governance, and the growing importance of digital interdependence. Subsequent sections examine key issues such as cyber norms, international law, cyber conflict management, digital trade, privacy, and cross-border data flows. Special attention is given to the role of international organizations, multilateral forums, and public-private partnerships in shaping global cyber policy.

The book also highlights case studies involving cyber incidents, diplomatic negotiations, and global cyber strategies adopted by different countries. Contemporary challenges—including misinformation, digital public diplomacy, artificial intelligence governance, and geopolitical competition in cyberspace—are explored to underline the complexity of modern diplomatic practice.

By integrating theory, policy discussions, and real-world examples, Cyber Diplomacy provides readers with the analytical tools needed to navigate and contribute to the international digital policy ecosystem. It serves as a valuable guide for understanding how diplomacy adapts to a world increasingly shaped by technology.

Folake Akinyemi

Asha Ali

Preface

Contents

CHAPTER 1

Introduction to Cyber-Diplomacy

1.1 DEFINING CYBER-DIPLOMACY

Cyber-diplomacy is a term used to describe the application of diplomatic techniques and negotiations in international relations that deal with and regulate cyberspace-related issues. According to some studies, cyber-diplomacy also covers cyber-warfare and agreements on the rules of engagement because without proper rules of engagement, 'the international community could end up in error with an unwanted conventional or nuclear war'.

Cyber-diplomacy is usually applied to managing the difficulties and obstacles presented by the cyber world and aims to promote responsible actions, preserve cyber-security, and ensure stability in cyberspace. Without cyber-diplomacy in developing national cyber-security policies, adversaries can apply complex social engineering tactics and present advanced persistent threats and even political threats for national cyber-security environments.

International cooperation is promoted in cyber-diplomacy to mitigate mutual threats and challenges. Nations collaborate on developing cyber-standards, guidelines, and agreements that support a safe and secure online environment. In 2024, this is specifically focused on artificial intelligence (AI), because AI is simply software, and we have longstanding concerns in regards to 'artificial intelligence methods in distributed denial of service (DDOS) assault and defense'.

Cyber-diplomacy is used to establish mutually beneficial agreements through diplomatic means of dialogue and to communicate between nations during situations of cyber disagreements between different nations. Cyber-diplomacy is a conflict resolution strategy that attempts to prevent conflicts in cyberspace from developing into bigger geopolitical problems. International cyber-governance, including the development of cyber laws, treaties, and regulations, is significantly influenced by cyber-diplomacy. Such governance structures are crucial for preserving order and reducing the risks connected to cyber activity. Establishing confidence-building measures is a common step in cyber-diplomacy, and this is crucial for reaching agreements between nations and fostering mutual trust, reducing scepticism, and increasing openness in individual cyber-activities. Such activities might involve information exchange, team training, and hotlines to avoid misunderstandings and errors in judgment. One of the major issues in cyber-security is the identification of cyber-attacks. Cyber-diplomacy aims to address the attribution problem by building mechanisms to make people accountable for hostile cyber-operations. To combat cyber-threats effectively, cyber-diplomacy promotes cooperation between governments and private corporations because the private sector plays a major part in cyberspace. Hence, public-private collaborations can make the exchange of knowledge and experience in cyber-security easier.

Cyber-diplomacy promotes capacity building in developing nations to improve their cyber-security skills and strengths. This assistance can come from sharing expertise, training, and technology transfer. Cyber-diplomacy also discusses topics relating to freedoms and rights in cyberspace, including decentralisation and internet governance, freedom of expression, ethics, and privacy. Cyber-diplomacy is aimed at creating a balance between individual rights in cyberspace and national security.

Table: Key Aspects of Cyber-Diplomacy

Component	Description of Activity
International Cooperation	Collaboration amongst nations to address common cyber-threats and challenges. Establishing norms and agreements for cyberspace.
Conflict Resolution	Seeking peaceful resolutions to cyber-incidents and disputes through diplomatic channels and negotiations.
Cyber-security Governance	Shaping international cyber-governance, including the development and implementation of cyber laws, treaties, and regulations.
Confidence Building Measures	Establishing agreements to build trust, reduce suspicion, and enhance transparency in cyber-activities.
Attribution and Accountability	Addressing the issue of identifying the true source of cyber-attacks and holding malicious actors accountable.
Public-Private Partnerships	Encouraging collaboration between governments and private companies to effectively tackle cyber-threats.
Capacity Building	Promoting cyber-security capabilities in less developed countries through technology transfer, training, and knowledge sharing.
Digital Rights and Freedoms	Balancing national security with individual rights in cyberspace, including issues of privacy, freedom of expression, and governance

1.2 THE EVOLUTION OF DIPLOMACY IN THE DIGITAL AGE

The evolution of diplomacy in the digital age reflects the broader transformation of global society. From slow-moving negotiations conducted in closed chambers, diplomacy has shifted into an open, immediate, and often unpredictable domain shaped by digital technologies. The rise of social media, the urgency of cyber-security, the expansion of public diplomacy, and the influence of non-state actors all testify to the profound changes in international engagement. While these changes present opportunities for greater transparency, inclusivity, and responsiveness, they also demand caution, adaptability, and resilience from diplomats and policymakers. In the years ahead, the success of diplomacy will depend on the ability of nations to harness digital tools while preserving the principles of respect, dialogue, and cooperation that have always been at the heart of international relations.

As technology continues to evolve, diplomacy will increasingly rely on digital innovation. Artificial intelligence may soon play a role in translation, negotiation analysis, and conflict prediction. Virtual reality and immersive technologies could be used for diplomatic training or cross-cultural exchanges. Blockchain may enhance transparency in aid distribution and treaty verification.

Despite these advancements, human interaction will remain at the core of diplomacy, as trust, empathy, and cultural understanding cannot be entirely replaced by machines. The challenge for future diplomacy lies in integrating digital tools without losing the essence of human-centered negotiation and dialogue.

1.2.1 Traditional Diplomacy and Its Foundations

Before the digital revolution, diplomacy was conducted through physical embassies, secret communications, and formal treaties. Ambassadors were the central actors, tasked with representing their nations abroad and reporting back to their governments. The pace of communication was often slow, as messages had to be delivered physically or via telegraphs. Confidentiality and exclusivity characterized these interactions, ensuring that only trained diplomats and political leaders shaped international discourse. The traditional model emphasized discretion, negotiation behind closed doors, and the maintenance of long-term state relationships. While this form of diplomacy continues to exist, the digital age has introduced new dimensions that both complement and challenge these foundations.

1.2.2 Emergence of Digital Diplomacy

Digital diplomacy, often called e-Diplomacy or cyber-diplomacy, refers to the use of digital technologies, particularly the internet and social media, in the conduct of foreign affairs. Its roots can be traced back to the early adoption of websites by foreign ministries in the 1990s. These online portals initially served as tools for information dissemination, allowing governments to share policies, press releases, and statements with broader audiences. Over time, however, digital platforms evolved into interactive spaces where dialogue and engagement could occur directly between governments and foreign publics. The digital transformation has blurred the boundary between official diplomacy and public relations, making communication more transparent and accessible.

1.2.3 Social Media as a Diplomatic Tool

Social media platforms such as Twitter, Facebook, and Instagram have become vital instruments of modern diplomacy. World leaders, foreign ministers, and embassies maintain active accounts, using them to make announcements, express solidarity, or even criticize rivals. The practice, often called Twiplomacy, has allowed leaders to bypass traditional media channels and speak directly to global audiences.

A single tweet from a head of state can influence stock markets, trigger diplomatic debates, or reassure citizens during a crisis. Social media has democratized diplomacy by enabling ordinary citizens to witness, comment on, and sometimes influence international relations. However, it has also brought challenges, as miscommunication or inflammatory statements can escalate tensions rapidly.

1.2.4 Cyber-security and Digital Threats

The digital age has not only expanded the opportunities for diplomacy but also introduced new threats. Cyber-security has become one of the central concerns of modern statecraft. Hacking, espionage, disinformation campaigns, and cyber-attacks on critical infrastructure have turned cyberspace into a new battlefield. Diplomacy must now address questions of sovereignty in the digital domain, the regulation of cyberspace, and the development of international norms for responsible behavior online. Countries must negotiate treaties and agreements on cyber-governance while simultaneously defending themselves from cyber-threats. As a result, diplomats are increasingly required to understand technical issues such as encryption, data protection, and artificial intelligence.

1.2.5 Role of Public Diplomacy in the Digital Era

Public diplomacy has gained unprecedented significance in the digital age. In the past, governments engaged with foreign populations through cultural exchanges, broadcasting services, and educational programs. Today, digital tools allow governments to interact with global audiences instantly. For example, embassies organize online cultural festivals, ministries launch digital awareness campaigns, and leaders engage in online question-and-answer sessions with citizens worldwide. This form of diplomacy helps shape perceptions, build soft power, and counter misinformation. The immediacy of digital communication also allows governments to respond quickly to crises, demonstrating empathy and solidarity in times of need.

1.2.6 Multilateral Diplomacy and Digital Platforms

International organizations and multilateral institutions have also adapted to digital tools. The United Nations, the European Union, and other bodies now conduct hybrid or fully virtual meetings, enabling participation across time zones and reducing the costs of diplomacy. Digital platforms have made global governance more inclusive by allowing smaller nations, which might otherwise lack resources, to participate more actively in international discussions. During the COVID-19 pandemic, digital diplomacy proved essential as negotiations, summits, and peace talks were conducted virtually. This shift has highlighted the flexibility and resilience of digital tools in ensuring continuity of international relations during crises.

1.2.7 Opportunities Created by Digital Diplomacy

The digital age has expanded the scope of diplomacy beyond government officials to include non-state actors such as NGOs, multinational corporations, and even individuals. Digital platforms empower activists, journalists, and citizens to influence international debates, pushing governments to adopt more transparent policies. Moreover, digital diplomacy allows for real-time monitoring of global issues such as climate change, humanitarian crises, and conflict zones. This immediacy enables faster coordination of aid, greater accountability, and the sharing of best practices. The use of artificial intelligence, big data, and geospatial technology further enhances the ability of diplomats to analyze trends and craft informed policies.

1.2.8 Challenges and Risks of Digital Diplomacy

While digital tools have enriched diplomacy, they also present significant challenges. The rapid pace of online communication can undermine the careful deliberation that traditional diplomacy requires. Public statements made in haste can damage relations or escalate disputes. Furthermore, the spread of fake news and disinformation campaigns complicates the ability of governments to communicate effectively. Authoritarian regimes have also exploited digital platforms to control narratives, engage in surveillance, and manipulate international opinion. Additionally, the digital divide remains a major barrier, as not all nations have equal access to advanced technologies. This inequality risks marginalizing certain voices in international dialogue and exacerbating global power imbalances.

1.3 WHY CYBER-ISSUES ARE A DIPLOMATIC PRIORITY

Cyber-issues have risen to the forefront of diplomatic agendas because they touch every aspect of modern society, from national security and economic stability to democratic governance and international cooperation. The interconnected nature of cyberspace makes unilateral solutions ineffective, compelling nations to engage in diplomatic negotiations to establish norms, prevent conflict, and promote stability. Cyber-security, cybercrime, disinformation, and digital inequality are among the many issues that require coordinated diplomatic responses. As the digital landscape continues to evolve, diplomacy will remain the primary means of addressing these challenges, ensuring that cyberspace serves as a platform for progress rather than conflict. Ultimately, cyber-issues are a diplomatic priority because the peace, security, and prosperity of the modern world depend on how nations cooperate in managing the digital frontier.

As technology continues to advance, the scope of cyber-diplomacy will only expand. Emerging technologies such as artificial intelligence, quantum computing, and the Internet of Things introduce new vulnerabilities that require international regulation and cooperation. The future of cyber-diplomacy will involve not only managing threats but also promoting opportunities, such as digital innovation, sustainable development, and inclusive growth.

States will need to balance national interests with collective responsibility, ensuring that cyberspace remains open, secure, and beneficial for all. Diplomats of the future must therefore be equipped with both technical knowledge and cultural sensitivity to navigate the complex challenges of the digital world.

1.3.1 Global Interconnectedness of Cyberspace

One of the fundamental reasons cyber-issues are at the forefront of diplomacy is the deeply interconnected nature of cyberspace. Unlike traditional territorial borders, cyberspace transcends geography, connecting individuals, businesses, and governments across nations in real time.

An attack launched in one country can have devastating consequences thousands of miles away, disrupting critical infrastructure, financial systems, or healthcare services. This borderless characteristic makes unilateral responses ineffective and necessitates international cooperation. Diplomacy provides the mechanism for establishing shared norms, agreements, and collaborations to ensure that states manage these interdependencies responsibly.

1.3.2 Cyber-security as a National Security Imperative

Cyber-security has become synonymous with national security, making it a top diplomatic agenda. Governments depend heavily on digital infrastructure to run essential services such as defense, power supply, communication, and healthcare. At the same time, adversaries exploit cyber vulnerabilities to carry out espionage, sabotage, and disinformation campaigns.

For example, the theft of classified information, ransomware attacks on hospitals, or cyber-intrusions into electoral systems pose risks to state sovereignty and democratic processes. As these threats cross national borders, diplomacy is required to establish international laws and conventions that protect against malicious cyber-activities. Thus, ensuring cyber-security is not merely a technical matter but a diplomatic responsibility that shapes alliances and global security strategies.

1.3.3 Rise of Cyber-warfare and State-Sponsored Attacks

The evolution of cyber-warfare has added urgency to diplomatic engagement. Nation-states increasingly use cyber-tools as instruments of power, either for intelligence gathering, political manipulation, or direct disruption of adversaries' systems. State-sponsored attacks often blur the lines between peace and conflict, as they may not involve conventional military aggression but can cause significant harm to economies and societies. The lack of universally accepted rules governing cyber-conduct raises the risk of escalation into broader conflicts. Diplomatic efforts aim to fill this gap by negotiating frameworks that define acceptable behavior, promote transparency, and prevent misunderstandings that could lead to war. International discussions at forums such as the United Nations are examples of how diplomacy seeks to establish norms for responsible state behavior in cyberspace.

1.3.4 Economic Implications of Cyber-threats

Cyber-issues are also a diplomatic priority because of their profound economic implications. The global economy relies heavily on digital networks for trade, banking, and supply chain management. Cyber-attacks targeting these systems can cost billions of dollars, undermine investor confidence, and destabilize economies. Moreover, intellectual property theft through cyber espionage directly affects innovation and competition, particularly in high-tech industries. Countries engage in diplomatic negotiations to protect digital trade, regulate cross-border data flows, and combat cybercrime. Agreements on cyber-security standards, digital taxation, and e-commerce rules are examples of how cyber-issues shape economic diplomacy in the digital era.

1.3.5 Protecting Critical Infrastructure

Critical infrastructure, such as energy grids, transportation systems, financial markets, and healthcare networks, has become a prime target for cyber-attacks. Disruptions in these sectors have far-reaching consequences that extend beyond national borders. For instance, a cyber-attack on a power grid in one country can disrupt energy supplies to neighboring regions, creating geopolitical tensions. Diplomacy is essential for building frameworks of cooperation that allow countries to share intelligence, establish rapid response mechanisms, and develop joint strategies for protecting critical infrastructure. Collaborative agreements between nations and regional organizations underscore the recognition that cyber-threats to infrastructure cannot be managed in isolation.

1.3.6 Cybercrime and Transnational Challenges

Cybercrime has emerged as a global phenomenon that transcends jurisdictions. Criminal networks exploit the anonymity of the digital world to conduct activities such as identity theft, financial fraud, ransomware, and trafficking in illegal goods. The transnational nature of cybercrime makes it difficult for individual states to pursue justice without international cooperation. Diplomacy is vital in creating agreements that facilitate cross-border law enforcement collaboration, evidence sharing, and extradition procedures. Institutions such as INTERPOL and regional cyber-security initiatives rely on diplomatic support to harmonize legal frameworks and strengthen collective responses to cybercrime.

1.3.7 Disinformation and the Challenge to Democracy

In addition to technical attacks, cyberspace has become a battleground for narratives and influence. Disinformation campaigns, often supported by foreign actors, threaten democratic institutions by manipulating public opinion, undermining trust in media, and influencing electoral outcomes. These activities pose significant diplomatic challenges, as they not only affect internal stability but also strain international relations. Nations increasingly turn to diplomacy to establish norms of responsible online conduct, counter disinformation, and enhance media literacy. Furthermore, partnerships between governments, technology companies, and international organizations are being negotiated to regulate digital platforms while balancing freedom of expression.

1.3.8 Role of International Norms and Governance

One of the greatest diplomatic challenges regarding cyber-issues is the absence of universally binding rules. While international law applies to cyberspace, its application is often contested. The ambiguity surrounding what constitutes a cyberattack, how states should respond, and what accountability measures exist has created uncertainty. Diplomacy plays a crucial role in addressing these gaps by promoting consensus on cyber-governance. Initiatives such as the Tallinn Manual and the efforts of the United Nations Group of Governmental Experts highlight attempts to clarify international law in the digital domain. Establishing norms of responsible state behavior is essential to prevent conflict and foster trust in cyberspace.

1.3.9 Digital Inequality and the Global Divide

The digital divide between developed and developing nations also makes cyber-issues a diplomatic concern. While advanced economies invest heavily in cyber-security, many developing nations lack the infrastructure and expertise to defend themselves effectively. This inequality creates vulnerabilities that can be exploited by cybercriminals or hostile states. Diplomacy provides a channel for capacity building, knowledge sharing, and technology transfer, ensuring that all nations can participate securely in the digital economy. International aid and cooperation programs focused on cyber-security are therefore central to bridging the digital divide and promoting equitable participation in global digital governance.

1.3.10 Cyber-diplomacy and Multilateral Engagement

Cyber-issues demand multilateral engagement because no single nation can address these challenges alone. International organizations such as the United Nations, NATO, and the European Union have prioritized cyber-diplomacy by creating frameworks for collective defense, information sharing, and cooperative action. Diplomatic negotiations also extend to bilateral and regional agreements that strengthen alliances in cyberspace. The inclusion of cyber chapters in trade agreements and security pacts reflects the growing recognition that cyber-issues permeate all aspects of international relations. In this way, cyber-diplomacy has become a cornerstone of modern foreign policy.

1.4 KEY STAKEHOLDERS IN CYBER-DIPLOMACY

1.4.1 Nation States

Nation-states remain the cornerstone of cyber-diplomacy, serving as the primary actors responsible for shaping the governance, security, and stability of cyberspace. Their sovereign authority grants them unique responsibilities, from developing national cyber-security strategies to negotiating international norms. As guarantors of national security, protectors of economic interests, and participants in global governance, states embody the central role in navigating the challenges and opportunities of the digital age. While other stakeholders such as corporations, civil society, and technical bodies contribute significantly, the leadership and authority of nation-states remain indispensable. Cyber-diplomacy ultimately reflects the balance of power, cooperation, and competition among states, making them the most critical stakeholders in defining the future of the digital world.

Sovereign Authority of Nation States

Nation-states are uniquely positioned in cyber-diplomacy because they possess sovereignty, which grants them authority over their territories, populations, and infrastructure. This authority extends into cyberspace, where states develop legal and institutional frameworks to safeguard national interests. Sovereignty in the digital domain involves regulating internet use, managing critical infrastructure, and defending against cyber-attacks. States must balance their right to control cyberspace within their jurisdiction with international responsibilities, such as respecting the principles of international law and human rights. As sovereign actors, they negotiate agreements that define acceptable behavior in cyberspace and ensure that state interests are safeguarded in global digital governance.

National Security and Cyber-defense

One of the most significant roles of nation-states in cyber-diplomacy lies in the protection of national security. The increasing reliance on digital infrastructure has created vulnerabilities that adversaries can exploit. Cyber-attacks on power grids, healthcare systems, and financial institutions highlight the strategic importance of securing cyberspace. Nation-states invest in building cyber-defense capabilities, often through specialized agencies and military units dedicated to cyber-security. They also establish national strategies that outline goals for protecting infrastructure, preventing espionage, and countering cyberterrorism. In diplomatic forums, states advocate for norms and agreements that reduce the risk of cyber conflict, such as prohibiting attacks on civilian infrastructure. By prioritizing cyber-defense, nation-states reinforce their central role as guarantors of national and international security.

Cyber-diplomacy as a Tool of Foreign Policy

For nation-states, cyber-diplomacy has become an essential component of foreign policy. States use diplomatic channels to build alliances, negotiate agreements, and manage conflicts in the digital sphere. Just as traditional diplomacy involves managing power dynamics and interests, cyber-diplomacy enables states to project influence, protect sovereignty, and pursue national objectives. Leading states such as the United States, China, and Russia integrate cyber-diplomacy into broader strategies of geopolitical competition. For example, initiatives to shape global internet governance or to export digital infrastructure technology are also acts of cyber-diplomacy that advance state interests. Smaller states, while lacking the same resources, use cyber-diplomacy to build partnerships and advocate for equitable participation in digital governance.

Establishing International Norms and Rules

A critical contribution of nation-states in cyber-diplomacy is their involvement in creating international norms, laws, and agreements for cyberspace. States participate in forums such as the United Nations, where discussions on the applicability of international law to cyberspace are ongoing. These efforts aim to establish principles that govern state behavior, such as non-interference, the prohibition of the use of force, and the protection of human rights online. States also negotiate regional agreements that harmonize cyber-security standards and promote cooperation. By shaping these frameworks, nation-states ensure that the global digital order reflects their strategic priorities and values. The development of such norms underscores the leadership role of states in steering cyber-diplomacy.

Nation States and Cyber Conflict

Cyber conflict has become a defining feature of international relations in the digital era, further highlighting the importance of states in cyber-diplomacy. State-sponsored cyber-operations, ranging from espionage to disinformation campaigns, illustrate the use of cyberspace as a tool of competition and warfare. Nation-states must manage these conflicts through both deterrence and diplomacy. They engage in negotiations to prevent escalation and establish confidence-building measures with other states. Diplomatic efforts also focus on attribution, where states work to hold perpetrators accountable for cyber-attacks. By managing cyber-conflicts, nation-states demonstrate their indispensable role in maintaining stability and reducing the risks of digital warfare.

Collaboration and Alliances among States

Another significant dimension of nation-states as stakeholders in cyber-diplomacy is their ability to collaborate through alliances and partnerships. No single state can address the complexity of cyber-threats alone, which makes cooperation a necessity. Alliances such as NATO have incorporated cyber-defense into their collective security commitments, emphasizing that an attack in cyberspace can be treated as an attack on all members.

Similarly, regional organizations such as the European Union promote collaborative cyber-security policies, including information sharing and joint exercises. Bilateral agreements between states also strengthen trust and cooperation in addressing shared challenges. Through these partnerships, nation-states enhance their resilience and capacity to respond to global cyber-threats.

Protecting Economic Interests in the Digital Age

The digital economy has become a cornerstone of national development, making the protection of economic interests another key priority for nation-states in cyber-diplomacy. States rely on cyberspace to facilitate trade, financial transactions, and innovation, all of which are vulnerable to cyber-attacks. Intellectual property theft, financial fraud, and disruptions in digital supply chains threaten economic stability. Through cyber-diplomacy, states negotiate trade agreements that include digital provisions, advocate for secure data flows, and address cyber-enabled economic crimes. By engaging in these efforts, nation-states safeguard their economic competitiveness while contributing to global stability in the digital marketplace.

Role of Developing Nations

While powerful states dominate many aspects of cyber-diplomacy, developing nations are also vital stakeholders. These states often face greater challenges in cyber-security due to limited resources and technical expertise, but their participation in global governance ensures inclusivity and fairness. Many developing nations advocate for bridging the digital divide, securing technology transfers, and ensuring equitable access to digital opportunities. Diplomatic initiatives provide these states with platforms to voice their concerns and contribute to shaping international norms. Their involvement reflects the global nature of cyberspace, where governance must consider the needs and perspectives of all states, not only the most powerful.

Balancing Security and Human Rights

Nation-states also face the challenge of balancing security concerns with human rights obligations in cyberspace. Issues such as surveillance, censorship, and data protection illustrate the tension between state authority and individual freedoms. In cyber-diplomacy, states negotiate agreements that address these tensions, such as those promoting freedom of expression online while ensuring security. States are held accountable for their practices by international institutions and civil society, making human rights an integral part of cyber diplomatic debates. This dual responsibility of protecting security while upholding rights further illustrates the complexity of the state's role in cyber-diplomacy.

1.4.2 International Organizations

International organizations are indispensable stakeholders in cyber-diplomacy, bridging the gap between national interests and global needs. They provide platforms for dialogue, establish norms and standards, mediate conflicts, and promote cooperation across borders. By addressing issues ranging from security to human rights, from cybercrime to capacity building, they contribute to a balanced and inclusive governance of cyberspace. Although challenges such as geopolitical rivalry and technological change persist, international organizations remain uniquely positioned to foster collective action in the digital domain. Their continued leadership and adaptability will ensure that cyber-diplomacy evolves in ways that promote peace, security, and shared prosperity in the digital age.

Looking ahead, international organizations will remain central to the future of cyber-diplomacy. As digital technologies evolve, issues such as artificial intelligence, quantum computing, and cyber-physical systems will pose new challenges requiring international coordination. International organizations will need to expand their roles, creating updated norms and facilitating cooperation in emerging areas. They will also need to enhance partnerships with non-state actors, including private companies, technical experts, and civil society, to ensure that cyber-governance is comprehensive and multi-stakeholder. Their ability to adapt and innovate will determine their effectiveness in guiding the international community through the complexities of cyberspace.

Role of International Organizations in Cyber-governance

International organizations play a fundamental role in cyber-governance by providing forums where states can negotiate, cooperate, and resolve disputes. Unlike nation-states, which act primarily in their national interests, international organizations are designed to represent collective goals and common concerns. Through structured dialogues, policy frameworks, and multilateral treaties, they work to establish guidelines for responsible behavior in cyberspace. By bringing together diverse stakeholders, they ensure that cyber-diplomacy does not remain the preserve of powerful states but reflects a broader global consensus. Their role in cyber-governance underscores their unique position as facilitators of international order in the digital domain.

United Nations and Cyber-diplomacy

Among all international organizations, the United Nations holds the most prominent role in cyber-diplomacy. The UN provides a global platform where states discuss the applicability of international law in cyberspace and negotiate norms of responsible state behavior.

The UN Group of Governmental Experts (GGE) and the Open-Ended Working Group (OEWG) have been particularly influential in outlining principles such as the prohibition of cyber-attacks on civilian infrastructure, the need for confidence-building measures, and the importance of cooperation in investigating cyber-incidents. The UN also integrates cyber-security into its broader agenda of peace and security, human rights, and development. Its efforts emphasize that cyber-issues are not isolated but interconnected with global stability, humanitarian values, and sustainable development.

Regional Organizations and Their Influence

Regional organizations complement the work of the UN by focusing on cyber-security within specific geopolitical contexts. The European Union, for instance, has developed comprehensive policies on cyber-security, including the General Data Protection Regulation (GDPR) and directives for protecting critical infrastructure. These initiatives not only safeguard European citizens but also influence global standards by setting benchmarks for data protection and privacy. Similarly, NATO has integrated cyber-security into its collective defense commitments, acknowledging that cyber-attacks can trigger Article 5 obligations. The African Union and ASEAN have also taken steps to create frameworks for regional cyber-cooperation. These regional bodies demonstrate that international organizations at multiple levels are crucial for addressing the diverse challenges of cyberspace.

Importance of Norm-Building and Standard Setting

One of the key contributions of international organizations to cyber-diplomacy is their role in norm-building and standard setting. In a domain where binding international treaties are difficult to achieve, soft law instruments such as norms, principles, and voluntary commitments play a critical role. International organizations provide the platforms where these norms are developed and promoted. They facilitate consensus on issues such as the protection of human rights online, the prevention of cybercrime, and the need for cooperation in responding to cyber-incidents. Standard-setting bodies such as the International

Telecommunication Union (ITU) also contribute by establishing technical norms that enhance interoperability and security across global networks. These efforts ensure that cyberspace is governed not only by power dynamics but also by shared rules and technical standards.

International Organizations as Mediators in Cyber-conflicts

As cyber-conflicts become more frequent and complex, international organizations serve as mediators and peacebuilders in the digital domain. They provide neutral platforms where states can discuss grievances, share information, and de-escalate tensions. For example, the Organization for Security and Cooperation in Europe (OSCE) has promoted confidence-building measures to reduce the risk of misunderstandings and unintended escalation in cyberspace. By encouraging transparency and dialogue, international organizations contribute to preventing cyber-conflicts from spilling over into broader geopolitical crises. Their impartiality and legitimacy enable them to act as trusted intermediaries in a field where attribution of cyber-attacks is often contested.

Cyber-security and Human Rights Protection

International organizations also play a vital role in ensuring that cyber-diplomacy incorporates human rights principles. The digital age has brought new challenges to rights such as freedom of expression, privacy, and access to information. Organizations like the UN Human Rights Council emphasize that the rights people enjoy offline must also be protected online. International organizations push states to align cyber-security policies with human rights obligations and to avoid using security as a justification for repression or censorship. This balance between security and rights illustrates the broader responsibility of international organizations in shaping cyber-diplomacy around principles of justice and fairness.

Addressing Global Cybercrime through Cooperation

Cybercrime is one of the most pervasive threats in the digital era, requiring cross-border cooperation for effective mitigation. International organizations have responded by creating frameworks that facilitate collaboration among law enforcement agencies. The Council of Europe's Budapest Convention on Cybercrime is a leading example, establishing guidelines for harmonizing laws, improving investigative capacities, and enabling international cooperation in cybercrime cases. Through such conventions, international organizations help states overcome jurisdictional challenges that criminals exploit in cyberspace. Their efforts ensure that cybercrime is treated not only as a national issue but as a global problem requiring collective action.

Capacity Building and Support for Developing Nations

Another important contribution of international organizations is their role in capacity building. Many developing nations lack the resources and expertise to address sophisticated cyber-threats or to participate fully in global cyber-governance. International organizations provide training, technical assistance, and funding to strengthen the cyber-security capacities of these nations. The ITU, for example, runs programs that assist member states in creating national cyber-security strategies and improving technical infrastructure. By enabling developing nations to engage more effectively in cyber-diplomacy, international organizations ensure that the global digital order is inclusive and not dominated solely by technologically advanced powers.

Challenges Facing International Organizations in Cyber-diplomacy

Despite their vital role, international organizations face significant challenges in cyber-diplomacy. One major obstacle is the geopolitical rivalry between powerful states, which often hampers consensus-building in multilateral forums. Disagreements over issues such as internet governance, data sovereignty, and attribution of cyber-attacks create divisions that weaken the effectiveness of international organizations. Another challenge is the rapid pace of technological change, which makes it difficult for institutions to adapt their policies and frameworks in time. Resource constraints and differing national priorities also limit the ability of international organizations to enforce agreements and norms. Nevertheless, their continued relevance lies in their ability to provide platforms for dialogue and to push forward incremental progress.

1.4.3 Private Sector and Civil Society

The private sector and civil society are indispensable stakeholders in cyber-diplomacy. The private sector provides the infrastructure, expertise, and innovation necessary for securing and governing cyberspace, while civil society ensures that digital governance remains inclusive, rights-based, and accountable. Together, they complement the efforts of nation-states and international organizations, bringing balance to the competing priorities of security, development, and human rights. Despite challenges, their active involvement in cyber-diplomacy is vital to shaping a digital future that serves not only states but humanity as a whole. As the digital age advances, the collaboration of private sector and civil society with governments will remain a cornerstone of global efforts to create a safer, fairer, and more cooperative cyberspace.

Private Sector's Critical Role in Cyberspace

The private sector plays a unique role in cyber-diplomacy because it owns and operates much of the world's digital infrastructure. From undersea cables to cloud computing services and from social media platforms to cyber-security software, private companies are the backbone of the digital ecosystem. Governments rely heavily on these companies for the functioning of their economies, communication systems, and even national security. This makes the private sector not just a stakeholder but a critical partner in cyber-diplomacy. Their participation ensures that diplomatic discussions on norms, policies, and regulations reflect the realities of technological development and implementation. Without their involvement, agreements risk being impractical or ineffective.

Technology Companies as Drivers of Cyber-diplomacy

Large technology companies such as Microsoft, Google, Meta, and Amazon have become powerful actors in cyber-diplomacy. These companies operate globally, often with influence that rivals that of nation-states. They provide platforms that facilitate global communication, commerce, and information sharing, but they also face challenges such as disinformation, cyber-attacks, and data privacy concerns. Recognizing their responsibility, many companies have launched initiatives that contribute directly to cyber-diplomacy. For example, Microsoft has called for a Digital Geneva Convention to establish rules for state behavior in cyberspace, reflecting the company's belief that the private sector must play a role in shaping international norms. By engaging with governments and international organizations, technology companies demonstrate their capacity to influence the rules and standards that govern the digital world.

Cyber-security Firms and Public-Private Partnerships

Another major private-sector stakeholder in cyber-diplomacy is the cyber-security industry. Firms specializing in threat detection, incident response, and cyber-defense often possess more up-to-date knowledge about cyber-threats than governments. Their expertise is critical in identifying vulnerabilities, attributing cyber-attacks, and developing innovative defense measures. Public-private partnerships have therefore become central to national and international cyber-security strategies. Governments work closely with private firms to share threat intelligence, respond to incidents, and build resilient digital infrastructure. This collaboration extends into diplomatic forums, where private companies provide technical advice and policy recommendations that help shape international agreements on cyber-security.

Influence of Data and Cloud Service Providers

Data has become the most valuable resource of the digital era, and companies that collect, process, and store data wield enormous power in cyber-diplomacy. Cloud service providers, for example, are responsible for hosting critical government and corporate data across the world. This gives them a unique perspective on the need for secure and interoperable digital systems. These companies are deeply involved in discussions about cross-border data flows, data sovereignty, and privacy protections. Their participation ensures that international agreements reflect both the economic value of data and the necessity of protecting individual rights in the digital domain.

Civil Society as a Guardian of Digital Rights

While the private sector brings technical infrastructure and expertise, civil society plays an equally important role as the guardian of digital rights. Civil society organizations include non-governmental organizations, advocacy groups, academic institutions, and grassroots movements that represent citizens' voices in cyber-diplomacy. Their involvement ensures that cyber-security policies are not solely focused on state security but also take into account the protection of human rights, such as freedom of expression, privacy, and access to information. Civil society advocates against government overreach, censorship, and mass surveillance, ensuring that cyberspace remains open, inclusive, and rights-based.

Role of Advocacy and Watchdog Organizations

Many advocacy organizations have become active participants in cyber-diplomacy by monitoring state and corporate behavior in the digital sphere. Groups such as Access Now and the Electronic Frontier Foundation push for stronger protections of privacy, digital freedoms, and internet neutrality. These organizations often provide valuable expertise to international forums by highlighting the human consequences of cyber policies.

Their presence ensures that cyber-diplomacy does not become overly technical or state-centric but remains grounded in broader societal values. Advocacy organizations serve as watchdogs, reminding governments and corporations alike of their responsibility to respect international human rights obligations in the digital age.

Academic and Research Institutions in Cyber-diplomacy

Academic and research institutions form another important part of civil society's role in cyber-diplomacy. Universities and think tanks conduct research on cyber-security, digital governance, and international law, providing evidence-based insights to policymakers. Their role is to generate knowledge, test new ideas, and provide neutral analysis that can guide diplomatic negotiations. Institutions such as the Carnegie Endowment for International Peace and the Oxford Internet Institute are deeply engaged in cyber-related studies and often collaborate with governments, private companies, and international organizations. Through publications, conferences, and expert networks, they influence the direction of cyber-diplomacy and ensure that decisions are informed by rigorous analysis.

Civil Society and Multi-Stakeholder Models of Governance

The importance of civil society is most visible in multi-stakeholder governance models, such as those used in internet governance. The Internet Governance Forum (IGF), for example, brings together governments, the private sector, technical experts, and civil society to discuss global internet policies. This inclusive approach ensures that no single actor dominates the governance of cyberspace. Civil society plays a vital role in these forums by representing the perspectives of users, communities, and marginalized groups that may otherwise be excluded from policy discussions. Their involvement strengthens the legitimacy and inclusiveness of cyber-diplomacy.

Synergy between Private Sector and Civil Society

While the private sector and civil society may appear to represent different interests, their collaboration is essential for effective cyber-diplomacy. The private sector ensures that policies are technically feasible and economically viable, while civil society ensures that they are socially just and rights-based. Together, they balance the priorities of security, innovation, and freedom. For example, initiatives to combat online disinformation often involve collaboration between technology companies, governments, and civil society organizations. While companies develop tools to detect and reduce misinformation, civil society monitors the potential for abuse and advocates for the protection of free speech. Such synergies demonstrate the complementary roles of these two stakeholders in cyber-diplomacy.

Challenges Faced by Private Sector and Civil Society

Despite their importance, the private sector and civil society face significant challenges in cyber-diplomacy. For private companies, one challenge is balancing profit motives with public responsibilities. Their global operations sometimes put them at odds with national regulations, leading to tensions over issues like taxation, data localization, and censorship. Civil society organizations, on the other hand, often face resource constraints and political pressures. In some countries, civil society actors advocating for digital rights face harassment, censorship, or restrictions on their activities. These challenges highlight the need for continued international support and recognition of their roles in cyber-diplomacy.

1.5 THE INTERSECTION OF TECHNOLOGY, SOVEREIGNTY, AND DIPLOMACY

The intersection of technology, sovereignty, and diplomacy is reshaping international relations in profound ways. Technology has created new oppor-tunities and vulnerabilities, challenging traditional notions of state authority while introducing new actors into the diplomatic arena. Sovereignty in the digital age is no longer limited to physical territory but extends into cyberspace, where states struggle to assert control without undermining the global nature of digital networks. Diplomacy has expanded to address these challenges, engaging with both state and non-state actors to build norms, rules, and cooperative frameworks for cyberspace governance. The future of international relations will be determined by how effectively the world manages this intersection, ensuring that technology serves as a tool for security, development, and human rights rather than conflict and division. The delicate balance between sovereignty and interconnectedness will remain at the heart of this evolving diplomatic landscape, shaping the destiny of global politics in the digital age.

The intersection of technology, sovereignty, and diplomacy points toward the emergence of a new diplomatic order. Traditional diplomacy is no longer sufficient to manage the complexities of the digital age. Instead, a multi-stakeholder approach is becoming the norm, where governments, international organizations, private companies, and civil society collaborate in shaping global digital governance. This new order requires flexibility, innovation, and inclusivity. It must balance the legitimate concerns of state sovereignty with the reality of a borderless cyberspace, while also ensuring that the rights and freedoms of individuals are protected. The future of diplomacy will increasingly revolve around technological issues, making digital literacy and cyber expertise essential tools of statecraft.

The intersection of technology, sovereignty, and diplomacy is not only about power and security but also about ethics and human rights. Technologies such as artificial intelligence, digital surveillance, and social media raise questions about privacy, freedom of expression, and the manipulation of information. States that assert strong digital sovereignty may justify surveillance and censorship in the name of security, while civil society advocates push for rights-based approaches to digital governance. Diplomacy plays a crucial role in reconciling these conflicting perspectives and ensuring that international agreements reflect shared values such as human dignity and democratic accountability. The ethical dimension of technology requires diplomacy to act not only as a tool of negotiation but also as a safeguard of universal principles in a rapidly evolving digital landscape.

1.5.1 Technology as a Global Force in International Relations

Technology has become a primary driver of change in global affairs. The internet, artificial intelligence, big data, and cloud computing have reshaped how societies function and how governments interact with one another. Unlike traditional resources, digital technologies transcend borders and diffuse rapidly, creating a shared space where states, private companies, and civil society interact. This shared space has created opportunities for economic growth and innovation but has also introduced vulnerabilities. Cyber-attacks, disinformation campaigns, and surveillance have become tools of statecraft, demonstrating that technology has geopolitical implications as significant as conventional military power. In this context, diplomacy has expanded to include technology as a central theme, and sovereignty has been forced to adapt to a new kind of contested domain.

1.5.2 Sovereignty in the Digital Age

Sovereignty has traditionally meant a state's supreme authority over its territory, population, and governance. However, in the digital era, sovereignty is increasingly challenged by technologies that operate across borders. The flow of data, the global reach of technology companies, and the transnational nature of cyber-threats make it difficult for states to exercise absolute control over their digital environments.

Governments are responding by asserting what is often termed "digital sovereignty," which refers to their ability to regulate, secure, and control the digital activities within their jurisdictions. This includes policies on data localization, internet governance, and restrictions on foreign technology companies. While digital sovereignty strengthens state control, it also creates tension with the open and interconnected nature of the internet, leading to new conflicts and negotiations in the realm of diplomacy.

1.5.3 Geopolitics of Digital Sovereignty

Digital sovereignty has become a central geopolitical issue. Countries such as China and Russia emphasize strong state control over the internet, enforcing strict regulations on digital platforms and prioritizing national security. In contrast, democratic nations often emphasize openness, privacy, and freedom of expression in their approaches to digital governance.

These divergent approaches to digital sovereignty create competing models of internet governance that have global implications. The debate is not only about technology but also about values, rights, and power. As states push for their preferred models, diplomacy becomes the arena where these competing visions are negotiated, and where the future of cyberspace governance is contested.

1.5.4 Diplomacy in the Age of Technology

Diplomacy, once focused on issues of borders, trade, and treaties, has expanded to include technology as a core dimension. Cyber-diplomacy has emerged as a distinct field that addresses issues such as cyber conflict, digital norms, data governance, and technological cooperation.

States now negotiate over rules for responsible behavior in cyberspace, the protection of critical infrastructure, and the prevention of cybercrime. These negotiations often take place in international organizations such as the United Nations or regional frameworks like the European Union, but also in informal settings involving private sector and civil society actors. The challenge for diplomacy in this context is to balance state sovereignty with the global nature of digital technologies, requiring unprecedented levels of multilateralism and inclusivity.

1.5.5 Technology Companies as New Power Brokers

One of the most striking aspects of the intersection of technology, sovereignty, and diplomacy is the rising influence of technology companies. Unlike traditional corporations, global technology giants such as Google, Microsoft, Amazon, and Meta control platforms and infrastructures that shape communication, commerce, and security worldwide. Their decisions on issues such as data privacy, platform governance, and content moderation affect millions of users and influence international relations. These companies often operate with power that rivals or even exceeds that of nation-states in certain domains. This creates complex challenges for sovereignty, as states must negotiate not only with each other but also with private actors that control critical aspects of the digital environment. Diplomacy has thus expanded to include engagement with non-state actors, further blurring the lines between public and private authority in international relations.

1.5.6 Cyber-security and National Sovereignty

The defense of cyberspace has become integral to the preservation of sovereignty. Cyber-attacks on critical infrastructure such as power grids, healthcare systems, and financial institutions can paralyze a state without the use of traditional military force. This has led to the recognition of cyberspace as a domain of conflict alongside land, sea, air, and outer space. States are investing heavily in cyber-security capabilities to defend their digital sovereignty, and at the same time, they are engaging in diplomatic efforts to establish norms of responsible state behavior in cyberspace. The attribution of cyber-attacks is particularly challenging, often creating tensions between states and complicating the application of international law. Diplomacy is crucial in building mechanisms for cooperation, confidence-building, and crisis management in the face of these evolving threats.

1.5.7 Data as a Resource and Diplomatic Issue

Data has become the most valuable resource of the digital era, often compared to oil in its economic significance. The control, flow, and protection of data are at the heart of both sovereignty and diplomacy. States seek to regulate how data is stored, processed, and transferred across borders in order to safeguard national security, economic interests, and citizens' privacy. For example, the European Union's General Data Protection Regulation has set a global standard for data protection and has influenced diplomatic negotiations with other regions and countries. Disputes over cross-border data flows highlight the tension between sovereignty and globalization, requiring diplomatic solutions that balance national interests with global interconnectivity.

CHAPTER 2

The Geopolitics of Cyberspace

2.1 CYBERSPACE AS A STRATEGIC DOMAIN

The twenty-first century has witnessed the rise of cyberspace as one of the most important strategic domains alongside land, sea, air, and space. Unlike the traditional physical domains of conflict and interaction, cyberspace is a man-made, virtual, and globally interconnected network that facilitates communication, commerce, governance, and military operations. Its significance lies not only in its vast reach but also in its role as the backbone of modern life. Cyberspace enables critical infrastructure, supports financial transactions, underpins defense systems, and shapes the information environment.

As technology evolves, the strategic significance of cyberspace will continue to grow. The rise of artificial intelligence, quantum computing, and the Internet of Things will expand the attack surface and create new vulnerabilities. Autonomous cyber weapons may change the pace and scale of cyber-conflicts, while quantum technologies could undermine current encryption systems.

At the same time, cyberspace will remain central to economic development, social connectivity, and global governance, making its security and stability a top priority. The future will require balancing innovation with resilience, openness with control, and competition with cooperation. Ultimately, the strategic domain of cyberspace will define the character of international relations in the digital age.

Cyberspace has emerged as a critical strategic domain that transcends traditional boundaries of geography and sovereignty. It is a realm where states, non-state actors, and private entities compete for power, influence, and security. Its significance lies not only in enabling modern life but also in shaping the dynamics of warfare, politics, and society.

The challenges of attribution, deterrence, governance, and hybrid threats make cyberspace a complex environment requiring constant adaptation and innovation. As the digital age deepens, the ability to secure, control, and strategically utilize cyberspace will be one of the defining features of national power and global order. In recognizing cyberspace as a strategic domain, humanity acknowledges that the future of conflict, cooperation, and competition will increasingly be written in digital code as much as on physical terrain.

2.1.1 Nature of Cyberspace

Cyberspace is a complex and multidimensional environment composed of physical, logical, and cognitive layers. The physical layer includes the hardware, cables, satellites, and servers that allow connectivity. The logical layer is the code, software, and protocols that structure and direct communication. The cognitive layer refers to the human users who create, share, and interpret information. This layered structure makes cyberspace unique because actions in one layer can ripple through the others, creating outcomes that may be beneficial or harmful. The virtual and borderless nature of cyberspace challenges traditional notions of geography, sovereignty, and control, which have historically defined strategic domains.

2.1.2 Cyberspace as the Fifth Domain of Warfare

The recognition of cyberspace as a domain of warfare came formally in the early 2000s when military establishments, particularly in the United States and NATO, began categorizing it alongside the traditional four domains. In this context, cyberspace is viewed not merely as a tool but as an operational environment where states can project power, conduct operations, and defend assets. Offensive cyber-operations can disable enemy infrastructure, disrupt communication, and sow confusion without the need for physical force. Defensive operations, meanwhile, are essential to protecting military command systems, critical infrastructure, and sensitive data from adversaries. The integration of cyberspace into strategic thinking has fundamentally altered the character of warfare, shifting from kinetic dominance to information superiority.

2.1.3 Strategic Importance for National Security

National security is increasingly intertwined with cyber-security. States depend on cyberspace for energy distribution, financial systems, healthcare networks, transportation, and military command and control. Any disruption in these areas can cripple a nation's ability to function, making cyberspace a critical security concern. For example, cyber-attacks on power grids, such as the one experienced by Ukraine in 2015, demonstrate how cyber-threats can cause real-world chaos. Similarly, ransomware attacks on hospitals and supply chains highlight the vulnerability of societies to disruptions in cyberspace. Thus, safeguarding cyberspace is as crucial as defending territorial borders, and states are investing heavily in building cyber-defense forces and establishing doctrines for cyber resilience.

2.1.4 Cyberspace and State Competition

The strategic domain of cyberspace is also an arena for geopolitical competition among states. Major powers such as the United States, China, and Russia have developed sophisticated cyber capabilities not only for defense but also for offensive purposes. Cyber espionage, intellectual property theft, and information manipulation have become common tools in statecraft. The ability to infiltrate networks, extract sensitive data, and influence public opinion has given states new methods of projecting influence without resorting to conventional military confrontation. This competition is not confined to great powers alone; smaller states and even non-state actors can exploit the asymmetrical nature of cyberspace to challenge stronger adversaries. This democratization of power in cyberspace makes it a domain of strategic uncertainty and constant rivalry.

2.1.5 Role of Non-State Actors

While states are central players, non-state actors also wield significant influence in cyberspace. Hacktivist groups, cybercriminal organizations, terrorist networks, and private corporations contribute to shaping the strategic environment. Cybercriminals conduct financial thefts and ransomware operations that destabilize economies, while terrorist groups exploit cyberspace for propaganda, recruitment, and coordination. Hacktivists engage in politically motivated cyber-attacks to challenge governments or corporations. At the same time, technology companies own and manage much of the infrastructure of cyberspace, giving them immense power over security, innovation, and regulation. This multi-actor involvement distinguishes cyberspace from other domains, where the monopoly of power largely rests with states.

2.1.6 Information Warfare and Influence Operations

Cyberspace has become the battlefield of ideas, perceptions, and narratives. Information warfare, which involves manipulating information to influence decision-making and public opinion, has grown exponentially in the digital age. Through disinformation campaigns, fake news, and social media manipulation, actors can destabilize societies, polarize populations, and undermine trust in institutions. The 2016 U.S. presidential election, influenced by coordinated disinformation campaigns, illustrated how cyberspace can be weaponized to affect political processes. Influence operations blur the line between war and peace, as they often occur below the threshold of armed conflict but can cause long-term strategic harm. In this sense, cyberspace is not only about technology but also about the contest for control over human cognition and perception.

2.1.7 Challenges of Attribution and Deterrence

One of the greatest challenges in treating cyberspace as a strategic domain is the difficulty of attribution. Unlike traditional attacks, cyber-attacks are often anonymous, routed through multiple countries, and concealed through sophisticated methods. This ambiguity makes it hard to identify perpetrators with certainty, complicating the application of deterrence strategies. States hesitate to retaliate when the origin of an attack cannot be conclusively proven. Moreover, the low cost of conducting cyber-attacks compared to the high cost of defense creates a persistent imbalance that encourages malicious behavior. Developing frameworks for attribution and credible deterrence in cyberspace is one of the central strategic challenges of the twenty-first century.

2.1.8 International Norms and Governance

The borderless nature of cyberspace requires international cooperation, yet consensus on rules and norms remains elusive. Efforts have been made through forums such as the United Nations Group of Governmental Experts (UNGGE) to establish norms of responsible state behavior in cyberspace, including the principle that critical infrastructure should not be targeted during peacetime. However, enforcement mechanisms are weak, and powerful states often prioritize national interests over collective agreements. The absence of universally accepted governance structures has created a fragmented cyberspace with competing visions of regulation, such as the open internet model advocated by liberal democracies versus the state-controlled cyberspace championed by authoritarian regimes. The future of cyberspace as a strategic domain depends heavily on whether cooperative frameworks or competitive rivalries dominate.

2.1.9 Cyberspace and Hybrid Warfare

Hybrid warfare combines conventional military power with cyber-operations, disinformation, and economic pressure to achieve strategic objectives. Cyberspace plays a central role in this strategy by enabling covert actions that complement traditional military campaigns. Russia's actions in Crimea and Ukraine demonstrated how cyber-attacks can paralyze communications, disrupt infrastructure, and spread propaganda in support of kinetic operations. Similarly, cyber-tools have been used to weaken adversaries before direct confrontation, making cyberspace an essential component of modern hybrid warfare. The integration of cyber-operations into hybrid strategies underscores the necessity of viewing cyberspace not as a separate sphere but as an interconnected domain of overall strategic competition.

2.2 CYBERPOWER AND GLOBAL INFLUENCE

The advent of the digital age has fundamentally transformed the nature of global power and influence, giving rise to the concept of cyberpower as a critical determinant of international standing. Cyberpower, defined as the ability to use digital technologies to achieve strategic objectives, encompasses a wide range of capabilities, from economic innovation and cultural dissemination to espionage and military operations. In the contemporary geopolitical landscape, nations no longer rely solely on traditional measures of power such as military might or economic resources; instead, digital prowess has become a pivotal element in shaping global influence. The integration of cyber capabilities into national strategy has redefined how states interact, compete, and cooperate, creating a new frontier where dominance is exercised through control over information, networks, and technologies. This shift has profound implications for international relations, security, and global governance, as states and non-state actors leverage cyber-tools to advance their interests, disrupt adversaries, and project power beyond physical borders.

As cyberpower continues to evolve, its impact on the global order will deepen, driven by advancements in technologies like artificial intelligence, quantum computing, and the Internet of Things. These innovations will expand the scope and scale of cyber capabilities, enabling more sophisticated forms of influence, coercion, and control. Nations that lead in these areas will gain significant advantages, while those that fall behind may face increased vulnerability and dependency. The future will likely see greater integration of cyber-tools into all aspects of statecraft, from economic policy to military operations, making digital literacy and resilience essential components of national power.

However, the unchecked pursuit of cyber dominance risks fragmenting the internet into competing spheres of influence, often described as the "splinternet." Different regulatory regimes, technological standards, and ideological visions could lead to a bifurcated digital world, where interoperability declines and geopolitical tensions are amplified. To avoid this outcome, renewed multilateral efforts are needed to build consensus on norms, enhance transparency, and foster cooperation. Civil society, private sector actors, and technical communities must also play a role in shaping an inclusive and secure digital future.

Cyberpower has emerged as a defining element of global influence, reshaping international relations in profound and irreversible ways. Its economic, military, and diplomatic dimensions provide states with unprecedented tools to project power, advance interests, and navigate the complexities of the 21st-century world. Yet, this digital revolution also brings significant risks, from heightened geopolitical competition to vulnerabilities in global stability. Navigating this new frontier requires a balanced approach that harnesses the benefits of cyber capabilities while addressing the challenges through cooperation, innovation, and responsible governance. As the digital age unfolds, the nations that succeed will be those that not only master the technologies of cyberpower but also uphold the principles of security, inclusivity, and ethical leadership in the pursuit of a stable and prosperous global order.

2.2.1 Dimensions of Cyberpower

Cyberpower manifests in multiple dimensions, each contributing uniquely to a nation's global influence. The economic dimension is perhaps the most visible, as digital economies drive growth, innovation, and competitiveness. Nations with advanced technological sectors, such as the United States, China, and members of the European Union, harness cyberpower to dominate global markets, set industry standards, and control supply chains for critical technologies like semiconductors, artificial intelligence, and 5G networks. This economic clout translates into geopolitical leverage, enabling these states to shape international norms, impose sanctions, and influence global financial systems. Moreover, the ability to innovate and adapt digitally fosters resilience, allowing economies to withstand shocks and capitalize on emerging opportunities in an interconnected world.

The military and security dimensions of cyberpower are equally significant. Cyber-warfare capabilities have become integral to national defense strategies, with states developing offensive and defensive tools to protect critical infrastructure, conduct espionage, and disrupt adversaries' operations. The use of cyber-tools for intelligence gathering, as seen in campaigns attributed to states like Russia and China, demonstrates how digital espionage can provide strategic advantages without direct confrontation. Similarly, offensive cyber-operations, such as the Stuxnet attack on Iran's nuclear facilities, illustrate how cyber capabilities can achieve kinetic effects, blurring the lines between traditional and digital warfare. These activities underscore the role of cyberpower in enhancing national security while simultaneously creating vulnerabilities that adversaries may exploit.

2.2.2 Cyberpower as a Tool of Soft Power and Diplomacy

Beyond economic and military applications, cyberpower serves as a potent instrument of soft power, enabling states to shape global narratives, promote cultural values, and build international alliances. Digital platforms like social media, streaming services, and news outlets allow nations to project their cultural influence worldwide, as demonstrated by the global reach of American tech giants like Google, Facebook, and Netflix. These platforms disseminate ideas, lifestyles, and ideologies, often reinforcing the dominance of Western values and norms. Conversely, states like China and Russia employ digital tools to advance alternative narratives through state-sponsored media outlets and disinformation campaigns, seeking to challenge Western hegemony and promote their own models of governance.

Diplomacy, too, has been transformed by cyberpower. Digital diplomacy, or e-diplomacy, involves the use of digital technologies to conduct foreign policy, engage with global audiences, and manage international crises. Social media platforms enable leaders and diplomats to communicate directly with foreign populations, bypassing traditional media channels and fostering greater transparency—or manipulation. Additionally, cyber capabilities facilitate multilateral cooperation on issues such as cyber-security, internet governance, and digital trade, where states must negotiate frameworks to manage shared challenges. However, the use of cyber-tools for malicious purposes, such as election interference or cyber-attacks, can undermine trust and escalate tensions, complicating diplomatic relations and fostering a climate of suspicion among nations.

2.2.3 Geopolitical Contest for Cyber Dominance

The pursuit of cyber dominance has ignited a fierce geopolitical contest, primarily between the United States and China, with other actors like Russia, the European Union, and emerging powers jostling for influence. This competition is driven by the recognition that leadership in digital technologies translates into long-term economic, military, and ideological advantages.

China's strategy, encapsulated in initiatives like "Made in China 2025" and the Belt and Road Initiative's digital component, aims to achieve technological self-sufficiency and global leadership in areas such as artificial intelligence, quantum computing, and telecommunications. By exporting its digital infrastructure and standards, China seeks to expand its sphere of influence, particularly in developing regions, while promoting an authoritarian model of internet governance that emphasizes state control and surveillance.

The United States, meanwhile, leverages its historical dominance in technology and innovation to maintain its competitive edge. Through partnerships with allied nations, advocacy for an open and free internet, and the formidable presence of its tech corporations, the U.S. promotes a vision of digital globalization that aligns with its values of democracy and capitalism. However, this vision faces challenges from rising competitors and growing concerns over privacy, monopolistic practices, and the weaponization of technology. The European Union positions itself as a regulatory superpower, using its market size to enforce stringent standards on data protection (e.g., GDPR), competition, and ethical AI, thereby shaping global norms and curbing the excesses of larger tech powers.

2.2.4 Challenges to Global Stability and Governance

The rise of cyberpower introduces significant challenges to global stability and governance. The asymmetric nature of cyber-threats allows small states and non-state actors, such as terrorist groups and hacktivists, to wield disproportionate influence by targeting critical infrastructure, spreading disinformation, or stealing sensitive data. This democratization of threat capabilities undermines traditional power hierarchies and creates a more volatile international environment. Moreover, the attribution of cyber-attacks remains difficult, fostering a culture of impunity and increasing the risk of miscalculation and escalation between states.The lack of robust international norms and agreements further exacerbates these risks. While efforts like the United Nations Group of Governmental Experts

(UNGGE) have sought to establish rules for state behavior in cyberspace, progress has been hampered by divergent national interests and ideological divides. Disagreements over issues such as sovereignty, human rights, and the role of the state in cyberspace prevent consensus on frameworks for accountability, conflict prevention, and cooperation. This regulatory vacuum allows malicious actors to operate with minimal constraints, threatening the stability of the global digital ecosystem.

2.3 DIGITAL SOVEREIGNTY AND NATIONAL INTERESTS

Digital sovereignty has become a cornerstone of national interests in the modern era. It encompasses the security of critical infrastructure, the economic control of data, the preservation of cultural identity, and the protection of democratic values. As cyberspace becomes more deeply integrated into every aspect of life, the stakes of sovereignty in the digital domain continue to rise.

Nations must confront challenges such as technological dependence, cyber-threats, and competing geopolitical visions while striving to build resilient digital infrastructures. Ultimately, digital sovereignty is not about isolation but about ensuring that states can make independent decisions in a digital world shaped by rapid change and global interconnection. Protecting digital sovereignty is therefore inseparable from protecting national interests, and it will remain a defining strategic priority for states in the decades to come.

Looking ahead, the significance of digital sovereignty will only intensify as new technologies emerge. Artificial intelligence, quantum computing, and the Internet of Things will expand the digital domain and increase the stakes of sovereignty. The control of algorithms, the security of connected devices, and the governance of emerging technologies will become central issues for national interests. States will need to cooperate internationally to set norms and standards while continuing to defend their sovereignty against external pressures. The future of digital sovereignty will thus involve a delicate balance between autonomy and interdependence, innovation and regulation, openness and protection. Those nations that successfully navigate this balance will be better positioned to safeguard their national interests in the digital age.

2.3.1 Concept of Digital Sovereignty

Digital sovereignty embodies the idea that a state must retain control over the digital space within its borders. This includes the regulation of internet infrastructure, data storage, cyber-security, and digital platforms. Unlike the early vision of the internet as a borderless and open network, the rise of cyber-threats, disinformation, and technological dependency has prompted governments to rethink the role of sovereignty in the digital domain. It is not merely a technical or legal concept but a strategic imperative that defines how nations engage with technology and defend their autonomy in an environment dominated by global corporations and powerful states. By asserting digital sovereignty, countries seek to reduce vulnerabilities, secure sensitive information, and maintain decision-making authority over technological ecosystems.

2.3.2 Digital Sovereignty and National Security

The national security dimension of digital sovereignty is one of its most pressing aspects. Cyber-attacks on government systems, military networks, and critical infrastructure pose direct threats to national defense and public safety. States cannot allow foreign actors to control or compromise these vital assets without undermining sovereignty itself. For instance, cyber espionage campaigns targeting defense contractors or attacks on energy grids demonstrate how digital vulnerabilities can translate into strategic risks. By exercising digital sovereignty, states aim to build resilient cyber-defenses, establish strong encryption standards, and regulate the use of foreign technologies that may harbor hidden security risks. In this way, safeguarding digital sovereignty becomes a form of modern national defense.

2.3.3 Economic Dimensions of Digital Sovereignty

Beyond security, digital sovereignty has profound economic implications. Data has been described as the new oil of the digital economy, and whoever controls it wields significant economic power. Multinational corporations such as Google, Amazon, and Facebook manage vast amounts of personal and commercial data, raising concerns about national dependency on foreign-controlled platforms. Countries asserting digital sovereignty often seek to ensure that data generated within their borders is stored and processed locally to maximize economic benefits and protect consumer rights. Moreover, by fostering indigenous digital industries and reducing reliance on external technologies, states can enhance their competitiveness in the global economy. Policies promoting digital sovereignty therefore serve both as protective measures and as strategies to stimulate domestic innovation and growth.

2.3.4 Role of Culture and Identity

Digital sovereignty also extends into the cultural and societal spheres, where information flows shape national identity and social cohesion. The internet and digital platforms are powerful channels for cultural expression, but they can also expose societies to external influence, disinformation, and cultural homogenization. For example, global social media platforms may promote narratives that challenge local traditions or political systems. In response, states may seek to regulate online content, promote national languages in digital spaces, and encourage the creation of local platforms that reflect cultural values. Protecting digital sovereignty in this context means safeguarding cultural identity against erosion while ensuring that citizens have access to diverse, reliable, and contextually relevant information.

2.3.5 Geopolitical Competition in the Digital Sphere

Digital sovereignty is increasingly tied to the broader geopolitical landscape. The rivalry between major powers such as the United States, China, and the European Union illustrates how digital sovereignty shapes international relations. The United States, with its dominance in global technology companies, champions an open and free internet model, while China promotes a vision of cyber sovereignty characterized by strict state control of digital infrastructure and information flows. The European Union, through initiatives like the General Data Protection Regulation (GDPR), emphasizes individual rights and data protection as central to its digital sovereignty. These competing models highlight how different interpretations of digital sovereignty reflect broader political values and strategic priorities. Smaller states are often caught between these visions, forced to navigate alliances and dependencies while striving to preserve their autonomy.

2.3.6 Digital Sovereignty and Technological Dependence

One of the central challenges to achieving digital sovereignty lies in technological dependence. Many countries rely on foreign technologies for hardware, software, and cloud services, creating vulnerabilities in terms of security and autonomy. For example, reliance on foreign 5G networks has raised concerns about surveillance and control. Similarly, dependence on global cloud service providers creates risks for the confidentiality of sensitive data. Achieving digital sovereignty requires developing domestic capabilities in critical technologies, investing in research and development, and supporting local tech industries. However, this is a resource-intensive endeavor, and many states struggle to balance the need for independence with the benefits of global integration.

2.3.7 Regulation, Governance, and Law

The pursuit of digital sovereignty often manifests in legal and regulatory frameworks that govern digital infrastructure and data. Laws requiring data localization, strict privacy protections, and oversight of foreign technology providers are common examples. The European Union's GDPR has set global benchmarks for data protection, influencing regulations worldwide. Similarly, countries like India have proposed data localization laws to ensure that information generated by citizens remains within national boundaries. While such measures strengthen sovereignty, they also raise questions about global interoperability and the free flow of information across borders. The challenge lies in finding a balance between safeguarding sovereignty and maintaining the benefits of a globally connected digital economy.

2.3.8 Digital Sovereignty and Democratic Values

In democratic societies, digital sovereignty is closely linked to the protection of citizen rights and freedoms. States must ensure that their efforts to control digital infrastructure do not infringe upon freedom of expression, privacy, or access to information. The regulation of digital platforms should be transparent and accountable, avoiding the risk of turning digital sovereignty into digital authoritarianism. Balancing security and freedom is essential for maintaining trust between governments and citizens. In this sense, digital sovereignty in democratic contexts is not simply about control but about empowering citizens to participate safely and confidently in the digital world.

2.4 MAJOR PLAYERS AND GLOBAL CYBER STRATEGIES

2.4.1 USA

The United States has emerged as a global leader in developing cyber strategies that address the multifaceted challenges of the digital age. From national security and critical infrastructure protection to combating cybercrime and fostering international cooperation, U.S. strategies reflect the central role of cyberspace in modern life. The establishment of agencies like USCYBERCOM and CISA, combined with proactive doctrines such as persistent engagement, demonstrates a commitment to both defense and deterrence.

At the same time, the recognition of the private sector's critical role and the need for global partnerships highlights the cooperative dimension of U.S. cyber strategy. As technology continues to advance, the ability of the United States to safeguard its digital environment while promoting openness and innovation will define its strategic position in the twenty-first century. Cyberspace has become a permanent domain of competition, and U.S. cyber strategies are designed to ensure that the nation not only survives but thrives in this new frontier.

Looking ahead, U.S. cyber strategies will continue to evolve in response to changing threats and technological developments. Greater emphasis is likely to be placed on resilience, meaning the ability to recover quickly from cyber-incidents rather than simply preventing them. Efforts to strengthen international norms and partnerships will remain central, as global cooperation is essential for addressing cross-border threats.

Domestically, enhancing the cyber-security workforce, investing in education, and fostering a culture of digital hygiene will be priorities. As the line between civilian and military infrastructures blurs, the integration of cyber strategies into every aspect of governance and national planning will deepen. The success of U.S. cyber strategies will depend on the ability to adapt quickly, innovate responsibly, and strike a balance between security, freedom, and economic growth.

Evolution

The early stages of U.S. cyber policy were primarily focused on information assurance and the protection of federal networks. As the internet became a critical enabler of economic and social activity, the scope of cyber strategies broadened to include private sector networks, critical infrastructure, and international cooperation.

The 2009 Cyberspace Policy Review under President Barack Obama marked a turning point, emphasizing cyber-security as a national priority and recommending stronger coordination between government and industry. Under President Donald Trump, the 2018 National Cyber Strategy placed greater emphasis on deterrence, offensive capabilities, and protecting American intellectual property. President Joe Biden's administration has continued to build on these foundations, with a focus on resilience, partnerships, and addressing emerging threats such as ransomware. The evolution of U.S. cyber strategies illustrates a steady recognition that cyberspace is not only a technical domain but a central element of national power.

National Security and Cyber-defense

A cornerstone of U.S. cyber strategies is the protection of national security interests against adversarial actions in cyberspace. Cyber-attacks from state and non-state actors target defense systems, government agencies, and critical infrastructure, posing threats to both military operations and civilian life. The Department of Defense has developed specific cyber strategies to ensure the security of military networks, safeguard command and control systems, and maintain the ability to operate in contested cyber environments.

The 2015 Department of Defense Cyber Strategy introduced the concept of defending forward, which involves identifying and disrupting malicious cyber activity at its source before it reaches U.S. networks. This proactive approach reflects the understanding that purely defensive measures are insufficient in a domain where adversaries can act quickly and covertly.

Cyber Deterrence and Offensive Capabilities

Unlike traditional domains, cyberspace presents challenges for deterrence due to the difficulties of attribution and the relatively low costs of launching attacks. The U.S. cyber strategy addresses this by combining defensive resilience with offensive capabilities. By maintaining the ability to respond to cyber-attacks with both cyber and non-cyber means, the United States seeks to impose costs on adversaries and discourage malicious activity. The establishment of U.S. Cyber Command (USCYBERCOM) in 2010 formalized the military's role in conducting offensive and defensive cyber-operations. Through its doctrine of persistent engagement, USCYBERCOM actively operates in cyberspace to deter adversaries by contesting malicious actions continuously. This marks a significant shift from reactive defense to a strategy of active competition in the digital domain.

Protection of Critical Infrastructure

Critical infrastructure such as energy grids, transportation systems, healthcare networks, and financial institutions forms the backbone of American society. U.S. cyber strategies recognize that these sectors are highly vulnerable to cyber-attacks, with potential consequences that extend beyond the digital realm into physical and economic harm. The establishment of the Cyber-security and Infrastructure Security Agency (CISA) in 2018 was a major step toward coordinating efforts to protect these vital assets. CISA works with both public and private sectors to identify risks, share threat intelligence, and enhance resilience against attacks. U.S. cyber strategy emphasizes that securing critical infrastructure requires not only technological defenses but also partnerships across federal, state, and local governments as well as private stakeholders who own and operate most of these systems.

Combating Cybercrime and Ransomware

In addition to state-sponsored threats, cybercrime has become a pressing challenge for the United States. Ransomware attacks on hospitals, schools, and private companies have underscored the disruptive potential of criminal actors in cyberspace. The 2021 Colonial Pipeline ransomware attack highlighted vulnerabilities in energy supply chains and demonstrated how criminal groups could cause nationwide disruptions. U.S. cyber strategies have therefore placed increasing emphasis on combating cybercrime through improved law enforcement capabilities, international cooperation, and stricter regulations on cryptocurrency transactions used for ransom payments. Addressing cybercrime is not only a matter of economic security but also of national resilience, as criminal attacks can erode public trust and confidence in digital systems.

International Cooperation and Cyber-diplomacy

Given the borderless nature of cyberspace, U.S. cyber strategies also prioritize international cooperation. The United States engages with allies and partners to promote norms of responsible state behavior, enhance collective defense, and respond to malicious activities. Through forums such as NATO, the G7, and the United Nations, the U.S. advocates for agreements that prohibit attacks on critical infrastructure and discourage cyber-enabled theft of intellectual property. At the same time, the U.S. engages in bilateral dialogues with nations such as China and Russia, though tensions often remain due to conflicting interests. Cyber-diplomacy is a vital component of U.S. strategy because global stability in cyberspace depends on collaboration, trust, and the establishment of shared rules.

Public-Private Partnerships in Cyber-Security

Unlike traditional security domains where the state exerts primary control, cyberspace is largely owned and operated by private entities. This reality makes public-private partnerships central to U.S. cyber strategies. Technology companies, internet service providers, and infrastructure operators play critical roles in securing digital systems. The U.S. government has increasingly sought to build frameworks for information sharing, incident reporting, and joint exercises with private industry. Executive orders and legislative initiatives have aimed to create stronger standards for cyber-security practices, while also respecting innovation and competition. The recognition that cyber-security cannot be achieved by government alone reflects a pragmatic understanding of the shared responsibilities in safeguarding cyberspace.

Role of Emerging Technologies

Emerging technologies such as artificial intelligence, quantum computing, and 5G networks are reshaping the cyber domain. U.S. cyber strategies acknowledge both the opportunities and risks posed by these developments. Artificial intelligence offers new tools for detecting and responding to cyber-threats but also creates possibilities for more sophisticated attacks. Quantum computing threatens to undermine current encryption methods, making it a potential game-changer for cyber-security. The rollout of 5G networks expands connectivity but also increases the attack surface. U.S. strategies therefore focus on maintaining leadership in technological innovation while ensuring that new technologies are developed and deployed with security at their core. This dual emphasis on innovation and resilience is central to maintaining long-term strategic advantage in cyberspace.

Challenges and Criticisms

Despite progress, U.S. cyber strategies face significant challenges. Attribution of cyber-attacks remains difficult, limiting the effectiveness of deterrence. The vast attack surface created by America's highly digitized economy makes it nearly impossible to protect all systems equally. The fragmented nature of federal and state responsibilities sometimes hinders coordinated responses, while debates over privacy, surveillance, and regulation complicate the balance between security and civil liberties. Critics argue that U.S. strategies have sometimes prioritized military and offensive approaches at the expense of broader diplomatic and cooperative measures. These challenges underscore the complexity of governing cyberspace and the need for constant adaptation.

2.4.2 China

China's cyber strategies reflect a comprehensive approach that integrates security, governance, economic development, and geopolitical influence. Anchored in the principle of cyber sovereignty, these strategies prioritize state control over digital infrastructure and information while promoting technological self-reliance and international expansion.

The combination of domestic censorship, cyber-security laws, military capabilities, and global initiatives such as the Digital Silk Road demonstrates the breadth of China's ambitions in cyberspace. At the same time, these strategies face criticism for limiting openness, fostering mistrust, and challenging established international norms. As digital technologies continue to reshape global politics, China's cyber strategies will remain a defining element of its rise as a world power. Whether seen as a model or a threat, they exemplify how cyberspace has become a central battleground for national interests and global influence in the twenty-first century.

Looking ahead, China's cyber strategies are likely to become more sophisticated and assertive. Domestically, the state will continue to strengthen its control over digital platforms and data flows, using emerging technologies like artificial intelligence and quantum computing to enhance both security and governance. Economically, China will intensify its pursuit of technological self-reliance, aiming to dominate key sectors of the global digital economy.

Militarily, the PLA will further integrate cyber-operations into its doctrine, viewing cyberspace as a decisive arena in great-power competition. Internationally, China will expand its efforts to shape global cyber norms and promote its vision of cyber sovereignty as a legitimate model for other countries. Whether these strategies succeed will depend on China's ability to navigate external pressures, technological challenges, and the growing demands of a digitally connected global society.

Cyber Sovereignty

At the core of China's cyber strategies is the principle of cyber sovereignty, which asserts that each state has the right to govern the internet within its borders according to its own laws and political system. This concept rejects the notion of a borderless and open internet, advocating instead for strict national control over digital activities. For China, cyber sovereignty means that the state has ultimate authority over data, digital platforms, and information that circulates in cyberspace. This principle not only provides the Chinese government with legitimacy to regulate and censor online content but also positions it against Western models of internet governance. Through international forums, Beijing actively promotes cyber sovereignty as an alternative vision, appealing to other states that seek greater control over their digital domains.

Domestic Control and the Great Firewall

China's cyber strategies are most visible in its domestic environment, where the state has built one of the most extensive systems of online control in the world.

Commonly referred to as the Great Firewall, this system combines technological filters, regulatory measures, and human oversight to restrict access to foreign websites and monitor online behavior. Platforms such as Google, Facebook, and Twitter are blocked, replaced by domestic alternatives like Baidu, WeChat, and Weibo, which operate under state supervision. This digital ecosystem allows the government to maintain tight control over public discourse, prevent the spread of dissent, and shape the narratives that dominate Chinese cyberspace. Beyond censorship, the state employs surveillance technologies powered by artificial intelligence and big data to track citizens' online activities, integrating them into broader systems of social management.

Cyber-security and National Security

For China, cyber-security is inseparable from national security. The leadership views cyberspace as a potential source of threats ranging from espionage and sabotage to ideological subversion. In 2014, President Xi Jinping established the Central Cyberspace Affairs Commission, underscoring the strategic importance of cyber-security. The 2017 Cyber-security Law codified strict requirements for network operators, mandating data localization, security reviews of foreign technologies, and real-name registration for internet users. These measures are designed not only to protect critical infrastructure and state secrets but also to limit foreign influence on domestic digital space. By equating cyber-security with regime security, China ensures that its cyber strategies are aligned with the Communist Party's overarching objective of political control.

Economic Ambitions and Technological Self-Reliance

China's cyber strategies are also closely linked to its economic ambitions. Recognizing that digital technologies are the drivers of future growth, Beijing has invested heavily in building a strong domestic technology sector. The "Made in China 2025" initiative and the more recent "Dual Circulation" strategy emphasize the importance of indigenous innovation in key areas such as artificial intelligence, 5G, semiconductors, and cloud computing. The goal is to reduce dependence on foreign technologies and achieve technological self-reliance, which is seen as essential for both economic security and national sovereignty. At the same time, China has promoted the concept of the "Digital Silk Road" as part of its Belt and Road Initiative, exporting its digital infrastructure, platforms, and standards to partner countries. In this way, cyber strategies serve as both domestic development policies and tools of global influence.

Cyber Espionage and Intellectual Property

China's cyber strategies have frequently been associated with cyber espionage and the theft of intellectual property from foreign companies and governments.

Reports from Western intelligence agencies and private cyber-security firms have attributed numerous cyber-intrusions to Chinese state-sponsored groups. These operations are believed to target sensitive technologies, defense contractors, and critical infrastructure in order to accelerate China's technological development and strengthen its competitive advantage. While Beijing consistently denies such allegations, cyber espionage has become a key dimension of how China is perceived in global cyber competition. It reflects a strategy that blends national security priorities with economic objectives, blurring the line between state and commercial interests.

Military Dimensions of Cyber Strategy

The military dimension of China's cyber strategy is embedded in its doctrine of informationized warfare, which emphasizes the centrality of information dominance in modern conflict. The People's Liberation Army (PLA) has established specialized units for cyber-operations, tasked with both defensive and offensive missions. Offensive cyber capabilities are seen as tools to disrupt adversary command systems, disable critical infrastructure, and weaken enemy resolve during crises or conflicts. Defensive operations focus on protecting China's own networks and ensuring the integrity of military communications. The integration of cyber-operations into overall military strategy highlights the PLA's recognition that future wars will be fought as much in cyberspace as in physical domains.

International Promotion of China's Cyber Vision

China's cyber strategies are not confined to its borders but extend to the global arena, where it seeks to shape international norms and standards. Through forums such as the World Internet Conference held annually in Wuzhen, Beijing advocates for cyber sovereignty and presents itself as a leader in digital governance. China also works through international organizations like the International Telecommunication Union to promote technical standards that align with its interests. By exporting digital infrastructure through initiatives like the Digital Silk Road, China extends its influence over how other countries build and manage their cyber domains. This international dimension of China's strategy reflects its ambition to position itself as a global power not only in traditional domains but also in the digital sphere.

Challenges and Criticisms

Despite its advances, China's cyber strategies face significant challenges and criticisms. Domestically, strict state control over cyberspace has raised concerns about innovation and freedom of expression. While censorship ensures stability, it may also stifle creativity and limit the global competitiveness of Chinese companies. Internationally, China's approach is often criticized as authoritarian and incompatible with the principles of an open internet. Allegations of cyber espionage have strained its relations with the United States, Europe, and other countries, leading to sanctions and restrictions on Chinese technology firms such as Huawei and ZTE. Furthermore, China's efforts to promote cyber sovereignty abroad face resistance from states that value openness and interoperability. These challenges illustrate the tensions inherent in China's cyber strategies, which must balance control with innovation and domestic priorities with global integration.

2.4.3 Russia

In the twenty-first century, cyberspace has emerged as one of the most critical domains of competition between nations. It is not merely a technological realm but a sphere of political, military, economic, and ideological struggle. Russia has positioned itself as a leading actor in cyber-operations, developing sophisticated strategies to project power, disrupt adversaries, and advance its geopolitical objectives. Russian cyber strategies are rooted in both historical doctrines of information warfare and modern technological innovations. They are marked by a hybrid approach that blends state-directed operations with proxy actors, creating a landscape where attribution is difficult and accountability is elusive.

Russia's cyber strategies represent a sophisticated blend of historical traditions, doctrinal innovation, and pragmatic opportunism. They encompass a wide range of activities, from disinformation and influence campaigns to critical infrastructure attacks and espionage. By leveraging both state and non-state actors, Russia maximizes its cyber capabilities while maintaining plausible deniability. These strategies are integral to its broader geopolitical ambitions, enabling Moscow to project power asymmetrically in a multipolar world.

As cyberspace becomes an increasingly contested domain, Russia's approach serves as both a model and a warning, illustrating how states can weaponize information and technology to reshape global politics. The challenge for the international community lies in crafting responses that deter aggression, protect democratic institutions, and establish norms that preserve stability in the digital realm.

Historical Foundations

Russia's cyber approach is deeply embedded in its Soviet-era traditions of information warfare, often referred to as "informatsionnaya voyna." The Soviet Union relied heavily on disinformation, propaganda, and psychological operations to undermine opponents during the Cold War. This legacy carried over into modern Russia, where cyber capabilities became a natural extension of older methods. The collapse of the Soviet Union did not diminish Moscow's emphasis on information control; rather, it intensified the need for asymmetric tools to compensate for economic and military weaknesses compared to the West. Cyber strategies allowed

Russia to offset conventional disadvantages by exploiting vulnerabilities in interconnected global systems.

Doctrinal Principles

Russia's cyber doctrine is guided by the principle of "information confrontation," which extends beyond mere hacking to include psychological influence, disinformation campaigns, and strategic deception. Unlike Western doctrines that often separate cyber-defense from cyber offense, Russia sees the cyber domain as a continuum where political, military, and social influence are intertwined. Russian military doctrine emphasizes preemptive operations, blurring the line between peace and war. Cyber capabilities are considered integral to hybrid warfare, where military action, covert operations, and digital tools are fused together. This holistic approach ensures that cyber-operations are not isolated activities but part of a comprehensive geopolitical strategy.

State Actors and Institutional Framework

Russia's cyber strategies are orchestrated by a combination of military, intelligence, and civilian agencies. The Federal Security Service (FSB), the Foreign Intelligence Service (SVR), and the Main Directorate of the General Staff (GRU) play central roles. The GRU, in particular, has been associated with some of the most aggressive cyber campaigns, including operations against NATO members, U.S. electoral systems, and critical infrastructure. These agencies do not operate in isolation but often cooperate with state-affiliated groups, academic institutions, and private actors. This ecosystem creates a multilayered structure that enhances both capacity and deniability, allowing Moscow to engage in cyber-operations while maintaining plausible deniability.

Use of Proxy Actors and Cybercriminals

A distinctive feature of Russia's cyber strategies is its reliance on proxy actors, including cybercriminal organizations and patriotic hackers. These groups often operate in a gray zone where criminal activities intersect with state objectives. While they may engage in independent operations for financial gain, they are tolerated, encouraged, or subtly directed by Russian authorities when their actions align with national interests. This arrangement provides the state with flexibility and cover, making it difficult for adversaries to draw clear lines of responsibility. The blending of state and non-state actors ensures that Russia can project cyber power globally without bearing the full cost of direct engagement.

Disinformation and Influence Campaigns

One of the most prominent aspects of Russian cyber strategy is its extensive use of disinformation and influence operations. Russia has mastered the art of manipulating public opinion through coordinated online campaigns that spread false narratives, amplify divisions, and erode trust in institutions. The use of social media platforms has allowed Russia to target audiences with precision, shaping perceptions on issues ranging from elections to international conflicts. The 2016 U.S. presidential election interference stands as a key example, where Russian-linked troll farms and bots were deployed to sow discord and polarize society. Such operations are not limited to the West; Russia uses similar tactics in its near abroad to undermine neighboring states and reinforce its regional dominance.

Cyber-operations against Critical Infrastructure

Beyond disinformation, Russia has demonstrated the capability and willingness to target critical infrastructure. Cyber-attacks on Ukraine's power grid in 2015 and 2016 highlighted the ability of Russian actors to disrupt essential services with precision. These operations served both as tactical tools to weaken adversaries and as strategic signals of Russian power. Critical infrastructure attacks create psychological effects by instilling fear and uncertainty, while also showcasing Russia's readiness to escalate conflicts into the digital domain. By targeting energy systems, transportation networks, and communication hubs, Russia aims to pressure adversaries without resorting to full-scale military confrontation.

Espionage and Data Theft

Espionage remains another central pillar of Russian cyber strategy. Through sophisticated hacking campaigns, Russian actors infiltrate government agencies, research institutions, and private corporations to steal sensitive information. This data is often used to inform state policy, strengthen industrial competitiveness, or manipulate diplomatic negotiations. Operations such as the SolarWinds breach in 2020 demonstrated the scale and stealth of Russian cyber espionage, compromising thousands of networks worldwide. Unlike disruptive attacks, espionage campaigns are typically long-term and clandestine, aimed at building a reservoir of intelligence for strategic use.

Cyber Strategies in Hybrid Warfare

Russia integrates cyber-operations into broader hybrid warfare tactics, particularly in conflicts within its geopolitical neighborhood. In the war with Georgia in 2008 and during the annexation of Crimea in 2014, cyber-attacks accompanied military campaigns and political maneuvers. These operations disrupted communications, paralyzed government websites, and spread disinformation, magnifying the confusion on the battlefield. The ongoing war in Ukraine has further underscored Russia's reliance on hybrid strategies, where cyber-operations complement kinetic warfare. This integration demonstrates how cyberspace has become inseparable from conventional military strategies in Russia's playbook.

Global Reach and Strategic Ambitions

While Russia prioritizes operations in its immediate neighborhood, its cyber strategies are global in scope. Russian cyber actors have been implicated in campaigns targeting the United States, European Union, Asia, and even international organizations. By extending operations beyond regional boundaries, Russia signals its status as a global cyber power capable of challenging Western dominance. The international reach of these campaigns also enables Moscow to destabilize adversaries far from its borders, distracting them from Russian activities closer to home. Through global cyber engagement, Russia seeks to reshape international norms and assert itself as a central player in defining the rules of cyberspace.

Challenges of Attribution and Response

One of the strengths of Russian cyber strategies lies in the ambiguity they create. The use of proxies, false flags, and layered operations makes attribution extremely difficult. Even when strong evidence links attacks to Russian actors, Moscow routinely denies involvement, framing accusations as political manipulation. This denial strategy complicates international responses, as states hesitate to escalate conflicts without undeniable proof. Moreover, Russia exploits divisions within the international community, using the lack of consensus to its advantage. The challenge of attribution ensures that Russia can continue cyber-operations with relatively low risk of direct retaliation.

Implications for International Security

Russia's cyber strategies have profound implications for international security and global governance. They challenge the stability of democratic institutions, undermine trust in digital infrastructure, and blur the lines between war and peace. By normalizing aggressive cyber behavior, Russia contributes to an environment of insecurity where norms and rules are difficult to establish. The global community faces the challenge of responding effectively to these strategies without escalating tensions into open conflict. For NATO, the European Union, and other organizations, Russian cyber-activities have prompted discussions on collective defense, resilience, and deterrence in the digital age.

2.4.4 EU

The European Union's journey toward a cohesive and robust cyber strategy is a testament to its evolving understanding of digital threats in an increasingly interconnected world. This journey did not begin with a single grand declaration but has been a process of gradual, yet accelerating, integration and response to a shifting threat landscape. The foundational recognition was that cyberspace knows no borders; a attack on one member state's critical infrastructure could have cascading effects across the single market, disrupting economies, democracy, and daily life. Early initiatives focused on establishing basic frameworks for network and information security, but it was the escalating sophistication of cybercrime, state-sponsored attacks, and the weaponization of disinformation that catalyzed a more strategic and unified approach. The EU's strategy has matured from a technical concern handled by IT departments to a paramount geopolitical and economic imperative, central to the Union's ambitions for strategic autonomy and digital sovereignty.

Cornerstone of Resilience: The NIS Directive and its Successor

A pivotal moment in the EU's cyber defence architecture was the adoption of the Directive on Security of Network and Information Systems (NIS Directive) in 2016. This legislation represented the first EU-wide law on cyber-security, mandating a baseline of security and incident reporting obligations across member states. Its primary objective was to achieve a high common level of cyber-security resilience and response.

The Directive identified operators of essential services in sectors such as energy, transport, banking, and healthcare, as well as key digital service providers, requiring them to take appropriate security measures and report significant incidents to national authorities. While the NIS Directive was a crucial first step, its implementation revealed challenges, including inconsistent application across member states and a scope that quickly became outdated with the rapid digitalization of society. This led to the development of a strengthened successor, the NIS2 Directive, which expanded the range of sectors covered, introduced more stringent supervisory measures, and harmonized enforcement mechanisms, including sanctions, across the Union. This evolution underscores a commitment to adaptive and forward-looking regulation.

Unified Front: The Role of the European Union Agency for Cyber-security (ENISA)

The institutional heart of the EU's cyber strategy is the European Union Agency for Cyber-security, known as ENISA. Initially established with a limited mandate, ENISA's role has been significantly strengthened over time, reflecting the growing importance of a centralized hub for expertise and coordination. Based in Athens, ENISA acts as a centre of expertise, providing advice and recommendations to EU institutions, member states, and private businesses.

It facilitates operational cooperation between member states, organizes large-scale cyber-security exercises to test preparedness, and plays a key role in developing the European cyber-security certification framework. This framework is essential for building trust in the digital single market, ensuring that products, services, and processes meet agreed-upon security standards. By fostering a community of shared knowledge and best practices, ENISA helps to level the cyber-security playing field across the EU, ensuring that smaller member states have access to the same high-quality expertise and threat intelligence as larger ones.

Securing the Digital Decade: The EU Cyber-security Act and Certification

The EU Cyber-security Act, which came into full force in 2021, marked another significant leap forward. This regulation permanently established ENISA and endowed it with a stronger mandate and more resources to fulfil its mission. More importantly, it created a framework for EU-wide cyber-security certification schemes for digital products, services, and processes. The logic is straightforward yet powerful: in a market where consumers and businesses use countless connected devices and cloud services, trust is paramount. A certified product with a CE cyber-security marking would provide assurance that it has been assessed against rigorous EU security standards. This not only protects consumers but also benefits European companies by providing a clear standard to meet, potentially giving them a competitive advantage in the global market as a symbol of quality and security. The certification framework is a concrete manifestation of the EU's drive for digital sovereignty, aiming to reduce dependence on uncertified and potentially vulnerable technology from outside the bloc.

From Defence to Deterrence: The Cyber-diplomacy Toolbox

Recognizing that not all threats originate within its borders, the EU has developed a sophisticated external dimension to its cyber strategy, often referred to as its Cyber-diplomacy Toolbox. Adopted in 2017, this framework establishes a set of measures the EU can deploy to prevent, deter, and respond to malicious cyber-activities that target the Union or its member states. The Toolbox operates on the principle of a proportionate response and is grounded in the belief that international law applies in cyberspace. The most significant measure within this arsenal is the framework for targeted restrictive measures, or cyber sanctions. This allows the EU to impose travel bans and asset freezes on individuals and entities responsible for significant cyber attacks, regardless of their nationality or location. This ability to attribute attacks and impose tangible costs represents a major step in the EU's evolution from a purely defensive posture to one that incorporates elements of deterrence, sending a clear message that malicious cyber-activities will have consequences.

Fortifying the Digital Economy: The Critical Entities Resilience Directive

The digital and physical worlds are inextricably linked, and the EU's strategy reflects this reality. The Critical Entities Resilience Directive (CER Directive) complements the NIS2 Directive by focusing on the physical resilience of entities that are essential for the functioning of society and the economy. While NIS2 deals with digital infrastructure and cyber-incidents, the CER Directive ensures that critical entities, from power grids and water works to financial infrastructure and public administration, have robust physical security and business continuity plans in place. The directive acknowledges that a cyber attack can have devastating physical consequences, and a physical attack can cripple digital networks. This holistic approach ensures that the EU's resilience is not siloed but is integrated across the digital and physical domains, creating a more comprehensive security posture for the Union's most vital services.

Horizon of Challenges: AI, Disinformation, and Strategic Autonomy

Looking ahead, the EU's cyber strategies must continuously evolve to address emerging challenges. The rapid development and deployment of Artificial Intelligence present both opportunities for enhanced security and new threats, such as AI-powered cyber attacks or vulnerabilities in AI systems themselves. The EU's pioneering AI Act seeks to mitigate these risks by classifying and regulating high-risk AI applications. Furthermore, the battlefield of information has become a central concern, with cyber strategies now explicitly addressing foreign information manipulation and interference. Initiatives like the Digital Services Act aim to create a safer online environment by holding platforms accountable for systemic risks. Underpinning all these efforts is the persistent theme of strategic autonomy—the desire to reduce the EU's dependency on foreign technology and to assert its values and standards in the global digital order. This involves investing in homegrown innovation, securing digital supply chains, and promoting a global, open, and stable cyberspace based on the rule of law. The EU's cyber strategy is, therefore, not a static document but a dynamic and expanding framework, a continuous effort to build a secure, resilient, and sovereign digital future for all its citizens.

2.4.5 India

India's cyber strategies reflect the scale and complexity of a vast digital economy that now touches almost every citizen and enterprise. From digital identity and instant payments to smart infrastructure and cloud-first governance, India's transformation has created immense opportunity alongside concentrated risk. The strategic vision guiding cyber-security is therefore pragmatic and layered: protect critical systems and citizen data, build resilient digital public infrastructure, grow indigenous capabilities, and shape norms internationally, all while keeping the internet open, interoperable, and secure. This vision is carried forward by a web of institutions, laws, and operational playbooks that continue to evolve as threat actors, technologies, and geopolitics change.

Governance Architecture and Institutional Roles

Cyber-governance in India is distributed but increasingly coordinated. The Ministry of Electronics and Information Technology drives civilian cyber-security policy and anchors the Indian Computer Emergency Response Team, which monitors threats, issues advisories, and coordinates incident response across sectors. The National Critical Information Infrastructure Protection Centre under the National Technical Research Organisation serves as the nodal body for securing critical information infrastructure, working with designated sector leads to enforce baseline controls and conduct readiness exercises. The National Security Council Secretariat provides top-level coordination and threat assessment, including through the National Cyber Coordination Centre, which enhances situational awareness. On law enforcement, the Ministry of Home Affairs runs the Indian Cyber Crime Coordination Centre, funds cyber forensics and training, and operates the 1930 helpline and the National Cyber Crime Reporting Portal to accelerate citizen relief and recovery in online fraud. State-level computer emergency response teams and sectoral security operations centers complement this federal backbone, bringing incident response closer to assets and users.

Legal and Policy Frameworks

The legal foundation for cyberspace remains the Information Technology Act, 2000, as amended in 2008, which establishes cyber offenses, electronic records, and intermediary liability. Its subordinate rules, including the Intermediary Guidelines of 2021, push platforms to remove unlawful content expeditiously, enable traceability for specific orders on significant messengers, and maintain grievance redress mechanisms. Complementing this regime, the Digital Personal Data Protection Act, 2023, defines lawful processing of personal data, rights of data principals, and duties of data fiduciaries, and is being operationalized through rules and the Data Protection Board. Sectoral regulators such as the Reserve Bank of India, the Securities and Exchange Board of India, and the Insurance Regulatory and Development Authority enforce cyber-security frameworks tailored to financial stability and consumer protection, demanding controls such as multi-factor authentication, continuous monitoring, and incident reporting. A proposed Digital India Act aims to modernize the core statute for an era of artificial intelligence, deepfakes, and immersive technologies, signaling a shift toward risk-based, accountability-centered regulation that can adapt to fast-moving threats.

Critical Infrastructure and National Resilience

Protecting critical information infrastructure is central, given the potential cascading effects of disruptions in power, finance, telecom, transport, healthcare, and government services. The NCIIPC's sectoral risk assessments inform minimum security baselines, while regular red team exercises and drills stress-test preparedness. Government cloud adoption through the MeghRaj initiative and empanelled providers is paired with strict security accreditation, identity and access controls, and continuous monitoring architectures. Telecom networks, now transitioning to 5G and beyond, are governed by a trusted vendor framework to mitigate supply chain risks, while machine-to-machine and IoT security guidelines promote secure device identity, firmware integrity, and patchability. Across ministries and states, security operations centers are migrating to zero-trust principles, deploying identity-centric controls, endpoint detection and response, and encrypted micro-segmentation to limit blast radius.

Incident Reporting and Operational Playbooks

Operational doctrine emphasizes early visibility and rapid containment. CERT-In's 2022 directions require covered entities to report specified cyber-incidents within six hours and to maintain synchronized system clocks, standardized log retention, and designated points of contact, allowing faster correlation across cases. Data centers, cloud and virtual private server providers, and VPN operators are obligated to retain certain subscriber information for investigatory purposes, while virtual asset service providers must maintain know-your-customer records and transaction footprints. These rules aim to reduce dwell time and enhance attribution, even as industry seeks clarity and harmonization across overlapping obligations. Sectoral computer emergency response teams and industry information-sharing cells round out the ecosystem, enabling joint advisories, threat intelligence exchange, and coordinated response to supply chain compromises and ransomware campaigns.

Cybercrime Mitigation and Citizen Protection

With hundreds of millions using mobile payments and social platforms daily, India's cybercrime strategy prioritizes citizen protection and fraud mitigation. The 1930 helpline and interconnected bank and wallet nodal teams enable quick freezing of funds in transit, often within the so-called golden hours after a scam. The Indian Cyber Crime Coordination Centre funds labs, training, and analytics capabilities to support state police units on investigations ranging from business email compromise to sextortion and investment scams. Public awareness has been scaled through national campaigns, monthly cyber awareness observances, and partnerships with schools and universities to promote safe digital habits. Technical countermeasures such as tokenization in card payments, secure-by-default UPI clients, and anomaly detection for suspicious transactions complement legal and educational measures.

Defense and Deterrence in Cyberspace

On the national security side, the Defence Cyber Agency provides tri-service integration for cyber-defense and, where authorized, offensive cyber-operations, working alongside technical intelligence capabilities. The focus is on defending command-and-control networks, securing weapon systems and logistics software, and integrating cyber effects into joint operations planning within clear legal and oversight frameworks. Deterrence is pursued through resilience, credible response options, and law enforcement action against cyber-enabled crime, balanced by adherence to international law and the desire to avoid escalation. Partnerships with trusted allies for malware analysis, vulnerability research, and supply chain assurance are expanding, especially as software-defined systems become central to military readiness and strategic infrastructure.

Data Protection, Trust, and Encryption Debates

Building digital trust requires reconciling privacy, security, and lawful access. The DPDP Act articulates core rights for individuals and accountability duties for organizations, with cross-border data transfer policies expected to be risk-based and interoperable with global regimes. Encryption remains a bedrock for securing data at rest and in transit across government and industry, even as debates continue over platform traceability, metadata retention, and exceptional access for serious offenses. India's approach seeks to preserve strong encryption while exploring privacy-preserving compliance mechanisms such as secure enclaves, auditable key management, and tightly scoped, judicially overseen requests.

Technology Frontiers: AI, 5G, and Cloud

Emerging technologies change both the attack surface and the defense toolkit. The rapid rollout of 5G catalyzes edge computing, network slicing, and industrial IoT, demanding secure orchestration, robust identity for devices, and continuous verification across software supply chains. Artificial intelligence powers both intrusion and defense, with attackers automating reconnaissance and phishing at scale while defenders leverage anomaly detection, large-scale log analytics, and autonomous response playbooks. Cloud adoption continues under a shared-responsibility model, driving deployment of configuration baselines, posture management, confidential computing for sensitive workloads, and automated compliance as code. India's digital public infrastructure—Aadhaar, UPI, DigiLocker, and beyond—continues to harden its security posture with layered controls, red teaming, and independent audits to sustain trust at population scale.

Capacity Building and Public-Private Collaboration

A durable cyber strategy invests in people and partnerships. Skill development programs across universities, specialized institutes, and industry consortia are expanding the pipeline of defenders, threat analysts, and digital forensics specialists. Government-industry initiatives such as Cyber Surakshit Bharat and the Cyber Swachhta Kendra combine awareness, hygiene tooling, and managed services to elevate baseline security for small and medium enterprises and government departments. Startups and research labs increasingly contribute to domestic capability in areas such as endpoint protection, crypto-agility, secure silicon, and threat intelligence platforms, reducing dependency on opaque supply chains and tailoring solutions to Indian threat realities.

International Engagement and Norms

India engages multilaterally to shape a stable and secure cyberspace. It participates in United Nations processes on responsible state behavior and cybercrime, pursues bilateral and plurilateral cyber-security arrangements with partners in the Quad and beyond, and signs operational memoranda between incident response teams to accelerate collaboration. While India is not a party to the Budapest Convention, it has pursued practical cooperation through mutual legal assistance, joint exercises, and capacity-building, and supports the development of interoperable legal frameworks that respect sovereignty while enabling swift action against transnational cybercrime.

Challenges and the Road Ahead

The road ahead is defined by scale, speed, and sovereignty. Threat actors will continue to probe the seams between legacy systems and modern platforms, target software supply chains, and exploit human factors. India's response hinges on deeper adoption of zero trust, continuous control validation, and secure-by-design procurement; clearer, risk-based harmonization of overlapping compliance regimes; greater investment in open standards and indigenous tooling; and relentless emphasis on user-centric safety and rapid restitution. With a whole-of-society approach that blends legal certainty, operational excellence, technological innovation, and international cooperation, India's cyber strategies aim not only to manage risk but to unlock the full potential of its digital century.

2.5 CYBERCONFLICT, ESPIONAGE, AND CYBERWARFARE

The digital revolution has redefined the way states and non-state actors compete, collaborate, and confront each other. Cyberspace, once perceived primarily as a domain of communication and commerce, has now become a central arena of political, military, and economic rivalry. Cyberconflict, espionage, and cyberwarfare are three interconnected aspects of this evolving landscape. They encompass everything from covert surveillance and intelligence collection to disruptive operations that target critical infrastructure and influence public opinion. Cyberconflict, espionage, and cyberwarfare illustrate how the digital age has transformed the nature of rivalry between states and other actors. Espionage has expanded dramatically through cyberspace, allowing for massive-scale intelligence collection and economic theft. Cyberconflict operates in a gray zone, constantly undermining adversaries without triggering open war. Cyberwarfare, while not yet fully realized on a global scale, represents the potential integration of digital attacks into conventional military strategies. Together, these phenomena challenge existing frameworks of law, ethics, and security, forcing the world to confront a new era of uncertainty. As technology continues to evolve, the boundaries of conflict will shift further, and the task of ensuring stability in cyberspace will remain one of the central challenges for the international community.

2.5.1 Defining Cyberconflict

Cyberconflict refers to confrontations between actors in cyberspace that involve the use of digital tools to pursue political, military, or strategic goals. Unlike conventional conflicts that are fought with physical weapons, cyberconflicts are often characterized by stealth, speed, and deniability. They may occur between states, between states and non-state actors, or even within societies. Cyberconflict does not always involve destruction; it may include disinformation campaigns, website defacement, or the disruption of services. The essence of cyberconflict lies in its ambiguity. It often takes place below the threshold of declared war, making it difficult for international law and traditional security frameworks to address effectively.

2.5.2 Espionage in the Digital Age

Espionage has always been a cornerstone of statecraft, but in the digital age, it has expanded dramatically in scale and sophistication. Cyber espionage allows actors to penetrate government networks, research institutions, corporations, and even individual devices to steal sensitive information. The motivations behind cyber espionage range from acquiring military secrets to gaining competitive advantages in trade and technology. Unlike conventional spying, which required human agents and physical infiltration, cyber espionage can be conducted remotely and at a massive scale. Tools such as malware, phishing campaigns, and zero-day exploits provide cyber spies with unprecedented capabilities to collect intelligence.

2.5.3 State-Sponsored Espionage

One of the most concerning trends in cyber espionage is the active involvement of state actors. Governments now invest heavily in cyber capabilities to monitor adversaries and gather intelligence. State-sponsored espionage campaigns often target defense agencies, diplomatic communications, and advanced technological research.

Notable examples include campaigns attributed to Russia, China, the United States, and Iran, each using cyber espionage to secure strategic advantages. These operations can alter the balance of power by providing insights into military planning, political strategies, and economic developments. Moreover, stolen intellectual property can accelerate technological development, giving the sponsoring state a competitive edge.

2.5.4 Corporate Espionage and Economic Motives

Cyber espionage is not limited to military and political domains. Corporations are increasingly targeted by cyber spies seeking to steal trade secrets, proprietary research, and financial data. Economic espionage undermines competitiveness by allowing rivals to bypass years of research and development.

Multinational companies in fields such as pharmaceuticals, aerospace, and information technology are particularly vulnerable. State involvement is often suspected in corporate espionage, as governments may encourage or even direct cyber actors to support national industries. This creates a blurred boundary between state interests and private competition, making the problem of cyber espionage particularly complex.

2.5.5 Cyberwarfare as a Military Domain

Cyberwarfare goes beyond espionage and conflict in the digital space by directly integrating cyber capabilities into military operations. It involves the use of offensive cyber-tools to disrupt, degrade, or destroy adversary systems during conflicts. Unlike traditional warfare, cyberwarfare is not confined to physical battlefields; it can reach across borders instantly, striking targets anywhere in the world. Military doctrines increasingly recognize cyberspace as a domain of warfare alongside land, sea, air, and space. Nations are building cyber commands, training specialized units, and investing in both defensive and offensive cyber arsenals to prepare for the possibility of digital battle.

2.5.6 Tactics of Cyberwarfare

The tactics of cyberwarfare are diverse and adaptable. They may include distributed denial-of-service attacks to paralyze communication systems, malware that disables industrial control systems, or operations that manipulate data to mislead adversaries.

Cyberwarfare may also involve psychological operations, where disinformation is spread to weaken morale or sow confusion among enemy populations. Unlike conventional attacks, cyberwarfare can be launched with relative anonymity, making retaliation and deterrence complicated. Furthermore, cyber-operations can be synchronized with kinetic attacks to maximize their effectiveness, as seen in conflicts where communication networks were disabled just as military offensives began.

2.5.7 Cyberconflict below the Threshold of War

One of the defining characteristics of cyberconflict is that it often operates below the threshold of open warfare. States engage in continuous low-intensity cyber-operations that cause disruption without triggering military responses.

For example, cyber-intrusions into electoral systems, disinformation campaigns during political crises, or minor attacks on infrastructure are designed to weaken adversaries without provoking full-scale retaliation. This "gray zone" of conflict allows states to pursue their goals while avoiding direct confrontation. It also creates an environment of constant tension, where peace and conflict coexist in a fluid and uncertain manner.

2.5.8 Role of Non-State Actors

Non-state actors also play an important role in cyberconflict, espionage, and warfare. Hacktivist groups may launch cyber-attacks for ideological reasons, targeting governments or corporations they oppose. Terrorist organizations may attempt to exploit cyberspace for recruitment, propaganda, and potentially even offensive operations. Cybercriminals, while often motivated by profit, sometimes intersect with political goals, especially when they operate from countries where governments tolerate or even encourage their activities. The involvement of non-state actors complicates the cyber landscape, as attribution becomes difficult and responses become fragmented.

2.5.9 Challenges of Attribution

Attribution is one of the greatest challenges in cyberconflict, espionage, and warfare. Unlike conventional attacks, which leave visible evidence, cyber-operations can be disguised through false flags, proxies, and layered obfuscation techniques. Determining who carried out an attack requires technical forensics, intelligence gathering, and often political judgment. Even when strong evidence exists, states may hesitate to assign blame publicly due to the risk of escalating tensions. The difficulty of attribution undermines deterrence, as adversaries believe they can act with relative impunity in cyberspace.

2.5.10 Legal and Ethical Dilemmas

Cyberconflict raises complex legal and ethical questions. International law struggles to define acceptable behavior in cyberspace. For instance, should a cyber-attack on a power grid be considered an act of war, or is it a form of sabotage below the threshold of armed conflict? The Tallinn Manual, a scholarly attempt to apply international law to cyber-operations, reflects ongoing debates about proportionality, sovereignty, and state responsibility. Ethical dilemmas also emerge when considering the collateral impact of cyber-operations, as attacks on civilian infrastructure may harm innocent populations. The lack of universally accepted norms makes cyberspace a domain of uncertainty and contestation.

2.5.11 Implications for International Security

The rise of cyberconflict, espionage, and warfare has significant implications for global security. Traditional deterrence models, based on nuclear or conventional weapons, do not apply neatly in cyberspace. States must invest in resilience, defense, and intelligence to counter ongoing cyber-threats. Alliances such as NATO now consider cyber-attacks as potential triggers for collective defense, signaling the seriousness with which digital threats are treated. However, the absence of clear red lines and the constant activity below the threshold of war mean that cyberspace is likely to remain an arena of persistent competition. The potential for escalation, miscalculation, and unintended consequences makes cyberconflict one of the most pressing security challenges of the twenty-first century.

Comparative Analysis of Cyberconflict, Espionage, and Cyberwarfare

When comparing cyberconflict, espionage, and cyberwarfare, it is useful to consider their definitions, objectives, methods, actors involved, and implications for international security. Though interconnected, each represents a distinct aspect of activity in cyberspace.

In terms of definition, cyberconflict refers broadly to hostile or competitive interactions in cyberspace that may involve disruption, propaganda, or influence campaigns. Cyber espionage, on the other hand, is the covert collection of sensitive information through digital means, typically focused on intelligence gathering rather than immediate disruption. Cyberwarfare is the most escalated form, involving offensive digital operations designed to degrade or destroy an adversary's systems in the context of military conflict. The objectives of these activities further differentiate them. The primary goal of cyberconflict is to undermine trust, destabilize societies, or gain political advantage without crossing the threshold of armed war. Espionage seeks knowledge—political, military, or economic—that provides long-term strategic benefit to the actor conducting it. Cyberwarfare, however, aims to achieve decisive outcomes on the battlefield by neutralizing command, control, communications, or infrastructure, thus complementing or even replacing conventional weapons.

Methods also vary across the three. Cyberconflict often employs tactics such as website defacement, disinformation campaigns, or low-level denial-of-service attacks that send political signals but avoid major destruction. Espionage relies on stealthy methods including phishing, malware implants, and exploitation of zero-day vulnerabilities, all designed to remain hidden while extracting information. Cyberwarfare employs highly destructive tools such as logic bombs, worms, or tailored malware like Stuxnet that can disable industrial control systems or cause large-scale operational paralysis. The actors involved reflect differing levels of organization. Cyberconflict can be initiated by both state and non-state actors, including hacktivists or ideological groups, as well as governments that seek plausible deniability. Cyber espionage is predominantly state-driven, often carried out by intelligence agencies or state-supported groups, though corporations and private actors also engage in it for economic gain. Cyberwarfare, in contrast, is almost exclusively conducted by nation-states, since it requires advanced resources, coordination with military operations, and significant technical sophistication.

The implications for international security also diverge. Cyberconflict complicates diplomacy and governance by creating constant low-level tensions, eroding trust among states and between governments and their populations. Espionage threatens both national security and economic competitiveness, as the theft of military secrets or intellectual property alters strategic balances and undermines innovation. Cyberwarfare has the gravest consequences, as it can lead to widespread societal disruption, potentially causing casualties, paralyzing economies, and escalating into full-scale armed conflict.

2.5.12 Notable Attacks and Their Diplomatic Fallout

The Estonia Cyber-attacks of 2007

One of the earliest large-scale examples of cyberconflict occurred in Estonia in 2007. Following a political dispute over the relocation of a Soviet-era war memorial, Estonia was hit by massive distributed denial-of-service attacks that crippled government websites, financial institutions, and media outlets. While Moscow denied direct involvement, the attacks were widely attributed to Russian actors. The diplomatic fallout was significant. Estonia, a NATO member, appealed to the alliance for support, sparking discussions about whether cyber-attacks could trigger collective defense under Article 5 of the NATO treaty. Although NATO did not invoke Article 5, the incident galvanized efforts to strengthen cyber-defense capabilities within the alliance and led to the establishment of the NATO Cooperative Cyber Defence Centre of Excellence in Tallinn. The Estonia case demonstrated how cyberconflict could escalate political disputes into international crises and reshape alliance strategies.

The Stuxnet Attack on Iran's Nuclear Program

A landmark in the history of cyberwarfare was the discovery of the Stuxnet worm in 2010. This highly sophisticated malware, attributed to a joint U.S.-Israeli operation, targeted Iran's Natanz nuclear facility, causing centrifuges to malfunction while reporting false data to operators. Stuxnet marked the first known instance of a cyber-weapon being used to cause physical destruction in a critical infrastructure system. The diplomatic fallout was multifaceted. Iran denounced the attack as an act of aggression, escalating its mistrust of Western powers, while the United States and Israel neither confirmed nor denied responsibility. The incident also raised alarm globally, as it highlighted how cyber-operations could be weaponized to sabotage industrial systems. In the aftermath, states accelerated their cyber-defense programs, and debates intensified at the United Nations about the applicability of international law to cyber-attacks. Stuxnet blurred the boundary between espionage and warfare, setting a precedent for state use of cyber-tools as instruments of coercive diplomacy.

The Sony Pictures Hack of 2014

The attack on Sony Pictures in 2014 illustrated how cyber-operations can intersect with cultural politics and freedom of expression. Hackers calling themselves the "Guardians of Peace" infiltrated Sony's networks, stealing sensitive data, releasing embarrassing internal communications, and leaking unreleased films. The attack was linked to North Korea and was seen as retaliation for the planned release of The Interview, a satirical film about an assassination plot against Kim Jong-un. The diplomatic fallout was immediate. The United States accused North Korea of conducting the attack, leading to increased sanctions against Pyongyang. President Barack Obama publicly condemned the assault as an attempt to suppress free expression, framing it as a direct challenge to democratic values. This incident showed how cyber-operations could be used by authoritarian regimes to extend censorship beyond their borders, raising questions about sovereignty, cultural diplomacy, and the vulnerability of private corporations to state-driven cyber coercion.

The Office of Personnel Management Breach of 2015

In 2015, the United States discovered a massive breach of the Office of Personnel Management (OPM) in which sensitive records of over 21 million individuals were stolen. The breach included fingerprints, security clearance data, and background investigation records, making it one of the largest compromises of personal information in history. The attack was attributed to actors linked to China, though Beijing denied responsibility. The diplomatic fallout centered on U.S.-China relations, already strained by disputes over trade and the South China Sea. The breach underscored the scale of state-sponsored cyber espionage and led to high-level negotiations between Washington and Beijing. In 2015, President Obama and President Xi Jinping announced an agreement that neither government would conduct or knowingly support cyber-enabled theft of intellectual property for commercial advantage. Although questions remain about its implementation, the OPM breach catalyzed efforts to establish cyber norms between major powers and demonstrated how espionage campaigns can become catalysts for diplomatic dialogue.

The Democratic National Committee Hack of 2016

The 2016 U.S. presidential election became a flashpoint in the intersection of cyberconflict and political warfare. Hackers linked to Russian intelligence services infiltrated the Democratic National Committee (DNC), stealing emails and releasing them through platforms like WikiLeaks. At the same time, Russia orchestrated widespread disinformation campaigns on social media to sow division and influence voter perceptions. The diplomatic fallout was profound. The United States accused Russia of interfering in its democratic process, leading to sanctions, the expulsion of diplomats, and heightened tensions between Washington and Moscow. The incident also triggered debates within NATO and the European Union about the resilience of democratic institutions against digital manipulation. Internationally, it raised alarm about the vulnerability of elections worldwide, with many states introducing new cyber-security measures to protect electoral systems. The DNC hack highlighted the fusion of cyber espionage, influence operations, and geopolitical rivalry, marking a turning point in how states perceive threats to democracy in the digital age.

The NotPetya Attack of 2017

In 2017, the world witnessed one of the most destructive cyber-attacks to date with the spread of the NotPetya malware. Initially disguised as ransomware, NotPetya was designed to cause irreversible destruction rather than financial gain. It originated in Ukraine, crippling banks, energy companies, and government institutions, but quickly spread globally, causing billions of dollars in damages to multinational corporations. Western governments, including the United States and the United Kingdom, attributed the attack to Russian military intelligence, though Russia denied involvement. The diplomatic fallout included coordinated condemnation by multiple states, renewed sanctions on Russia, and calls for stronger international cooperation in cyber-security. NotPetya underscored the risks of cyber-attacks spiraling out of control, affecting states and corporations far beyond their intended targets. It also reinforced the idea that cyberwarfare has global consequences, potentially destabilizing international commerce and economic security.

The SolarWinds Supply Chain Compromise of 2020

The SolarWinds attack, discovered in late 2020, represented a new level of sophistication in cyber espionage. Hackers inserted malicious code into updates of SolarWinds' Orion software, which was used by thousands of organizations, including U.S. government agencies, Fortune 500 companies, and critical infrastructure providers. The operation, attributed to Russian intelligence, went undetected for months and provided access to vast amounts of sensitive data. The diplomatic fallout was significant. The United States accused Russia of orchestrating the breach, imposing sanctions and expelling diplomats in retaliation. The incident also sparked global concern about the vulnerability of supply chains and the interconnectedness of digital ecosystems. Unlike disruptive attacks, SolarWinds highlighted the long-term strategic dimension of espionage, demonstrating how patient and covert infiltration could yield enormous intelligence dividends. Diplomatically, it reinforced calls for international norms on cyber espionage, though divisions between major powers remain unresolved.

Broader Diplomatic Consequences of Cyber-attacks

The cumulative effect of these notable cyber-incidents has been to elevate cyber-security to a central issue in international diplomacy. Cyber-attacks now feature prominently in bilateral and multilateral discussions, from U.S.-Russia summits to United Nations debates. They have led to sanctions, expulsions of diplomats, and in some cases, limited agreements on cyber norms. However, the ambiguity of cyberspace complicates diplomacy, as states often deny involvement and exploit attribution challenges to avoid accountability. Moreover, cyber-attacks have exposed the lack of comprehensive international law governing digital operations. While frameworks such as the Tallinn Manual attempt to apply existing legal principles, there remains no universally accepted treaty defining the rules of engagement in cyberspace.

CHAPTER 3

Norms, Laws, and Ethics in Cyber-Diplomacy

3.1 INTERNATIONAL LAW IN CYBERSPACE

3.1.1 The UN Charter and Cyber Norms

The UN Charter and emerging cyber norms together form the foundation of international law in cyberspace. While the Charter provides enduring principles of sovereignty, non-intervention, and prohibition of force, its application to digital operations is fraught with ambiguity. Cyber norms developed through UN processes and regional initiatives offer guidance but remain non-binding and contested. The diplomatic fallout from notable cyber-incidents underscores both the urgency and the difficulty of establishing clear rules of the road.

As states continue to grapple with cyberconflict, espionage, and warfare, the interplay between the UN Charter and cyber norms will remain central to shaping order and stability in the digital age. Building consensus, enhancing attribution capabilities, and reinforcing accountability will be essential for ensuring that cyberspace develops not as a lawless frontier but as a domain governed by shared principles of responsibility and restraint.

Looking ahead, the evolution of cyber norms and the application of the UN Charter to cyberspace will continue to shape global security. The challenge lies in balancing flexibility with clarity. Too rigid a legal framework may become obsolete in the face of technological change, while excessive ambiguity allows states to exploit loopholes. Multilateral dialogue, confidence-building measures, and incremental agreements are likely pathways forward. Efforts to harmonize national and regional strategies with UN principles may gradually build a more coherent system. Ultimately, the effectiveness of international law in cyberspace will depend not only on legal texts but also on the political will of states to respect and uphold them.

UN Charter as a Legal Foundation

The UN Charter, signed in 1945, establishes the principles of sovereignty, territorial integrity, and non-interference that govern relations among states. It sets out the prohibition on the use of force under Article 2(4), the right to self-defense under

Article 51, and the role of the Security Council in maintaining international peace and security. While drafted in a pre-digital era, the Charter provides a framework that many argue applies equally to cyberspace. Cyber-attacks that cause physical damage or loss of life may fall under the prohibition of force, while less destructive operations raise questions about whether they constitute violations of sovereignty or unlawful intervention. The challenge lies in interpreting the Charter's provisions in light of new technological realities, as cyberspace often operates in a legal and political gray zone.

Sovereignty and Non-Intervention in Cyberspace

One of the most contentious issues is the principle of sovereignty in the digital domain. States traditionally enjoy exclusive authority over activities within their territory, but cyber-operations often traverse borders in milliseconds. Questions arise about whether a cyber intrusion into another state's networks, even without physical damage, constitutes a violation of sovereignty. Similarly, the principle of non-intervention prohibits coercive interference in the internal affairs of another state, particularly in areas such as political independence. Cyber-operations targeting elections, media ecosystems, or political institutions have been widely criticized as breaches of this principle. Yet there is no consensus among states on the threshold at which a cyber-operation becomes unlawful under international law. Some states argue that only actions causing significant harm to essential functions violate sovereignty, while others consider any unauthorized intrusion a breach.

Prohibition of the Use of Force

Article 2(4) of the UN Charter prohibits the use of force against the territorial integrity or political independence of any state. Applying this provision to cyberspace has generated significant debate. Cyber-operations that disable power grids, sabotage industrial systems, or cause casualties may clearly amount to uses of force. However, operations that result only in temporary disruption or financial loss are more difficult to categorize. The Tallinn Manual on the International Law Applicable to Cyber-operations, produced by an independent group of experts, suggests that cyber-operations can constitute a use of force if their scale and effects are comparable to traditional kinetic attacks. Yet this interpretation is not universally accepted. The ambiguity surrounding the use of force in cyberspace creates both flexibility and risk, as states may exploit the uncertainty to pursue aggressive actions without triggering legal accountability.

Right of Self-Defense

Article 51 of the UN Charter affirms the inherent right of states to self-defense in the event of an armed attack. Whether cyber-attacks qualify as armed attacks is a matter of intense debate. If a cyber-operation results in destruction, casualties, or severe disruption, many argue that it would justify defensive measures, including potentially kinetic responses. However, the vast majority of cyber-incidents fall short of such catastrophic consequences, leaving states uncertain about when they can legally invoke self-defense. This ambiguity complicates deterrence and escalation management, as adversaries may calculate that their actions will not provoke a forceful response. At the same time, the prospect of states interpreting cyber-intrusions as armed attacks raises the danger of disproportionate responses, potentially escalating conflicts into broader confrontations.

Role of the UN Security Council

The Security Council is tasked with maintaining international peace and security, including the authority to determine threats and authorize collective measures. Yet its role in cyberspace remains limited. The Council has occasionally discussed cyber-threats, particularly in relation to critical infrastructure and terrorism, but it has not developed binding resolutions specific to cyber-operations. The political divisions among permanent members, many of whom are themselves leading cyber powers, hinder consensus. Nevertheless, the Security Council remains a potential platform for addressing large-scale cyber-attacks that threaten international stability. Its inaction highlights the broader challenge of applying traditional institutions to the rapidly evolving cyber domain.

Emergence of Cyber Norms

Beyond formal international law, states have sought to establish norms of responsible behavior in cyberspace. Cyber norms represent voluntary, non-binding principles that shape expectations and reduce the risk of conflict. The United Nations has played a central role in this process through its Groups of Governmental Experts (GGE) and Open-Ended Working Group (OEWG) initiatives. These forums have produced reports affirming that existing international law applies to cyberspace and recommending norms such as refraining from attacking critical infrastructure during peacetime, avoiding interference with computer emergency response teams, and cooperating on incident response. While these norms lack binding force, they contribute to building shared understanding and confidence among states, laying the groundwork for future legal frameworks.

Divergent Views on International Law in Cyberspace

Despite progress in developing cyber norms, states remain divided over how international law applies. Western countries, particularly the United States and European Union members, generally affirm that the UN Charter applies fully to cyberspace and emphasize norms of restraint and accountability. Russia and China, however, advocate for greater state control over the internet and propose new international treaties specifically addressing information security. These differences reflect broader geopolitical rivalries and competing visions of cyberspace governance. The lack of consensus hampers the development of binding rules, leaving cyberspace as an arena of contested interpretations and strategic ambiguity.

Regional Approaches and National Strategies

In addition to UN efforts, regional organizations and individual states have developed their own approaches to cyber law and norms. NATO has declared cyberspace a domain of operations and affirmed that cyber-attacks could trigger collective defense. The European Union has advanced regulatory measures to improve resilience and promote responsible state behavior. Meanwhile, countries such as the United States, China, and Russia have articulated national cyber strategies that reveal differing priorities, from defending critical infrastructure to asserting sovereignty over information flows. These regional and national efforts contribute to a fragmented but evolving legal landscape, where multiple frameworks interact with UN principles.

Challenges of Attribution and Enforcement

Even with norms and legal principles, enforcement in cyberspace faces major hurdles. Attribution of cyber-attacks is technically and politically challenging, as attackers often conceal their identity or use proxies. Without clear attribution, holding states accountable under international law is difficult. Furthermore, the decentralized nature of cyberspace complicates enforcement, as attacks can be launched from anywhere in the world and may involve non-state actors. Sanctions, diplomatic protests, and public attributions are common responses, but they lack the consistency and authority of binding legal judgments. This enforcement gap undermines the effectiveness of international law in deterring malicious cyber behavior.

3.1.2 The Tallinn Manual on International Law and Cyber-operations

The advent of the digital age presented a profound challenge to the international legal order: how does centuries-old law, designed for a world of physical borders and kinetic weapons, apply to the nebulous and borderless realm of cyberspace? This question became increasingly urgent for NATO members and their allies as they faced a rising tide of sophisticated state-sponsored cyber-operations. In response to this legal lacuna, following significant cyber-incidents against Estonian infrastructure in 2007, the NATO Cooperative Cyber Defence Centre of Excellence (CCDCOE), based in Tallinn, initiated a groundbreaking project. The goal was not to create new law but to clarify how existing international law, particularly the law governing the use of force (jus ad bellum) and international humanitarian law (IHL) or the law of armed conflict (jus in bello), applies to cyber-operations.

Threshold of Force: The Prohibition of Intervention and the Use of Force

A central and highly consequential contribution of the Tallinn Manual is its analysis of when a cyber-operation violates the prohibition of intervention in the sovereign affairs of another state or even rises to the level of an unlawful "use of force" as prohibited by Article 2(4) of the UN Charter. The manual affirms that the core legal principles of sovereignty and non-intervention apply in cyberspace. A cyber-operation that interferes with inherently governmental functions, such as the conduct of elections or the operation of critical national infrastructure, could constitute a violation of international law, even if it does not cause physical damage or injury.

The manual's examination of what constitutes a "use of force" is particularly nuanced. The experts agreed that while espionage alone typically does not qualify, cyber-operations that cause death, serious injury, or significant destruction would likely cross this threshold. More difficult are the cases in between, such as a operation that cripples a nation's financial system for weeks. The manual provides factors for consideration, including the severity of the operation, its immediacy, directness, invasiveness, and measurability of effects, offering a crucial, though sometimes debated, framework for states to assess the legality of hostile cyber acts.

Most Serious Acts: Cyber-operations and the Law of Armed Conflict

The manual's most detailed guidance pertains to the application of International Humanitarian Law, the legal regime that governs the conduct of parties during an armed conflict. The Tallinn Manual 2.0, the updated and expanded edition, makes a critical distinction between the law that applies to cyber-operations below the threshold of armed conflict and the law that applies during an actual armed conflict. It confirms that IHL only applies to cyber-operations that are part of an ongoing armed conflict, whether international or non-international in character.

A pivotal concept it addresses is the definition of a "cyber-attack" within the meaning of IHL. Contrary to colloquial use, an IHL "attack" is defined by its consequences: it must be an act of violence, whether in offense or defense, whose primary purpose is to cause death, injury, or destruction. Therefore, a cyber-operation that causes a widespread electrical blackout would qualify as an attack, while one that temporarily defaces a government website would not. This distinction carries immense operational significance, as the rules of distinction, proportionality, and precaution only attach fully to operations qualifying as "attacks."

Principles on the Digital Battlefield: Distinction, Proportionality, and Precautions

Within an armed conflict, the Tallinn Manual meticulously applies the core principles of IHL to cyber-warfare. The principle of distinction, which requires combatants to always distinguish between civilians and combatants and between civilian objects and military objectives, is paramount. The manual states that cyber weapons must be designed and used to avoid indiscriminate effects and that directly targeting civilian cyber infrastructure is prohibited unless it is being used for military purposes. The manual also affirms that the principle of proportionality applies fully to cyber-attacks. This prohibits launching an attack that may be expected to cause incidental loss of civilian life, injury to civilians, or damage to civilian objects that would be excessive in relation to the concrete and direct military advantage anticipated. This is particularly complex in cyberspace due to the interconnected nature of networks, where an attack on a military target could cascade into catastrophic civilian disruption. Furthermore, the manual outlines the obligation to take constant precautions in attack, including verifying targets are not civilian and choosing means and methods of cyber-warfare to minimize collateral damage.

Sovereign Responses: The Law of State Responsibility and Countermeasures

Beyond the law of armed conflict, the Tallinn Manual provides essential guidance on the peacetime law of state responsibility. It establishes that a cyber-operation is attributable to a state if it is conducted by state organs or by actors acting under the state's instructions or under its effective control. This attribution is the essential first step for holding a state legally accountable for a malicious cyber-operation. For acts that violate international law but do not rise to the level of an armed attack, the manual outlines the legal pathway of countermeasures. A state that is the victim of an internationally wrongful cyber act may, under strict conditions, take proportionate countermeasures that would otherwise be unlawful. These measures must be designed to induce the wrongdoing state to comply with its legal obligations and must be temporary and reversible. The manual's rules on countermeasures provide a legal justification for a victim state to, for example, launch a disruptive cyber-operation back against the aggressor state's infrastructure as a form of lawful retaliation, a concept that provides states with a critical tool short of war.

Manual's Legacy: Influence, Critique, and the Future of Cyber Norms

The Tallinn Manual's influence extends far beyond academic circles. It has become a foundational reference point for military lawyers, diplomats, and policymakers worldwide, providing a common vocabulary and a structured legal framework for discussing state behaviour in cyberspace. Many nations, including the United States and the United Kingdom, have publicly stated that they view the manual as an authoritative reflection of how international law applies and have incorporated its principles into their own military doctrines and cyber strategies. However, the manual is not without its critics. Some states, including China and Russia, argue that it represents the views of a Western-centric group of experts and that new binding treaties, rather than the application of existing law, are needed to govern cyberspace.

Others note that the manual's experts did not always achieve consensus, leaving certain issues, like the legality of countermeasures that infringe upon third-party states, unresolved. Despite these critiques, the Tallinn Manual's greatest achievement is its undeniable role in launching and structuring the global conversation on international law in cyberspace. It stands as the first and most comprehensive effort to build a bridge between the analog foundations of international law and the digital realities of the 21st century, providing an indispensable guide for navigating this uncharted and increasingly contested domain.

3.2 GLOBAL NORMS DEVELOPMENT

3.2.1 UN Group of Governmental Experts (UNGGE)

The United Nations Group of Governmental Experts on developments in the field of information and telecommunications in the context of international security was created to help states navigate the strategic, legal, and practical implications of state behavior in cyberspace. Its roots trace back to a 1998 General Assembly resolution that first placed information security on the multilateral agenda. From that foundation, the UN Secretary-General has periodically convened small, geographically balanced groups of national experts to study emerging threats, consider cooperative measures, and advise the General Assembly on how international security principles translate to the digital domain. The UNGGE operates under the First Committee on disarmament and international security, which situates cyberspace alongside other strategic stability issues and underscores that peace and stability increasingly depend on reliable digital infrastructure and responsible state conduct online.

Evolution of the Process

Over two decades, the UNGGE process has moved from cautious exploration to substantive convergence. Early groups helped establish shared terminology and mapped the contours of risk as more state functions migrated into networked systems. A pivotal shift occurred in the 2012–2013 cycle when the group reached consensus that international law, and in particular the UN Charter, applies to state behavior in cyberspace. That seemingly simple statement had far-reaching implications because it anchored cyberspace within existing rules governing sovereignty, non-intervention, and the prohibition on the use of force. The 2014–2015 group built on this momentum, producing a landmark consensus report that set out voluntary, non-binding norms of responsible state behavior, along with recommendations on confidence-building measures and capacity-building. A subsequent cycle in 2016–2017 could not reach consensus on its report, reflecting deep debates over how specific legal doctrines apply to cyber-operations. The process resumed and culminated in a 2019–2021 report that reaffirmed earlier understandings, offered guidance on implementing norms, and developed common understandings on how international law applies, even while acknowledging ongoing differences in interpretation.

Norms of Responsible State Behavior

The 2015 report is best known for articulating a set of voluntary norms that define what responsible conduct by states looks like in peacetime. Without listing them exhaustively, the norms coalesce around protecting civilian critical infrastructure that provides essential services, maintaining the integrity of computer emergency response teams by refraining from targeting them, fostering secure supply chains, promoting responsible vulnerability disclosure, and assisting other states in investigating and mitigating malicious activity that emanates from one's territory.

These norms do not replace international law, nor do they give license to malicious conduct that falls below armed conflict thresholds. Instead, they reduce risk by setting expectations for restraint, cooperation, and transparency, and by creating a vocabulary that states and regional organizations can translate into practical measures. The 2019–2021 report did not reopen the norms but elaborated how states might implement them, for example by developing processes for coordinated vulnerability disclosure, safeguarding electoral infrastructure, and improving cross-border incident communication.

International Law and Legal Debates

A central contribution of the UNGGE has been to situate cyberspace within existing international law. The 2013 consensus affirmed applicability of the UN Charter, which in turn implicates bedrock principles such as sovereignty, the prohibition of the use of force, peaceful settlement of disputes, and non-intervention in the internal affairs of other states. Subsequent reports grappled with how doctrines like due diligence, state responsibility, and attribution operate in practice when activity may be covert, deniable, or routed through third countries.

The 2019–2021 report recorded common understandings and a diversity of views on topics including when a cyber-operation might violate sovereignty, how countermeasures and necessity principles might apply, what thresholds distinguish unlawful intervention from permissible influence, and how international humanitarian law and international human rights law bear on cyber-operations in situations of armed conflict. Rather than codifying new law, the UNGGE has clarified that existing frameworks are relevant and has encouraged states to publish national positions that deepen shared understanding and signal how they interpret and intend to apply the law.

Confidence-Building and Risk Reduction

Beyond norms and law, the UNGGE has consistently promoted practical measures that reduce the risk of misperception and escalation. Confidence-building proposals encourage transparency about national strategies and doctrine, exchanges of points of contact among relevant agencies, voluntary incident communication channels, and joint exercises that test procedures before crises occur. These recommendations have influenced regional arrangements in organizations such as the Organization for Security and Co-operation in Europe, the Organization of American States, and the ASEAN Regional Forum, where states have created directories of cyber-diplomacy contacts, shared best practices, and run cyber incident tabletop exercises. While these steps are modest compared to treaty obligations, they can be consequential at moments of tension by providing trusted pathways for clarification and assistance and by building habits of cooperation that make hostile miscalculations less likely.

Capacity-Building and Inclusivity

The UNGGE has underscored that global stability depends on all states being able to prevent, detect, and respond to malicious cyber activity. Capacity-building is framed as demand-driven, sustainable, and respectful of human rights and national priorities, rather than as a vehicle for geopolitical leverage. The reports encourage sharing of technical expertise, development of national strategies and incident response capabilities, establishment of computer emergency response teams, and wider participation in international exercises and information-sharing networks. Attention has increasingly turned to the needs of developing countries and small states that face acute exposure but limited resources, with an emphasis on aligning capacity-building with the norms framework so that assistance simultaneously improves security and advances responsible behavior.

Relationship to the Open-Ended Working Group

In parallel with the UNGGE, the General Assembly established an Open-Ended Working Group that is open to all Member States, reflecting a desire for inclusivity in a domain that affects every country. The first OEWG concluded in 2021 with a consensus report broadly aligned with the UNGGE's outcomes, and a second OEWG is continuing work on norms implementation, confidence-building, capacity-building, and regular institutional dialogue. The two tracks have increasingly been described as complementary, with the UNGGE offering focused, expert-level negotiation and the OEWG providing a forum for wider participation and transparency. Building on this convergence, many states have advocated a permanent, action-oriented Program of Action to move beyond episodic mandates and provide a standing platform for implementation and cooperation.

Critiques and Legitimacy

Despite its achievements, the UNGGE has drawn criticism on several fronts. Its limited membership and closed-door negotiations have raised concerns about legitimacy and representation, especially among states that were not at the table but are expected to implement outcomes. The non-binding character of the norms and the absence of dedicated compliance mechanisms have prompted questions about real-world impact, particularly as high-profile incidents, ransomware campaigns, and supply chain compromises continue to proliferate. Differing legal interpretations persist, and geopolitical tensions can spill into the process, complicating consensus. The group has responded in part by encouraging national legal positions, inviting informal stakeholder consultations, and focusing on implementation guidance, but sustained progress ultimately depends on states translating commitments into policy, doctrine, and operational restraint.

Implementation in Practice

The test of the UNGGE's value lies in how states and regional bodies operationalize its guidance. Many have integrated the norms into national strategies, developed vulnerability disclosure programs, and strengthened the institutional independence and protection of incident response teams. Regional points-of-contact networks now exist to facilitate rapid communication during incidents, and transparency measures such as publishing national cyber strategies and legal positions contribute to predictability. International organizations and research institutes have created repositories to track state practice, which in turn informs future negotiations and helps identify gaps. While implementation is uneven and sometimes symbolic, the steady accumulation of practices aligned with the norms framework creates expectations of behavior and provides reference points for diplomatic engagement when those expectations are breached.

3.2.2 Open-Ended Working Group (OEWG)

The Open-Ended Working Group on security of and in the use of information and communications technologies emerged from a recognition that cyber stability cannot be built by a small circle alone. While earlier expert groups advanced vital groundwork, many Member States sought a forum that reflected the universality of the UN, where every country could table views, test proposals, and share concerns. The General Assembly responded by mandating an inclusive process to examine how international law applies in cyberspace, to refine norms of responsible state behavior, and to promote practical measures that reduce risks of miscalculation and conflict. The OEWG's open format was intended not only to broaden legitimacy but also to bring a wider range of experiences to the table, particularly from regions where digital transformation is rapid but defensive capacity is still maturing.

Mandate and Scope

The OEWG's mandate spans the core pillars of the international cyber stability framework. It considers voluntary, non-binding norms that guide state behavior in peacetime, examines the application of the UN Charter and wider international law to cyber-operations, and develops confidence-building measures and capacity-building approaches tailored to national and regional needs. It also explores modalities for regular institutional dialogue, recognizing that threats and technologies evolve too quickly for sporadic processes. Importantly, the OEWG's remit is distinct from negotiations on cybercrime, which proceed in a separate track focused on criminal law cooperation. By centering security and stability among states, the OEWG addresses the strategic layer of cyberspace where misperception or reckless action could have systemic consequences.

First OEWG: Establishing a Baseline

The first OEWG cycle concluded with a consensus report that accomplished three foundational tasks. It reaffirmed that international law applies to state conduct in cyberspace, anchoring the discussion in existing principles rather than inventing a parallel legal universe. It endorsed and elaborated the voluntary norms previously articulated by expert groups, translating abstract principles into suggested practices such as protecting the integrity of computer emergency response teams and cooperating across borders to mitigate malicious activity. It also brought a broader set of states into the conversation, experimenting with modalities to hear from industry, civil society, and the technical community. This early success showed that inclusivity and consensus could coexist, even amid divergent geopolitical views.

Ongoing OEWG: From Principles to Practice

A subsequent, multi-year OEWG has focused on implementation and operationalization. Meeting in regular sessions and intersessional consultations, it has produced annual progress reports that track convergence and record areas of continuing debate. The group has encouraged states to publish national positions on international law, to stand up or strengthen national computer emergency response capabilities, and to identify points of contact for crisis communication. It has explored how coordinated vulnerability disclosure can be institutionalized, how elections infrastructure should be safeguarded, and how to promote security in supply chains without fragmenting global markets. The chair has prioritized transparency and constructive engagement, seeking to transform agreed norms into sustained habits of responsible behavior.

Norms, Law, and the Emerging Acquis

A central output of the OEWG is an emerging acquis that blends non-binding norms with shared legal understandings. States have converged on protecting critical infrastructure that delivers essential services to the public, refraining from targeting incident response teams, and cooperating to address malicious activity emanating from their territory consistent with domestic and international law.

Legal discussions have probed how sovereignty, non-intervention, due diligence, and state responsibility apply when cyber-operations are covert, cross-jurisdictional, or routed through compromised systems. While not every interpretive question has been settled, the OEWG has encouraged states to articulate positions in public, creating transparency that helps manage expectations and reduces the risk of escalation borne of misunderstanding.

Confidence-Building and Points of Contact

Risk reduction in cyberspace begins with communication. The OEWG has prioritized confidence-building measures that increase transparency and create channels for clarification during incidents. Proposals have included establishing a global directory of national points of contact for cyber-incidents, encouraging states to publish doctrines and strategies, and running tabletop exercises that test crisis communication before a real emergency occurs.

These measures draw on successful regional practices and seek to globalize them. The logic is simple but compelling: when systems fail or indicators suggest a hostile act, rapid dialogue between designated counterparts can distinguish accident from intent, coordinate mitigation, and prevent political reactions that exacerbate technical problems.

Capacity-Building and Bridging the Digital Divide

For many states, the immediate challenge is not abstruse legal doctrine but the practical capacity to prevent, detect, and respond to cyber-threats. The OEWG has emphasized that capacity-building should be demand-driven, transparent, and aligned with human rights and development priorities. It encourages assistance that helps countries develop national strategies, establish incident response capabilities, adopt best practices for risk management, and participate in information-sharing communities. The group has also highlighted the need for sustainable financing, regional hubs of excellence, and mechanisms to measure the impact of assistance. By integrating capacity-building into the stability agenda, the OEWG links security with inclusion, recognizing that vulnerabilities anywhere can become risks everywhere.

Multi-Stakeholder Participation

Although the OEWG is intergovernmental, it acknowledges that states alone cannot secure the digital ecosystem. The private sector builds and operates much of the internet's infrastructure, the technical community sets standards, and civil society brings expertise on rights and accountability. The group has therefore experimented with consultations that allow non-state stakeholders to share research, operational insights, and implementation ideas. Participation remains a contested space, with some delegations advocating broader access and others favoring tighter controls, but the trajectory is toward greater transparency and engagement. When stakeholders can present evidence on real-world attack trends, supply chain risks, or effective disclosure practices, the resulting recommendations tend to be more grounded and actionable.

Relationship with UNGGE and the Program of Action Proposal

The OEWG does not supplant the work of the Group of Governmental Experts; rather, the two tracks have become mutually reinforcing. Expert groups distilled principles and identified norms, while the OEWG widened participation and emphasized implementation. Building on this complementarity, many states have rallied around the idea of a permanent, action-oriented Program of Action to carry the agenda forward beyond episodic mandates. A Program of Action could provide predictable cycles of reporting, peer exchange, and targeted assistance, anchored in the acquis of norms, law, confidence-building, and capacity-building. The OEWG has provided a forum to refine this proposal, debate its governance, and consider how to align it with existing regional and global efforts.

Challenges, Politics, and Contested Concepts

Progress has not been linear. Deep differences persist over how sovereignty applies to cyber-operations, whether and how to reference international humanitarian law in peacetime-focused discussions, and how to balance national security with the free flow of information. Some states argue for stronger emphasis on content regulation and information integrity, while others insist the OEWG remain focused on technical and operational security. Multi-stakeholder access has been uneven, and geopolitical tensions have occasionally spilled onto the negotiating floor. Even so, the OEWG has repeatedly found consensus language that preserves space for continued cooperation, demonstrating that pragmatic risk reduction can advance even amid strategic rivalry.

Measuring Impact and Practical Outcomes

The OEWG's value is ultimately judged by what changes on the ground. Indicators of progress include the growing number of states publishing national legal positions, the expansion of national and sectoral incident response capabilities, and the translation of norms into operational policies such as vulnerability disclosure programs or protections for emergency response teams. Regional organizations have borrowed and adapted OEWG recommendations, standing up directories of points of contact and running cross-border exercises. International research institutes maintain repositories that track state practice, creating feedback loops between policy and implementation. These steps are incremental and sometimes uneven, but over time they build expectations of behavior that enable more precise diplomatic responses when those expectations are breached.

3.3 ETHICS OF STATE BEHAVIOR IN CYBERSPACE

3.3.1 Proportionality

Proportionality in cyberspace is not merely a legal requirement but a moral imperative for states seeking to maintain stability in an increasingly digital world. The principle demands that states carefully weigh the necessity, scope, and potential consequences of their cyber-operations, ensuring that responses to threats do not inflict disproportionate harm. While legal frameworks provide a foundation, ethical considerations—rooted in just war theory, human rights, and the prevention of unnecessary suffering—must guide state behavior. As cyber-threats evolve, so too must the application of proportionality, adapting to new technologies and geopolitical realities while upholding the fundamental goal of minimizing harm and preserving global digital security. The challenge for policymakers, legal scholars, and ethicists is to refine these principles in ways that are both practical and principled, ensuring that the digital domain remains governed by restraint as much as by capability.

As cyber capabilities advance, the ethical and legal debates around proportionality will only intensify. The rise of artificial intelligence in cyber-warfare, for instance, introduces new complexities—autonomous cyber weapons may act faster than human decision-makers can assess proportionality, raising concerns about unintended escalation. Similarly, the increasing interdependence of global digital infrastructure means that even localized cyber-operations could have far-reaching consequences, demanding greater foresight in proportionality assessments. Future international discussions must address these challenges, potentially through new norms, transparency measures, or even treaty-based limitations on certain types of cyber-operations to ensure that state behavior remains both effective and ethically sound.

Legal Foundations of Proportionality

Proportionality is deeply embedded in international law, particularly in the principles governing the use of force and armed conflict. The United Nations Charter prohibits the use of force except in self-defense or when authorized by the

Security Council, and even then, responses must be proportionate to the threat faced. The law of armed conflict, including the Geneva Conventions, further refines this principle by requiring that military actions avoid excessive harm to civilians and civilian infrastructure. In cyberspace, these legal frameworks apply, but their interpretation is contested. Some states argue that cyber-operations must meet the same thresholds of proportionality as kinetic attacks, while others contend that the unique characteristics of cyber-warfare—such as reversibility, non-destructive effects, and indirect consequences—demand a nuanced application of the principle.

Ethical Dimensions of Proportionality

Beyond legal obligations, proportionality in cyberspace is fundamentally an ethical question. States must consider not only whether an action is lawful but also whether it is morally justifiable. Ethical proportionality requires weighing the intended benefits of a cyber-operation against its potential collateral damage, including unintended disruptions to civilian life, economic stability, and global digital infrastructure. For example, a cyber countermeasure against a state-sponsored hacking group might be legally permissible, but if it risks destabilizing financial systems or healthcare networks in third countries, its ethical justification weakens. Ethical frameworks such as just war theory, which emphasizes discrimination (distinguishing combatants from non-combatants) and proportionality, provide a useful lens for evaluating state behavior in cyberspace, even if the digital domain complicates traditional distinctions.

Challenges in Applying Proportionality to Cyber-operations

One of the greatest challenges in applying proportionality to cyber-operations is the difficulty in predicting and measuring their effects. Unlike a missile strike, where the blast radius and immediate casualties can be estimated, a cyberattack's impact may unfold unpredictably—disrupting unintended systems, spreading beyond initial targets, or triggering secondary effects in interconnected networks. Additionally, the attribution problem—where identifying the true origin of a cyber-operation is often uncertain—makes it difficult to determine whether a response is proportionate to the original act. States may also struggle with defining what constitutes a "proportionate" response when dealing with non-state actors, such as criminal hacking groups or proxy forces, where traditional state-to-state proportionality frameworks may not neatly apply.

Proportionality in Cyber Deterrence and Retaliation

Cyber deterrence strategies often rely on the threat of retaliation to discourage hostile actions. However, ensuring that retaliatory measures remain proportionate is critical to preventing escalation. A disproportionate response—such as a massive cyber-attack in retaliation for a minor intrusion—could provoke further conflict rather than restore stability. Some states have adopted "defend forward" strategies, where they preemptively disrupt adversary cyber-operations before they materialize. While such measures may be framed as defensive, they risk being perceived as disproportionate if they exceed the scale of the anticipated threat. The ethical and strategic challenge lies in calibrating responses that are strong enough to deter future attacks but restrained enough to avoid unnecessary harm or unintended escalation.

Role of Norms and International Agreements

International norms and agreements play a crucial role in shaping how states interpret and apply proportionality in cyberspace. The United Nations Group of Governmental Experts (UNGGE) and the Open-Ended Working Group (OEWG) have emphasized that states should refrain from cyber-operations that intentionally damage critical infrastructure or disrupt essential services. These norms, while non-binding, help establish expectations for what constitutes proportionate behavior. Additionally, bilateral and multilateral agreements on cyber-security cooperation—such as those between NATO allies or regional organizations—often include proportionality considerations in their frameworks for response and retaliation. By codifying shared understandings of what is acceptable, these agreements reduce the risk of miscalculation and excessive responses.

Case Studies: Proportionality in State Cyber-operations

Historical examples illustrate both the successes and failures of proportionality in state cyber behavior. The 2010 Stuxnet attack, widely attributed to the U.S. and Israel, targeted Iran's nuclear facilities but reportedly spread beyond its intended scope, affecting unrelated industrial systems. While some argued that the operation was a proportionate response to Iran's nuclear ambitions, others criticized its lack of containment as ethically and strategically problematic. Conversely, Estonia's measured response to the 2007 cyber-attacks on its government and financial institutions—focusing on resilience and international legal recourse rather than immediate retaliation—has been cited as an example of proportional restraint. These cases demonstrate how states navigate the tension between effective deterrence and ethical restraint in their cyber-operations.

3.3.2 Attribution

The unique architecture of the internet, designed for robustness and openness rather than for accountability, has provided a near-perfect medium for state-sponsored cyber-operations to flourish under a veil of anonymity. This inherent characteristic of cyberspace presents the international community with its most persistent and consequential ethical dilemma: the problem of attribution. Unlike a traditional military incursion across a geographically defined border, a cyber-operation can be launched from anywhere in the world, routed through a series of compromised computers in neutral countries, and designed to mimic the tactics of unrelated actors. This ability to operate with plausible deniability undermines the very foundations of the international legal order, which is predicated on the ability to identify the perpetrator of a wrongful act and hold them accountable. The ethical challenge of attribution, therefore, extends far beyond the technical forensics of tracing an IP address; it sits at the heart of regulating state behavior, deterring malicious activity, and upholding a rules-based order in a domain seemingly designed for impunity.

Technical and Analytical Labyrinth: The Process of Attribution

Attribution is not a single act but a multi-layered process, a complex mosaic where technical evidence forms only the first piece. The initial phase involves digital forensics, where analysts examine malware code, log files, network traffic, and infrastructure used in the attack. They look for unique signatures, code similarities to past operations, domain registration details, and other technical indicators that can point to a specific group or country. However, sophisticated state actors are adept at planting false flags—elements deliberately inserted into the code or infrastructure to implicate another nation or to create confusion. Consequently, technical evidence alone is rarely deemed sufficient for a high-confidence public attribution. This leads to the second, more nuanced layer: intelligence gathering. Signals intelligence, human intelligence, and geopolitical analysis provide the crucial context that technical data lacks. Intelligence agencies might intercept communications planning the operation, have sources within foreign institutions, or be able to correlate the attack's timing and target with a state's strategic interests. The final and most critical layer is the political decision, where a government weighs the technical and intelligence findings against broader strategic considerations, such as the desire to avoid escalation, protect intelligence sources and methods, or maintain diplomatic relationships.

Ethical Imperative for Accuracy: Consequences of Erroneous Attribution

The immense difficulty of attribution carries with it a profound ethical responsibility for states considering publicly naming another sovereign nation as the perpetrator of a malicious cyber act. The consequences of erroneous attribution are severe and far-reaching. A false accusation can irreparably damage diplomatic relations, trigger unwarranted and destabilizing retaliatory measures, and shatter the credibility of the attributing state, making future justified attributions less likely to be believed by the international community. It can also play directly into the hands of malicious actors who seek to sow discord and distrust among nations. Therefore, the ethical bar for public attribution must be set exceedingly high, demanding a high degree of confidence supported by a preponderance of evidence from both technical and intelligence sources. The decision to attribute should be governed by principles of accuracy, responsibility, and a commitment to stability, not by political expediency. This ethical burden necessitates robust internal vetting processes within governments, often involving legal advisors, intelligence analysts, and senior policymakers to ensure that any public attribution is sound, justified, and serves a clear strategic purpose beyond mere naming and shaming.

Strategic Calculus: The Purposes and Ethics of Public Attribution

The decision to publicly attribute a cyber-operation is a deliberate political act with multiple strategic objectives, each with its own ethical dimensions. One primary purpose is deterrence. By systematically and credibly exposing malicious activity, a state seeks to impose a cost on the aggressor's reputation and undermine its strategy of plausible deniability. The theory is that by removing the veil of anonymity, the state raises the calculus of risk for the adversary, potentially deterring future attacks. A second purpose is to enable accountability and facilitate countermeasures. Public attribution is often the necessary precursor to imposing diplomatic sanctions, economic penalties, or indicting specific individuals. It provides the public justification for such responses, aligning them with the international law of state responsibility. Ethically, this links attribution to the principle of justice and the right of a victim state to take lawful measures in its own defense. A third purpose is to build collective resilience and solidarity. By sharing attribution information with allies and partners, a state can help others defend against similar threats, foster a shared understanding of malicious actors, and work towards a coordinated international response. This aligns with an ethical commitment to collective security and the strengthening of the global community's defenses.

Normative Frontier: Attribution and the Shaping of State Behavior

Beyond its immediate tactical goals, the practice of attribution is playing a crucial, albeit gradual, role in shaping the ethical norms of state behavior in cyberspace. The consistent and credible attribution of major malicious campaigns, such as those targeting critical infrastructure or democratic processes, serves to establish a global consensus on what constitutes unacceptable behavior. It creates a form of informal adjudication, where the court of world opinion can judge a state based on the evidence presented. This process helps to stigmatize certain activities, pushing them beyond the pale of acceptable statecraft even in the absence of a formal treaty prohibition. For instance, the widespread attribution of the NotPetya attack to Russia, which caused billions in collateral damage to global businesses, helped solidify a norm against reckless cyber-operations that spill over to affect neutral parties. In this sense, attribution is not merely a reactive tool but a proactive instrument of norm entrepreneurship. It is a mechanism through which responsible states can collaboratively define and enforce red lines, fostering an environment where predictability and restraint are valued over chaos and impunity.

Path Forward: Towards a More Responsible and Stable Cyberspace

The ethics of attribution remain a work in progress, fraught with challenges but also filled with potential. The current system, reliant on unilateral declarations by victim states, is inherently imperfect and susceptible to charges of bias. To enhance the legitimacy and impact of attribution, the international community must strive for greater collaboration. This includes strengthening channels for sharing technical evidence among allies, developing multilateral attribution mechanisms through organizations like the European Union or groups of like-minded states, and supporting the work of independent cyber-security firms whose analyses can provide valuable corroboration.

Furthermore, states must continue to engage in difficult diplomatic dialogues to establish clearer expectations and potentially even agreements on what types of targets are off-limits and what constitutes a proportional response. The ultimate ethical goal of attribution is not to foster a new cyber cold war of constant accusation but to create a system of accountability that promotes stability, discourages destabilizing behavior, and upholds the fundamental principles of sovereignty and peaceful interstate relations. By wielding the tool of attribution with accuracy, restraint, and a commitment to the collective good, responsible states can slowly peel away the veil of anonymity and build a more secure and ethical digital future.

3.3.3 Due Diligence

The digital revolution has transformed the way states interact, compete, and defend their interests. Cyberspace is no longer a peripheral concern but a central arena of national security, economic growth, and political influence. However, the borderless and decentralized nature of cyberspace has made it difficult to apply traditional legal and ethical principles that regulate state conduct. One of the most significant concepts to emerge in the debate over responsible behavior in cyberspace is the principle of due diligence. Rooted in international law and adapted to the digital era, due diligence requires states to prevent their territory from being used for actions that harm other states. When applied to cyberspace, this principle raises critical ethical and legal questions about the extent of state responsibility, accountability, and the moral obligations that should govern behavior in the interconnected digital environment.

- **Concept of Due Diligence in International Law:** Due diligence is not new to international law. It has historically been invoked in contexts such as environmental law, where states are expected to prevent transboundary harm, and in counterterrorism, where governments must ensure their territory is not used as a base for attacks against others. The principle essentially means that states have a duty to act with reasonable care to prevent, mitigate, and address harmful activities that originate within their jurisdiction. In cyberspace, due diligence extends this obligation to digital infrastructure, requiring states to ensure that their networks are not exploited for malicious activities that impact the rights and interests of other nations. This adaptation of a traditional legal principle to cyberspace highlights the continuity of international law across domains, even as technology evolves.

- **Due Diligence and State Sovereignty:** The relationship between due diligence and sovereignty is particularly complex in cyberspace. Sovereignty grants states supreme authority within their territory, but it also entails responsibilities toward other states. The ethical dimension of sovereignty suggests that with power comes responsibility, including the responsibility to prevent harm emanating from one's networks. When cyber-attacks are launched from servers located within a state's jurisdiction, even without the direct involvement of that state, questions arise about whether the state failed in its duty of due diligence. Ethically, ignoring such activities undermines trust among states and contributes to a perception of complicity. Therefore, due diligence serves as a bridge between the rights of states to control their digital infrastructure and their obligations to respect the security and stability of others.
- **Ethical Imperative of Responsibility:** The ethical foundation of due diligence in cyberspace lies in the principle of responsibility. In an interconnected digital ecosystem, the actions or inactions of one state can have cascading effects across the globe. Allowing malicious actors to exploit domestic networks for cybercrime, espionage, or sabotage without taking preventive measures undermines the collective security of the international community. From an ethical standpoint, due diligence represents more than a legal obligation; it is a moral duty to uphold fairness, accountability, and mutual respect. Just as states are expected to prevent their territory from becoming a haven for armed groups or polluters, they are equally expected to ensure that cyberspace under their control is not weaponized against others.
- **Challenges in Implementing Due Diligence:** Despite its importance, applying due diligence in cyberspace faces significant challenges. The technical complexity of cyberspace makes it difficult to detect, attribute, and mitigate harmful activities. States may lack the technological capacity or resources to monitor all activities within their networks

effectively. Moreover, the decentralized nature of the internet, where malicious traffic can be routed through multiple jurisdictions, complicates the identification of responsibility. Politically, some states resist the imposition of due diligence obligations, arguing that it infringes on their sovereignty or that attribution standards are too uncertain to justify action. These challenges highlight the tension between ethical imperatives and practical realities, leaving due diligence a contested and unevenly applied principle.

- **Due Diligence and Non-State Actors:** A defining feature of cyberspace is the role of non-state actors, including hackers, criminal groups, and private companies. Unlike traditional warfare, where the state is the primary actor, cyber-operations are often conducted by individuals or groups outside direct government control. Due diligence requires states to regulate these actors within their jurisdiction and ensure they do not conduct harmful operations against others. Ethically, this aligns with the principle that states should not tolerate lawlessness within their borders, whether physical or digital. However, some states deliberately harbor or tolerate cybercriminals for strategic or economic benefits, undermining the ethical commitment to due diligence. This creates friction in international relations, as victim states view such tolerance as a breach of moral and legal obligations.
- **Role of Attribution in Accountability:** Attribution plays a central role in the ethics of due diligence. Without the ability to accurately identify the source of cyber-attacks, it becomes difficult to hold states accountable for failing in their obligations. Attribution requires technical evidence, intelligence gathering, and political consensus, which are often elusive. States may deny responsibility or claim insufficient capacity to act, exploiting ambiguity to avoid accountability. From an ethical standpoint, the absence of reliable attribution undermines justice and perpetuates impunity in cyberspace. Strengthening international cooperation on attribution, transparency, and information-sharing is therefore essential to operationalizing due diligence and ensuring that states cannot shirk their responsibilities.
- **Due Diligence as a Confidence-Building Measure:** Beyond legal and technical considerations, due diligence plays an important role in building trust among states. By demonstrating a commitment to preventing harmful activities from their territory, states can signal goodwill and contribute to stability in cyberspace. This ethical commitment enhances cooperation, reduces suspicion, and fosters

collective security. International norms, such as those advanced by the United Nations Group of Governmental Experts (GGE) and the Open-Ended Working Group (OEWG), emphasize due diligence as a cornerstone of responsible state behavior. These initiatives reflect a growing recognition that ethical principles, when institutionalized, can reduce the risk of conflict and escalation in the digital domain.

- **Divergent Perspectives on Due Diligence:** Despite broad agreement on the importance of due diligence, states interpret its scope and application differently. Western countries often emphasize due diligence as a binding obligation under international law, rooted in the principles of sovereignty and non-intervention. Russia, China, and some other states, however, resist this interpretation, framing cyberspace as an area requiring new treaties and greater state control. These divergent perspectives reflect deeper geopolitical rivalries, where legal and ethical principles become tools of strategic positioning. The lack of consensus hampers the development of a universal framework, leaving due diligence more aspirational than enforceable. Nonetheless, the ethical weight of the principle continues to influence diplomatic discourse and shape expectations of state behavior.

3.4 HUMAN RIGHTS AND DIGITAL FREEDOMS

The rise of digital technology has profoundly reshaped societies, economies, and politics worldwide. The internet and digital platforms have created new spaces for expression, information sharing, and civic engagement. At the same time, these technologies have introduced novel risks and challenges to fundamental human rights. The concept of digital freedoms has emerged as a central theme in the contemporary discourse on rights, encompassing access to the internet, freedom of expression online, the right to privacy, and the protection of personal data. As technology becomes more integrated into daily life, the boundary between traditional human rights and digital rights is increasingly blurred.

Recognizing and safeguarding these freedoms is essential to ensuring that technology empowers rather than undermines humanity. Human rights and digital freedoms are inseparable in the twenty-first century. The digital environment has become the primary arena in which individuals express themselves, connect with others, and access opportunities. Yet this environment is also fraught with risks, including censorship, surveillance, inequality, and authoritarian abuse. Safeguarding digital freedoms means extending the principles of human rights into cyberspace and adapting them to the challenges of new technologies. It requires states to uphold their obligations, corporations to respect ethical responsibilities, and the international community to promote equitable access and accountability.

Ultimately, the defense of digital freedoms is about more than protecting online spaces; it is about ensuring that technology serves humanity and that the digital revolution strengthens rather than diminishes the universal rights and freedoms that define human dignity.

The future of human rights and digital freedoms depends on building frameworks that place human dignity at the center of technological development. This requires collaboration among states, corporations, and civil society to create rules and norms that uphold rights while fostering innovation. International cooperation on issues such as privacy standards, cyber-security, and access to the internet is essential to creating a fair and just digital order. Ethically, the goal is not only to protect individuals from harm but also to ensure that digital technologies enhance freedom, equality, and participation. A human-centered approach demands vigilance, accountability, and an ongoing commitment to aligning technological progress with universal values.

3.4.1 Human Rights in the Digital Age

Human rights, as enshrined in international instruments such as the Universal Declaration of Human Rights and the International Covenant on Civil and Political Rights, are universal, indivisible, and inalienable. They include the rights to life, liberty, expression, privacy, and participation in public affairs. In the digital age, these rights extend into cyberspace, where they are exercised and challenged in new ways.

For example, freedom of expression now takes place on social media platforms, and the right to assembly is often realized through online movements and digital activism. The universality of rights means that states are obligated to uphold them in the digital domain as much as in the physical one. However, technological change has outpaced legal and regulatory frameworks, leaving many rights inadequately protected in digital environments.

3.4.2 Digital Freedoms as an Extension of Human Rights

Digital freedoms refer to the liberties individuals must enjoy in order to fully exercise their human rights online. This includes the freedom to access the internet without undue restriction, the freedom to share and receive information, and the freedom from unwarranted surveillance or censorship. These freedoms are not separate from human rights but extensions of them into the digital context. For example, freedom of expression is directly linked to the ability to communicate on digital platforms, while the right to privacy is tied to the protection of personal data from intrusive monitoring. The recognition of digital freedoms underscores the idea that human dignity and autonomy must be respected regardless of the medium through which individuals live their lives.

3.4.3 Right to Internet Access

Access to the internet has increasingly been recognized as a prerequisite for exercising many other rights. Education, employment, healthcare, and civic participation now rely heavily on digital connectivity. Denying access to the internet effectively excludes individuals from opportunities for personal development and social engagement. During crises such as the COVID-19 pandemic, the centrality of internet access to basic human needs became even more apparent. Some governments and international organizations have argued that internet access should be considered a human right in itself, as it enables the realization of other rights. Yet disparities in infrastructure, affordability, and digital literacy perpetuate a global digital divide, raising ethical questions about equity and justice in the digital era.

3.4.4 Freedom of Expression Online

Freedom of expression, a cornerstone of democratic societies, has been both empowered and endangered by digital technologies. On the one hand, social media and online platforms allow individuals to share their voices with global audiences, fostering creativity, activism, and political engagement. On the other hand, online expression faces new restrictions through government censorship, corporate content moderation, and the spread of disinformation. While it is legitimate to restrict harmful speech such as incitement to violence, overly broad measures risk silencing dissent and curbing legitimate debate. The ethical challenge lies in striking a balance between protecting users from harm and preserving the open exchange of ideas that underpins democratic life.

3.4.5 Privacy and Data Protection

The right to privacy has become one of the most contested issues of the digital age. Vast amounts of personal data are collected, stored, and processed by governments and private companies, often without meaningful consent. Surveillance technologies, data breaches, and targeted advertising raise concerns about individual autonomy and dignity. The ethical principle underlying privacy is the right of individuals to control their own information and protect themselves from intrusion. Legal frameworks such as the European Union's General Data Protection Regulation (GDPR) represent attempts to safeguard this right, but global enforcement remains inconsistent. The erosion of privacy not only threatens individuals but also undermines trust in digital ecosystems and democratic governance.

3.4.6 Cyber-security and Human Rights

Cyber-security is often framed in terms of protecting states and institutions from attacks, but it also has profound implications for human rights. Insecure networks expose individuals to identity theft, financial loss, and breaches of personal information. State-sponsored cyber-attacks may target hospitals, schools, or utilities, directly harming civilians and infringing on their rights to security and health. At the same time, cyber-security measures themselves must be designed with human rights in mind, as overly intrusive practices can compromise freedom and privacy. The ethical imperative is to ensure that digital safety and human dignity are mutually reinforcing rather than mutually exclusive goals.

3.4.7 Digital Freedoms and Authoritarianism

The digital age has created new tools for authoritarian regimes to monitor, control, and repress populations. Technologies such as facial recognition, artificial intelligence, and big data analytics can be used to surveil citizens, silence dissent, and manipulate public opinion. Internet shutdowns and censorship are increasingly deployed to suppress protest movements or control information flows. These practices represent clear violations of digital freedoms and broader human rights. They also illustrate how digital technologies, while empowering, can be weaponized against populations. Defending digital freedoms in such contexts becomes an ethical and political struggle for accountability, transparency, and the preservation of democratic values.

3.4.8 Corporate Responsibility and Digital Freedoms

Private companies, especially technology giants, play an outsized role in shaping digital freedoms. Platforms such as Google, Facebook, and Twitter serve as the new public squares where expression and association occur. Their policies on content moderation, data collection, and algorithmic curation directly affect the enjoyment of human rights. Ethically, corporations have responsibilities to respect human rights, even if they are not bound by international treaties. Initiatives like the UN Guiding Principles on Business and Human Rights provide a framework for corporate accountability. However, profit motives often conflict with ethical responsibilities, as seen in controversies over misinformation, algorithmic bias, and data exploitation. The tension between corporate power and human rights underscores the need for stronger regulation and ethical leadership in the private sector.

3.4.9 Digital Divide and Inequality

The enjoyment of digital freedoms is not uniform across the globe. Stark disparities in access to technology create a digital divide that mirrors and exacerbates existing inequalities. Rural communities, developing countries, and marginalized populations often lack the infrastructure or resources to benefit from digital connectivity. This inequality denies them not only the advantages of the digital economy but also the full exercise of human rights online. Bridging the digital divide is therefore both a developmental and ethical imperative. Ensuring universal access, affordability, and digital literacy are critical steps toward making digital freedoms a reality for all rather than a privilege for a few.

3.5 BRIDGING THE LEGAL AND DIPLOMATIC DIVIDE IN CYBER-ISSUES

The rapid evolution of cyber conflict has exposed a fundamental and dangerous schism in how nations approach state behavior in the digital realm. On one side lies the legal domain, a world of precise definitions, established thresholds, and rules-based accountability, striving to apply frameworks like international humanitarian law and the law of state responsibility to a borderless and abstract battlespace.

On the other side resides the diplomatic domain, a realm of political nuance, strategic ambiguity, and the perpetual pursuit of stability through dialogue and deterrence, often wary of the escalatory potential of rigid legal pronouncements. This is not merely an academic disagreement but a operational chasm that creates significant uncertainty, hampers effective response, and allows malicious actors to exploit the gap between what is clearly unlawful and what is politically actionable.

Bridging this legal-diplomatic divide is the most critical challenge in developing a stable and secure cyberspace, requiring a nuanced understanding that law and diplomacy are not opposing forces but complementary instruments of statecraft that must be wielded in concert.

3.5.1 Lawyer's Dilemma: The Rigor and Limitations of Legal Frameworks

The legal project, exemplified by scholarly works like the Tallinn Manual, has made commendable progress in articulating how existing international law applies to cyber-operations. Lawyers seek clarity: they work to define the threshold at which a disruptive cyber-operation constitutes a prohibited "use of force" under Article 2(4) of the UN Charter, or when such an operation rises to the level of an "armed attack" triggering the right to self-defence under Article 51.

They meticulously apply principles of distinction, proportionality, and precaution to cyber-warfare within the context of an armed conflict. However, this rigor encounters profound limitations in the murky reality of cyberspace. Most damaging state-sponsored activity—such as pervasive espionage, election interference, or critical infrastructure prepositioning—intentionally operates below these high legal thresholds. A lawyer may conclude that such acts violate the principle of sovereignty but must also acknowledge that the law provides few clear, lawful response options for these "below-the-threshold" coercive acts. This creates a perception, particularly among diplomats and military strategists, that the law is either irrelevant or insufficient to address the daily reality of cyber competition, leaving a vast grey zone of malicious activity unchallenged by legal frameworks.

3.5.2 Diplomat's Dilemma: The Necessity and Perils of Strategic Ambiguity

Conversely, diplomats often operate from a position of strategic ambiguity, which they view as a necessary tool for maintaining stability and avoiding escalation. Publicly attributing a cyber attack to another state is not merely a legal finding of fact but a deliberate political act with potentially severe diplomatic consequences.

A diplomat must weigh the benefits of public shaming and deterrence against the risks of provoking a cycle of retaliation, damaging bilateral relations on a range of unrelated issues, or exposing sensitive intelligence sources and methods. This calculous often results in a cautious, delayed, or entirely absent public response, even when private demarches are made.

This diplomatic caution, while prudent from a narrow bilateral perspective, creates a significant accountability gap. When states consistently fail to impose tangible costs for malicious behavior below the threshold of war, they inadvertently reinforce a permissive environment where adversaries face no consequences for their actions. This diplomatic silence can be misread as acquiescence or weakness, emboldening aggressors and undermining the development of deterrence.

3.5.3 Attribution Gap: Where Law and Diplomacy Most Often Diverge

Nowhere is the divide between law and diplomacy more apparent than in the complex process of attribution. From a legal perspective, attribution is a objective requirement for invoking the law of state responsibility; a state must be able to credibly demonstrate that a cyber-operation is attributable to another state under the rules of effective control before countermeasures or other responses can be legally justified.

The legal standard, while complex, strives for an evidence-based conclusion. Diplomacy, however, treats attribution as a political weapon to be deployed selectively. A government may have intelligence confirming attribution with high confidence but choose to withhold it publicly to manage escalation or preserve a broader strategic relationship. Alternatively, a state might publicly attribute an attack with minimal evidence for geopolitical reasons unrelated to the incident itself.

This politicization of attribution creates confusion and cynicism, eroding trust in the process and making it difficult to build the consistent, credible international consensus required to reinforce legal norms. When attribution is inconsistent, the legal rules that depend on it become difficult to enforce in practice.

3.5.4 Forging a Complementary Relationship: Norms as a Bridging Mechanism

The path forward requires a conscious effort to reframe the relationship between law and diplomacy from one of tension to one of synergy. The most promising mechanism for bridging this divide is the sustained development and promotion of voluntary peacetime norms of responsible state behavior.

Unlike binding international law, norms are politically negotiated expectations of conduct that can address the very grey zone activity that law struggles to encompass. Diplomatic forums, particularly the United Nations Group of Governmental Experts (UNGGE) and the Open-Ended Working Group (OEWG), have made progress in articulating such norms, including the consensus that states should not knowingly allow their territory to be used for malicious cyber activity and should protect the integrity of the critical infrastructure of other states.

These norms serve as a crucial bridge. They provide a diplomatic foundation for calling out bad behavior using a shared vocabulary, even when that behavior is not strictly illegal. This, in turn, strengthens the legal regime by creating a broader framework of expected conduct, building a political consensus that can eventually inform the interpretation of legal principles like sovereignty and due diligence.

3.5.5 Towards an Integrated Strategy: Fusing Legal Clarity with Diplomatic Statecraft

Ultimately, bridging the divide requires states to develop integrated national strategies that consciously fuse legal analysis with diplomatic action. This means empowering legal advisors within foreign ministries and national security councils to provide real-time counsel on the legal boundaries of state response, not as a veto on action but as a guide for crafting proportionate and legitimate responses.

Conversely, diplomats must better communicate their political and strategic constraints to legal teams, ensuring that legal opinions are informed by the realities of geopolitics. Operationally, this integration could take several forms. It could involve developing a graduated classification system for cyber-incidents that clearly links the legal characterisation of an event to a menu of predetermined diplomatic, economic, and legal response options. It also necessitates greater investment in multilateral coalition-building for attribution, where like-minded states jointly investigate and publicly attribute attacks, thereby sharing the political burden and lending greater credibility to the findings, insulating them from charges of politicization.

The future of cyber stability depends on states learning to wield law and diplomacy not as separate tools but as two hands working together. Law provides the essential framework for legitimacy, defining the red lines of armed conflict and establishing the rules of accountability. Diplomacy provides the essential tools for daily management, building coalitions, managing escalation, and negotiating the norms of behavior that fill the gaps in the legal architecture. By consciously integrating these disciplines, the international community can move from a reactive posture of confusion to a proactive strategy of deterrence, where the boundaries of acceptable state behavior are clearer, and violations—whether legal or normative—are met with a predictable and proportionate cost. Closing the legal-diplomatic divide is the necessary step to transforming cyberspace from a lawless frontier into a domain governed by predictable rules and responsible statecraft.

CHAPTER 4

Cyber-Security and Diplomacy

4.1 CYBER-SECURITY AS A FOREIGN POLICY ISSUE

In the twenty-first century, cyber-security has evolved from being a technical concern of governments and private organizations into a central pillar of international relations. The increasing digitization of societies and economies has transformed cyberspace into a domain of geopolitical contestation, where state and non-state actors interact in ways that directly affect national security, economic growth, and diplomatic relations. Cyber-attacks on critical infrastructure, intellectual property theft, disinformation campaigns, and espionage have all underscored the importance of cyber-security as a foreign policy issue. Unlike traditional domains of conflict, cyberspace is borderless, fast-moving, and asymmetric, which challenges existing frameworks of diplomacy and security. For states, cyber-security is no longer merely a domestic issue of protecting networks but a matter of strategic interaction in the international system.

Cyber-security has become one of the defining foreign policy issues of our time. It touches on national security, economic prosperity, human rights, and global governance, making it an indispensable part of international relations. The borderless nature of cyber-threats demands international cooperation, while the geopolitical competition over cyberspace reflects deeper rivalries among states. Foreign policy must address not only the technical aspects of cyber-security but also its ethical, political, and social dimensions. By integrating cyber-security into diplomacy, trade, security alliances, and international law, states can build frameworks that reduce risks and promote stability. Ultimately, the challenge for foreign policy is to ensure that cyberspace evolves as a domain that supports peace, prosperity, and human dignity rather than one dominated by conflict and division.

As technology advances, cyber-security will become even more deeply embedded in foreign policy agendas. The rise of artificial intelligence, quantum computing, and the Internet of Things will create new vulnerabilities and new opportunities for both cooperation and conflict. States will need to develop foreign policy strategies that are adaptive, inclusive, and ethically grounded to navigate the evolving challenges of cyberspace. International cooperation will remain essential, but so too will competition, as states vie for dominance in the digital realm. The ethical question that underpins these developments is whether states can create a stable, secure, and rights-respecting cyberspace, or whether cyberspace will remain a theater of conflict and mistrust.

4.1.1 Globalization of Cyber-threats

Cyber-security has become a foreign policy concern largely because cyber-threats do not respect territorial boundaries. A malicious cyber campaign launched in one country can instantly affect systems in another, disrupting global financial networks, supply chains, and governance structures. The global nature of cyber risks means that no state can address them alone. Attacks such as the NotPetya incident in 2017, which crippled businesses and institutions worldwide, revealed the interconnected vulnerabilities of modern societies. This interdependence compels states to incorporate cyber-security into their foreign policy agendas, not only to defend themselves but also to cooperate with allies and international organizations. The globalization of cyber-threats thus pushes governments to balance competition and collaboration in an increasingly contested digital arena.

4.1.2 Cyber-security and National Security

Cyber-security is closely tied to national security, and foreign policy is the vehicle through which states project and defend this security internationally. Modern militaries depend on digital systems, and critical infrastructure such as energy grids, transportation networks, and healthcare systems are prime targets for cyber-attacks. Foreign policy strategies must therefore include cyber-defense commitments, deterrence measures, and alliances that extend into the digital realm. For example, NATO has recognized cyberspace as a domain of operations, affirming that a severe cyber-attack could trigger collective defense mechanisms under Article 5 of its treaty. This demonstrates how cyber-security has become integral to security policies and international commitments. States are increasingly using diplomacy to strengthen cyber resilience while signaling their willingness to respond to threats as they would to physical aggression.

4.1.3 Cyber-diplomacy and International Engagement

Diplomacy has become one of the most important tools for addressing cyber-security challenges. Cyber-diplomacy refers to the use of diplomatic channels to promote norms, agreements, and cooperative measures in cyberspace. Through bilateral and multilateral negotiations, states attempt to reduce the risks of conflict, enhance trust, and establish rules of responsible behavior. The United Nations has played a central role in fostering discussions through its Group of Governmental Experts and Open-Ended Working Group, both of which have affirmed that international law applies to cyberspace. Similarly, regional organizations like the European Union and ASEAN have developed initiatives to coordinate cyber policies. Cyber-diplomacy also involves building partnerships with the private sector and civil society, recognizing that cyber-security is a shared responsibility across multiple actors.

4.1.4 Cyber Espionage and Foreign Policy Tensions

One of the most contentious areas of cyber-security in foreign policy is cyber espionage. States use digital tools to steal intellectual property, gather intelligence, and monitor adversaries, often blurring the line between acceptable intelligence activities and hostile acts. Incidents such as the SolarWinds breach in 2020, attributed to Russian-linked actors, highlighted how cyber espionage can compromise government systems and strain diplomatic relations. While espionage has long been a part of international affairs, its digital form raises new ethical and security dilemmas because of its scale, reach, and potential to undermine trust in global institutions. States frequently respond to cyber espionage with sanctions, indictments, and public attributions, using foreign policy instruments to deter and punish malicious activities. The ethical and political tensions created by cyber espionage underscore the need for clearer rules and stronger diplomatic engagement.

4.1.5 Cyber-security, Trade, and Economic Policy

Cyber-security has also become deeply intertwined with trade and economic policy, making it a critical foreign policy issue. Digital technologies underpin global commerce, from financial systems to e-commerce platforms, and disruptions in cyberspace can lead to enormous economic losses. Intellectual property theft through cyber-attacks has been a source of significant diplomatic friction, particularly between the United States and China, where allegations of state-sponsored theft of trade secrets have strained relations. Cyber-security also plays a role in debates over technology supply chains, with controversies surrounding companies such as Huawei raising questions about trust, espionage, and sovereignty. Foreign policy must therefore balance the promotion of free trade and innovation with the protection of national interests in an era of digital competition.

4.1.6 Geopolitics of Cyberspace

Cyberspace is increasingly viewed as a domain of geopolitical competition, where states project influence, contest power, and shape norms to reflect their values. The United States and its allies generally promote an open, free, and secure internet, while Russia and China advocate for state sovereignty over digital information and infrastructure. These competing visions have profound implications for global governance and human rights. Foreign policy strategies in cyberspace are therefore not only about security but also about promoting ideological models of internet governance. This geopolitical struggle extends to forums such as the International Telecommunication Union and the UN, where states advocate for rules that align with their strategic interests. The geopolitics of cyberspace illustrate how cyber-security is inseparable from broader foreign policy debates about power, sovereignty, and values.

4.1.7 Cyber Norms and International Law

The development of cyber norms and the application of international law to cyberspace are central to cyber-security as a foreign policy issue. Norms are voluntary principles of responsible state behavior, such as refraining from attacking critical infrastructure during peacetime or cooperating to prevent malicious activity. International law, particularly the UN Charter, provides a framework for addressing issues such as the prohibition of the use of force and the principle of sovereignty. However, states disagree on how these principles apply in cyberspace, creating uncertainty and opportunities for exploitation. Foreign policy plays a vital role in negotiating these norms, promoting interpretations of international law, and building coalitions to hold violators accountable. The establishment of norms is not only a legal task but also an ethical one, as it reflects shared values about how states should act in the digital age.

4.1.8 Public Diplomacy and Information Warfare

Cyber-security is also linked to foreign policy through the rise of information warfare and public diplomacy. Disinformation campaigns, election interference, and the manipulation of social media platforms have become tools of statecraft, designed to influence public opinion and destabilize democratic institutions. These activities blur the line between traditional propaganda and cyber-operations, posing unique challenges for foreign policy. States must defend against foreign interference while promoting their own narratives in the digital sphere. The ethical dimension of information warfare makes it especially difficult, as responses must protect free expression without resorting to censorship. In this way, cyber-security has become a central arena for both conflict and communication in international relations.

4.2 NATIONAL CYBER-SECURITY STRATEGIES AND INTERNATIONAL ENGAGEMENT

In an increasingly interconnected digital ecosystem, the concept of cyber-security can no longer be confined within national borders. While the primary responsibility for protecting a nation's critical infrastructure, citizens, and economic interests from cyber-threats rests with the state, the transnational nature of these threats necessitates a paradigm that blends robust domestic action with deliberate international engagement. A National Cyber-security Strategy (NCS) is the foundational document through which a government articulates its vision, objectives, and principles for securing its digital domain. However, the efficacy of any strategy is contingent upon recognizing that malicious actors operate from abroad, supply chains are global, and the stability of the internet itself is a collective good. Therefore, a modern NCS cannot be an insular document; it must explicitly integrate international engagement as a core pillar, viewing diplomacy, cooperation, and the shaping of global norms not as secondary concerns but as essential components of national resilience and security. The most effective strategies understand that national security in the digital age is paradoxically dependent on international collaboration.

4.2.1 Domestic Foundation: Building a Resilient National Posture

The first and most critical function of a National Cyber-security Strategy is to establish a coherent and whole-of-nation approach to domestic cyber-security. This involves the articulation of clear roles and responsibilities across government agencies, critical infrastructure operators, the private sector, and the general public. A comprehensive NCS will typically outline strategic objectives such as enhancing the protection of critical national infrastructure, fostering a skilled cyber-security workforce, promoting research and development in cyber technologies, and raising public awareness about digital risks.

It establishes the legal and regulatory frameworks necessary to enable information sharing between the public and private sectors, mandate baseline security requirements for vital sectors, and empower national cyber-security agencies like Computer Security Incident Response Teams (CSIRTs). This domestic fortification is the necessary precondition for meaningful international action. A state that lacks internal coordination and a clear understanding of its own national assets and vulnerabilities cannot effectively represent its interests or contribute credibly on the global stage. The strength of a nation's international voice in cyber-diplomacy is directly proportional to the robustness of its internal cyber-security governance.

4.2.2 Diplomatic Arsenal: International Engagement as a Strategic Tool

Beyond domestic defense, a sophisticated NCS proactively outlines a framework for international engagement, transforming diplomacy into a strategic tool for enhancing national security. This external dimension serves several interconnected purposes. Firstly, it is a mechanism for building collective capacity.

Cyber capabilities are unevenly distributed globally, and many nations lack the resources to defend themselves effectively. Through bilateral and multilateral aid programs, developed nations can assist partners in building their own CSIRTs, developing national strategies, and improving their legal frameworks. This is not merely altruistic; it reduces the number of vulnerable nodes in the global network that can be hijacked and used as launchpads for attacks against others, thereby improving everyone's security. Secondly, international engagement is crucial for operational cooperation. Formal and informal channels for sharing threat intelligence, best practices, and early warnings with allies and partners significantly enhance the situational awareness of all participating states. This allows for a faster and more coordinated response to ongoing campaigns, disrupting adversaries and mitigating damage across jurisdictions.

4.2.3 Shaping the Rules-Based Order: Norms, Law, and Standard-Setting

A paramount objective of international engagement articulated in a National Cyber-security Strategy is the active participation in the development of the global rules-based order for cyberspace. This involves engaging in multilateral forums such as the United Nations Group of Governmental Experts (UNGGE) and the Open-Ended Working Group (OEWG) to negotiate and build consensus around voluntary peacetime norms of responsible state behavior.

These norms, which include commitments not to target critical infrastructure or to hinder emergency response teams, create expectations of conduct and provide a political basis for calling out and condemning malicious activities that may fall below the threshold of armed conflict. Furthermore, states use their engagement to promote a common understanding of how existing international law applies to state-on-state cyber-operations, a complex but vital endeavor for maintaining stability and preventing escalation.

Beyond these political and legal efforts, strategies also prioritize involvement in international technical standard-setting bodies. By influencing global standards for technologies like 5G, IoT security, and artificial intelligence, nations can proactively bake security and trust into the very fabric of the global digital economy, protecting their industries and citizens by design rather than through retrospective remediation.

4.2.4 Deterrence and Accountability: The Role of Attribution and Cost-Imposition

A crucial, and often most sensitive, element of an NCS's international engagement pillar is the framework for deterrence through attribution and cost-imposition. A strategy must define the state's approach to attributing malicious cyber-activities to their perpetrators, a process that blends technical forensics with intelligence and geopolitical analysis. The public attribution of attacks to specific state or non-state actors is a powerful diplomatic tool that strips away the veil of anonymity that aggressors rely upon. However, attribution alone is not deterrence; it must be linked to consequences. Therefore, a robust NCS will outline a holistic toolkit for imposing costs on malicious actors, which extends beyond cyber retaliation to include a range of diplomatic, economic, and legal measures. This can involve expelling diplomatic personnel, enacting targeted sanctions against individuals or entities, initiating criminal indictments, or assembling coalitions of like-minded states to condemn and sanction bad behavior collectively. By clearly communicating in its strategy a commitment to a policy of credible and proportionate cost-imposition, a state contributes to a broader deterrence posture, signaling to potential adversaries that their actions will be identified and will incur a meaningful price.

4.3 CYBER CAPACITY BUILDING AND TECHNICAL COOPERATION

Cyber capacity building and technical cooperation are essential to creating a more secure and resilient global digital environment. By strengthening national cyber-security frameworks, fostering international collaboration, and leveraging public-private partnerships, nations can better defend against cyber-threats while contributing to collective security.

The challenges are significant, but the progress made by leading initiatives demonstrates that coordinated, demand-driven efforts can yield meaningful results. As cyber-security becomes a defining issue of the 21st century, sustained investment in capacity building will be crucial to ensuring that all nations—regardless of their current capabilities—can participate in and benefit from a secure digital future. The path forward requires not only technological solutions but also a commitment to shared responsibility, trust, and long-term cooperation among all stakeholders.

As cyber-threats continue to evolve, so too must approaches to capacity building. Emerging technologies such as artificial intelligence, quantum computing, and the Internet of Things (IoT) will introduce new vulnerabilities and require updated defense strategies. Future capacity-building efforts must prioritize adaptability, ensuring that nations can continuously upgrade their cyber-security postures in response to technological shifts. Additionally, there is a growing need for standardized frameworks to measure the effectiveness of capacity-building programs, enabling better resource allocation and accountability. Finally, as cyber-security becomes increasingly intertwined with geopolitical competition, technical cooperation must remain grounded in principles of neutrality, inclusivity, and mutual benefit to prevent fragmentation of the global digital ecosystem.

4.3.1 Cyber Capacity Building

Cyber capacity building refers to the process of enhancing a nation's ability to manage cyber-security risks through a combination of policy frameworks, technical skills, institutional structures, and international partnerships. It is not merely about acquiring advanced technologies but also about developing the human expertise, legal frameworks, and operational procedures necessary to sustain cyber resilience. Effective capacity building involves multiple dimensions, including the establishment of national cyber-security strategies, the training of cyber-security professionals, the creation of incident response teams, and the fostering of public-private collaboration. It also requires alignment with international norms and standards to ensure interoperability and collective defense against transnational cyber-threats.

4.3.2 Role of Technical Cooperation

Technical cooperation is a cornerstone of cyber capacity building, enabling countries to share expertise, resources, and best practices in cyber-security. Unlike traditional aid models, technical cooperation in cyber-security often involves peer-to-peer learning, joint exercises, and collaborative research. Advanced cyber powers frequently engage in technical cooperation by providing training programs, threat intelligence sharing, and assistance in establishing national Computer Emergency Response Teams (CERTs). Regional organizations, such as the African Union, ASEAN, and the Organization of American States, also facilitate technical cooperation through workshops, policy dialogues, and joint cyber-security drills. This collaborative approach helps build trust, fosters mutual understanding of cyber-threats, and ensures that capacity-building efforts are tailored to local needs rather than imposed as one-size-fits-all solutions.

4.3.3 Key Components of Effective Cyber Capacity Building

A successful cyber capacity-building program must address several interrelated components. First, it requires the development of a national cyber-security strategy that aligns with a country's broader security and economic objectives. Second, it necessitates the establishment of legal and regulatory frameworks that define cybercrime, protect critical infrastructure, and enable cross-border cooperation. Third, it demands investment in education and workforce development to cultivate a skilled cyber-security workforce capable of managing evolving threats. Fourth, it involves the creation of operational capabilities, such as national CERTs and Security Operations Centers (SOCs), to monitor and respond to cyber-incidents in real time. Finally, it requires international collaboration to ensure that capacity-building efforts are sustainable, scalable, and responsive to global cyber-security trends.

4.3.4 Challenges in Cyber Capacity Building

Despite its importance, cyber capacity building faces significant challenges. One major obstacle is the rapid pace of technological change, which often outstrips the ability of governments to adapt their policies and defenses. Many developing nations also struggle with limited financial resources, making it difficult to invest in advanced cyber-security tools and training programs. Additionally, there is often a mismatch between donor-driven capacity-building initiatives and the actual needs of recipient countries, leading to inefficiencies or unsustainable outcomes. Political and bureaucratic hurdles can further impede progress, as cyber-security efforts may be fragmented across multiple agencies without clear coordination. Finally, the lack of standardized metrics to measure the effectiveness of capacity-building programs makes it difficult to assess progress and justify continued investment.

4.3.5 Role of International Organizations and Initiatives

International organizations play a pivotal role in facilitating cyber capacity building through technical cooperation. The United Nations, through its Open-Ended Working Group (OEWG) and other forums, promotes norms and best practices that guide national cyber-security efforts. The International Telecommunication Union (ITU) provides technical assistance and training to help countries develop their cyber-security frameworks. Regional bodies, such as the European Union's Cyber-security Agency (ENISA) and the African Union's Cyber-security Program, offer tailored support to member states. Additionally, initiatives like the Global Forum on Cyber Expertise (GFCE) bring together governments, private sector entities, and civil society to coordinate capacity-building efforts and avoid duplication of resources. These organizations help ensure that technical cooperation is demand-driven, inclusive, and aligned with global cyber-security standards.

4.3.6 Public-Private Partnerships in Cyber Capacity Building

The private sector is an indispensable partner in cyber capacity building, given that much of the world's digital infrastructure is owned and operated by private companies. Public-private partnerships enable governments to leverage industry expertise in threat detection, incident response, and cyber-security innovation. Technology firms often provide training programs, threat intelligence sharing, and cyber-security tools to governments at reduced costs or through corporate social responsibility initiatives. Meanwhile, governments can offer regulatory clarity, incentives for investment, and frameworks for collaboration that benefit both national security and private sector interests. Successful models, such as those seen in financial cyber-security alliances or telecom sector collaborations, demonstrate how joint efforts can enhance national cyber resilience while fostering economic growth.

4.3.7 Case Studies in Successful Cyber Capacity Building

Several countries and regions have made notable progress in cyber capacity building through targeted technical cooperation. Estonia, for example, transformed its cyber-security posture after the 2007 cyber-attacks by establishing a robust national CERT, integrating cyber-security into education, and fostering a thriving cyber-security industry. In Africa, the African Union's collaboration with the ITU and other partners has led to the creation of regional CERTs and cyber-security training hubs. Singapore's Cyber-security Agency has become a model for integrating public and private sector efforts, while also providing technical assistance to neighboring ASEAN nations. These examples highlight how a combination of strategic vision, international support, and domestic investment can significantly enhance a nation's cyber-security capabilities.

4.4 INCIDENT RESPONSE, CRISIS MANAGEMENT, AND CONFIDENCE-BUILDING MEASURES (CBMS)

Incident response, crisis management, and confidence-building measures represent three complementary pillars of cyber-security governance in the international system. Incident response provides the technical expertise to address immediate threats, crisis management offers the strategic and diplomatic tools to navigate high-stakes incidents, and CBMs build the trust necessary to prevent misperceptions and escalation. Together, they form a holistic approach to managing cyber risks in a borderless and interconnected domain. While challenges of attribution, capacity, and political mistrust remain, the continued development and integration of these practices are essential to securing cyberspace. By investing in incident response capabilities, strengthening crisis management frameworks, and expanding CBMs, states can move toward a more stable, cooperative, and secure digital future.

Looking ahead, the effectiveness of incident response, crisis management, and CBMs will depend on sustained international cooperation and innovation. Strengthening CERT-to-CERT cooperation, investing in capacity-building for developing countries, and fostering public-private partnerships are essential for improving incident response capabilities. Enhancing crisis management requires building trusted diplomatic channels, clarifying thresholds for response, and integrating cyber-incidents into broader national security planning.

For CBMs, the future lies in expanding participation and deepening commitments. Regional and global organizations can play a central role in promoting CBMs, but political will and trust among states are crucial. Confidence-building measures must also adapt to new challenges, including artificial intelligence-driven threats and the increasing role of non-state actors in cyberspace. Ultimately, the goal is to create a cyber-environment where transparency, communication, and mutual accountability reduce the risks of conflict and foster a stable digital order.

4.4.1 Incident Response: The First Line of Defense

Incident response refers to the coordinated efforts to detect, analyze, contain, and recover from cyber-incidents. It is often the first line of defense when malicious activity occurs, as timely and effective response can limit damage and restore systems. Incident response teams, commonly known as Computer Emergency Response Teams (CERTs) or Computer Security Incident Response Teams (CSIRTs), play a vital role in this process. These teams analyze incoming threats, share information with relevant stakeholders, and recommend actions to neutralize vulnerabilities.

The importance of incident response lies not only in its technical function but also in its role as a foundation for trust and accountability. When states and organizations demonstrate that they are prepared to handle cyber-threats responsibly, they signal their commitment to stability in cyberspace. International cooperation in incident response, such as the sharing of indicators of compromise and best practices, strengthens global resilience. However, challenges remain, including limited resources in developing countries, the complexity of attributing attacks, and the speed at which threats evolve. Addressing these obstacles is crucial for ensuring that incident response can effectively contain the risks of cyber-operations.

4.4.2 Crisis Management in Cyberspace

While incident response addresses immediate threats, crisis management involves handling cyber-incidents that escalate to the level of national or international concern. Cyber crises can arise when critical infrastructure is disrupted, when sensitive data is compromised, or when geopolitical tensions are heightened by malicious digital activity. Unlike routine incident response, crisis management requires coordination among technical experts, policymakers, diplomats, and security agencies. Crisis management in cyberspace shares similarities with traditional crisis management but also has unique characteristics. The speed and ambiguity of cyber-operations can create uncertainty about the scale of damage and the identity of perpetrators.

This complicates decision-making, as governments must weigh how to respond without escalating conflicts. Furthermore, the global interconnectedness of cyberspace means that a cyber-incident in one country can have cascading effects across borders. Effective crisis management therefore requires mechanisms for communication, de-escalation, and international coordination. Diplomatic channels are central to cyber crisis management, as they allow states to clarify intentions, share information, and negotiate responses. In some cases, cyber-incidents have been defused through backchannel communication or multilateral dialogue, preventing escalation into open conflict. Crisis management is therefore not only a technical exercise but also a diplomatic necessity, requiring states to engage with one another to prevent misunderstandings and unintended escalation.

4.4.3 Confidence-Building Measures: Building Trust in Cyberspace

Confidence-building measures (CBMs) are diplomatic and cooperative initiatives designed to reduce mistrust and prevent conflict among states. Originally developed in the context of arms control and military security during the Cold War, CBMs have been adapted to cyberspace. Their primary purpose is to increase transparency, foster communication, and promote predictable behavior in the digital domain. CBMs in cyberspace include a range of practices, such as the exchange of information about national cyber policies, the establishment of hotlines between states for cyber-incidents, and joint training exercises among CERTs. These measures help reduce the risk of misperception and miscalculation, as states can clarify their actions and intentions.

For example, a sudden surge in cyber activity might otherwise be interpreted as a hostile act, but CBMs provide mechanisms to seek clarification before escalating tensions. International organizations, including the Organization for Security and Co-operation in Europe (OSCE) and the United Nations, have played a significant role in promoting cyber CBMs. The OSCE, for instance, has developed a set of voluntary measures to enhance transparency and cooperation in cyberspace, including information-sharing and communication protocols. These initiatives reflect a recognition that trust in cyberspace cannot be achieved solely through deterrence and defense; it must also be built through dialogue and collaboration.

4.4.4 Interconnection of Incident Response, Crisis Management, and CBMs

Incident response, crisis management, and CBMs are interconnected elements of a broader framework for managing cyber-threats. Effective incident response provides the technical basis for understanding and containing cyber-incidents, which in turn informs crisis management strategies. Without accurate and timely information from incident response teams, policymakers may lack the data needed to make informed decisions in times of crisis. Crisis management, in turn, relies on diplomatic engagement and communication channels, many of which are institutionalized through CBMs. The existence of hotlines, agreed protocols, and information-sharing mechanisms established through CBMs enables states to manage crises more effectively. In this way, CBMs serve as the bridge between routine incident response and high-level crisis management, ensuring that states can move from technical analysis to political dialogue in a coordinated manner. Together, these elements contribute to stability in cyberspace. Incident response mitigates immediate threats, crisis management prevents escalation, and CBMs foster long-term trust. The integration of these components is essential to reducing the risks of conflict in the digital domain and ensuring that cyberspace remains a space for cooperation rather than confrontation.

4.4.5 Challenges and Limitations

Despite the importance of incident response, crisis management, and CBMs, significant challenges limit their effectiveness. One of the most persistent issues is attribution. Identifying the perpetrators of cyber-attacks is technically and politically complex, and uncertainty often hinders effective response. Without attribution, it is difficult to hold actors accountable or to engage diplomatically with the appropriate parties.

Resource disparities also pose challenges, as not all states have the capacity to develop robust incident response teams or participate meaningfully in international CBMs. This creates an uneven playing field where some states are more vulnerable to cyber-threats. Moreover, geopolitical rivalries and mistrust can undermine CBMs, as states may be reluctant to share information or cooperate with perceived adversaries. Another challenge is the evolving nature of cyber-threats. As technology advances, new vulnerabilities and attack vectors emerge, requiring constant adaptation of incident response and crisis management practices. This dynamic environment makes it difficult to establish stable and universally accepted norms, leaving CBMs as voluntary and often fragile commitments.

4.5 PUBLIC-PRIVATE PARTNERSHIPS IN GLOBAL CYBER-SECURITY

Public-private partnerships are indispensable in the fight against cyber-threats, offering a collaborative approach that leverages the strengths of both sectors. By fostering information sharing, joint defense initiatives, and policy co-development, these partnerships enhance global cyber-security resilience and reduce systemic risks. However, their success depends on overcoming challenges such as misaligned incentives, legal barriers, and trust deficits. As cyber-threats grow in sophistication and scale, the need for structured, sustainable, and internationally coordinated partnerships will only intensify. The future of cyber-security lies in the ability of governments and private entities to work together—not as adversaries or competitors, but as allies in safeguarding the digital infrastructure that underpins modern society. Through continued innovation, trust-building, and shared commitment, public-private partnerships can pave the way for a more secure and resilient global cyber landscape.

As cyber-threats continue to evolve, public-private partnerships must adapt to remain effective. The rise of artificial intelligence, quantum computing, and the Internet of Things (IoT) will introduce new vulnerabilities and require innovative defense strategies. Future partnerships will likely emphasize automation in threat detection, AI-driven incident response, and predictive cyber-security analytics. Additionally, there will be a growing need for standardized frameworks that enable seamless information sharing across borders and sectors. Governments and private entities must also address the ethical implications of cyber-security measures, ensuring that defense strategies do not infringe on privacy or civil liberties. Sustaining these partnerships will require continuous investment in trust-building, clear legal frameworks, and mechanisms for equitable resource allocation to ensure that all stakeholders benefit from collective cyber-security efforts.

4.5.1 The Evolution

The concept of public-private collaboration in cyber-security has evolved significantly over the past two decades. Initially, interactions between governments and private entities were ad hoc, often limited to crisis response or regulatory compliance. However, as cyber-threats grew in scale and complexity—particularly with the rise of state-sponsored cyber espionage, ransomware attacks, and supply chain vulnerabilities—structured partnerships became necessary. Early models, such as information-sharing initiatives in the financial sector, demonstrated the value of joint efforts in mitigating risks. Today, PPPs encompass a broad spectrum of activities, including threat intelligence sharing, joint cyber-defense exercises, policy co-development, and coordinated incident response frameworks. This evolution reflects a growing recognition that cyber-security is a shared responsibility requiring continuous engagement rather than sporadic cooperation.

4.5.2 Key Models

Several models of public-private partnerships have proven effective in strengthening cyber-security. One prominent example is the establishment of Information Sharing and Analysis Centers (ISACs), where private sector entities within specific industries—such as finance, energy, and healthcare—collaborate with government agencies to exchange threat intelligence and best practices. Another model involves joint cyber-security operations centers, where public and private stakeholders work side by side to monitor threats and coordinate responses in real time. Additionally, some governments have formalized partnerships through memoranda of understanding (MoUs) with technology firms, enabling faster threat mitigation and policy alignment. These models vary in structure but share a common goal: to bridge the gap between public oversight and private sector agility in cyber-defense.

4.5.3 Role of Information Sharing

One of the most critical functions of public-private partnerships is the exchange of threat intelligence. Governments often possess classified information about emerging threats, while private companies have real-time visibility into attacks targeting their networks. Effective information sharing ensures that both sectors can act swiftly to mitigate risks. Initiatives such as the U.S. Cyber-security and Infrastructure Security Agency's (CISA) Automated Indicator Sharing (AIS) program enable near-instantaneous dissemination of threat data between government and industry. Similarly, the European Union's Cyber-security Act encourages structured collaboration through its cyber-security certification framework. However, challenges remain, including concerns over data privacy, competitive sensitivities, and the need for standardized formats to ensure actionable intelligence. Overcoming these barriers requires trust-building mechanisms and clear legal frameworks that protect shared information while enabling rapid response.

4.5.4 Joint Cyber-defense and Incident Response

Public-private partnerships are particularly vital in the realm of incident response, where speed and coordination can mean the difference between containment and catastrophic damage. Governments and private entities often conduct joint cyber-defense exercises, simulating large-scale attacks to test response protocols and improve coordination. For instance, the U.S. Department of Homeland Security's Cyber Storm exercises bring together international partners, federal agencies, and private sector stakeholders to simulate cyber crises and refine response strategies. Similarly, the NATO Industry Cyber Partnership (NICP) facilitates collaboration between alliance members and private companies to enhance collective defense. These exercises not only improve technical readiness but also foster relationships that prove invaluable during actual cyber-incidents.

4.5.5 Policy Co-Development and Regulatory Frameworks

Beyond operational collaboration, public-private partnerships play a crucial role in shaping cyber-security policies and regulations. Governments rely on industry expertise to craft practical, effective laws that balance security with innovation. For example, the development of the U.S. National Institute of Standards and Technology (NIST) Cyber-security Framework involved extensive input from private sector stakeholders to ensure its applicability across industries. Similarly, the EU's General Data Protection Regulation (GDPR) and Network and Information Security (NIS) Directive were shaped by consultations with technology firms and cyber-security experts. This co-development ensures that regulations are both enforceable and adaptable to real-world cyber-security challenges, reducing compliance burdens while enhancing security postures.

4.5.6 Challenges

Despite their benefits, public-private partnerships face several challenges that can hinder their effectiveness. One major issue is the misalignment of incentives—governments prioritize national security and public safety, while private companies focus on profitability, market competition, and shareholder interests. This can lead to reluctance in sharing sensitive information or investing in collective defense measures. Additionally, legal and jurisdictional barriers often complicate cross-border cooperation, particularly when dealing with multinational corporations operating under different regulatory regimes. Trust deficits between sectors can also impede collaboration, as private entities may fear government overreach, while public agencies may distrust corporate motives. Addressing these challenges requires clear governance structures, liability protections, and mechanisms for equitable burden-sharing in cyber-defense efforts.

4.5.7 Role of International Public-Private Partnerships

Cyber-threats are inherently transnational, making international public-private partnerships essential for global cyber-security resilience. Initiatives such as the World Economic Forum's Partnership Against Cybercrime and the Global Cyber Alliance bring together governments, corporations, and civil society to tackle cybercrime and improve digital hygiene. Similarly, the Paris Call for Trust and Security in Cyberspace, endorsed by numerous nations and private entities, promotes norms of responsible behavior and collective action against malicious cyber-activities. These international collaborations help harmonize cyber-security standards, facilitate cross-border threat intelligence sharing, and coordinate responses to large-scale cyber-incidents that affect multiple jurisdictions. By fostering a unified approach, they reduce fragmentation in global cyber-security efforts and enhance collective defense capabilities.

4.5.8 Case Studies

Several real-world examples demonstrate the effectiveness of public-private partnerships in cyber-security. In the United States, the Financial Services Information Sharing and Analysis Center (FS-ISAC) has been instrumental in helping banks and financial institutions defend against cyber-threats by facilitating rapid intelligence exchange with government agencies. In Europe, the European Cyber-security Organisation (ECSO) works closely with EU institutions to drive innovation and standardize cyber-security practices across member states. Meanwhile, in Asia, Japan's Cyber-security Strategic Headquarters collaborates with private firms to enhance national cyber-defenses, particularly in critical infrastructure sectors. These cases illustrate how structured collaboration can lead to measurable improvements in threat detection, incident response, and overall cyber resilience.

CHAPTER 5

Multilateral and Regional Approaches

5.1 UN AND INTERGOVERNMENTAL CYBER NORMS INITIATIVES

The development of cyber norms under the auspices of the United Nations and other intergovernmental organizations represents a crucial step toward managing the complexities of the digital age. Initiatives such as the GGE and OEWG provide a foundation for applying international law in cyberspace, while organizations like the OSCE, NATO, and the EU operationalize these principles within their regions. Despite challenges of rivalry, enforcement, and technological change, the pursuit of norms reflects a shared recognition that stability in cyberspace requires cooperation and shared rules of the road. By fostering dialogue, promoting transparency, and building capacity, UN and intergovernmental initiatives contribute to the gradual emergence of a global framework for responsible state behavior in cyberspace.

Looking ahead, the trajectory of UN and intergovernmental cyber norms initiatives will depend on building greater consensus and operationalizing principles into practice. Strengthening the inclusivity of forums like the OEWG is essential for ensuring that all states, regardless of size or capacity, have a voice in shaping norms. At the same time, regional organizations will continue to adapt global principles to their specific security and political contexts, creating a multi-layered governance framework. There is also a growing recognition that norms must be complemented by practical measures, such as capacity-building programs, joint exercises, and information-sharing platforms. These measures help translate abstract commitments into concrete actions that enhance stability. Moreover, the future of cyber norms will increasingly involve public-private partnerships, as technology companies and civil society organizations play indispensable roles in securing cyberspace.

5.1.1 Role of the United Nations in Cyber Norms

The United Nations has emerged as the central forum for deliberating cyber norms due to its universal membership and legitimacy in international law. The UN Charter, which enshrines principles of sovereignty, non-intervention, and the prohibition of the use of force, is considered applicable to cyberspace. However, translating these principles into practical guidelines for digital activities requires consensus-building among diverse states with differing interests. The UN has primarily advanced its work on cyber norms through two key mechanisms: the Group of Governmental Experts (GGE) and the Open-Ended Working Group (OEWG).

5.1.2 Group of Governmental Experts (GGE)

The UN Group of Governmental Experts, first established in 2004, brought together small groups of states to deliberate on how international law applies to cyberspace. The GGEs made significant contributions to the normative framework by affirming that existing international law, particularly the UN Charter, applies to state conduct in cyberspace. The 2013 GGE report highlighted the applicability of sovereignty and the prohibition of the use of force in cyberspace, while the 2015 report went further by outlining eleven voluntary, non-binding norms of responsible state behavior. These norms included commitments such as refraining from attacking critical infrastructure, cooperating to mitigate malicious cyber-activities, and respecting the work of Computer Emergency Response Teams. Although the GGE faced challenges, especially in achieving consensus during its 2017 round, its contributions provided a foundation for future discussions on norms and set benchmarks for international expectations.

5.1.3 Open-Ended Working Group (OEWG)

The Open-Ended Working Group was established in 2018 through a resolution proposed by Russia and adopted by the UN General Assembly. Unlike the GGE, which was limited in membership, the OEWG was open to all UN member states, thereby making it a more inclusive forum for cyber norms discussion. The OEWG emphasized capacity-building, transparency, and dialogue among states, including the participation of non-governmental stakeholders such as civil society and private industry. Its reports reinforced the applicability of international law in cyberspace and reiterated the need for responsible state behavior, aligning in many ways with the GGE outcomes. The OEWG demonstrated the UN's role not only in legal clarification but also in fostering inclusivity in the norm-building process. This shift toward inclusivity reflects the recognition that cyberspace is not controlled by states alone but is a shared domain involving multiple actors.

5.1.4 Intergovernmental Initiatives Beyond the UN

While the United Nations provides a universal platform, other intergovernmental organizations have also played crucial roles in shaping cyber norms. The Organization for Security and Co-operation in Europe (OSCE), the North Atlantic Treaty Organization (NATO), and the European Union (EU) are prominent examples. These organizations complement UN efforts by introducing regional or alliance-based initiatives tailored to their constituencies. The OSCE has pioneered the adoption of confidence-building measures in cyberspace, aimed at reducing misperceptions and fostering communication among states. These measures include information-sharing on national policies, establishing contact points, and ensuring transparency in state conduct. The OSCE's role highlights the importance of regional frameworks in operationalizing norms developed at the UN level.

NATO has taken a more security-oriented approach, declaring cyberspace as a domain of operations in 2016 and committing to collective defense mechanisms against cyber-attacks. While NATO's initiatives do not establish global norms, they demonstrate how intergovernmental organizations adapt international principles to alliance security needs. The EU, meanwhile, has emphasized regulatory measures, promoting norms of accountability, data protection, and digital rights. By imposing strict legal frameworks, such as the General Data Protection Regulation (GDPR), the EU influences not only member states but also global digital practices.

5.1.5 Key Themes in UN and Intergovernmental Norms Initiatives

Across the UN and intergovernmental bodies, several themes emerge as central to cyber norms initiatives. First, the principle of sovereignty remains contested, with debates over whether cyber-operations that cross borders without causing physical harm constitute violations of sovereignty. Second, there is a shared commitment to protecting critical infrastructure, as disruption in sectors such as energy, healthcare, or transportation can have catastrophic effects. Third, the issue of attribution complicates accountability, as technical and political hurdles make it difficult to identify perpetrators of cyber-incidents with certainty. Norms initiatives therefore focus on encouraging transparency and cooperation to mitigate these challenges.

Another recurring theme is the importance of capacity-building, particularly for developing countries that lack the resources to defend against cyber-threats. Both the GGE and the OEWG have underscored the need for international assistance to ensure that all states can implement cyber norms effectively. This reflects a recognition that global security in cyberspace is only as strong as its weakest link. Finally, confidence-building measures are emphasized across initiatives, with the aim of reducing mistrust and preventing escalation. These measures serve as practical tools for implementing broader normative commitments.

Challenges

- Despite progress, the development of cyber norms faces significant obstacles. One major challenge is geopolitical rivalry. Different states have diverging visions for cyberspace governance, with some emphasizing state sovereignty and control, while others advocate for openness and multistakeholder participation. These differences manifest in disagreements over issues such as data localization, internet governance, and acceptable uses of cyber-operations.

- Another challenge is the voluntary and non-binding nature of most norms. While the GGE and OEWG reports have outlined important principles, their lack of legal enforcement mechanisms limits their effectiveness. States may endorse norms rhetorically while continuing to engage in activities that undermine them. Furthermore, the rapid pace of technological innovation means that new challenges, such as artificial intelligence-driven cyber-attacks or quantum computing vulnerabilities, outpace the ability of international frameworks to adapt.
- The involvement of non-state actors also complicates norm-building. Private companies own and operate much of the global digital infrastructure, while cybercriminal groups and hacktivists are significant players in cyberspace. While intergovernmental initiatives acknowledge the importance of multistakeholder engagement, integrating these actors into formal decision-making processes remains a challenge.

5.2 NATO, OSCE, AND REGIONAL CYBER-DEFENSE COOPERATION

The borderless nature of cyberspace presents a fundamental challenge to traditional national security models. No state, regardless of its resources or technical prowess, can unilaterally defend against the sophisticated and pervasive cyber-threats emanating from a globalized digital ecosystem. This reality has catalyzed the emergence of regional organizations as critical platforms for collective cyber-defense, offering a framework to pool resources, harmonize policies, and present a unified front against malicious actors.

Among these, the North Atlantic Treaty Organization (NATO) and the Organization for Security and Co-operation in Europe (OSCE) stand as two of the most significant, albeit distinct, models for regional cooperation. Their approaches, shaped by their founding mandates and membership structures, offer complementary pathways toward enhancing regional stability in cyberspace. Analyzing their respective strategies and initiatives reveals a complex tapestry of efforts aimed at transforming a domain of strategic competition into one of managed cooperation and collective resilience.

The future of regional cyber-defense cooperation will depend on the ability of these organizations to evolve and, where possible, synergize their efforts. For NATO, this means continuing to integrate cyber capabilities into all alliance operations and exercises, while deepening practical cooperation with partner nations and the

European Union. It must also continue to refine its deterrence posture to address grey-zone activities that fall below the threshold of armed conflict. For the OSCE, the path forward involves patiently working to preserve existing communication channels and seeking incremental progress on CSBMs, even in the face of political hostility.

Its role as a facilitator for dialogue is arguably more important during periods of tension than during times of peace. The ultimate goal for the broader region should be to foster a security environment where NATO's deterrence discourages the most egregious forms of cyber aggression, while the OSCE's dialogue mechanisms provide the tools to manage and de-escalate the constant daily competition in cyberspace. This multi-layered, multi-stakeholder approach, leveraging the unique strengths of each institution, represents the most promising model for achieving a stable and secure digital future for the region.

5.2.1 NATO: From Collective Defense to Operationalizing Cyber as a Domain

NATO's journey in cyber-defense is a definitive case of a military alliance adapting its core principles to a new battlespace. The cornerstone of NATO, Article 5's collective defense clause, which stipulates that an attack on one member is an attack on all, required careful consideration in the cyber context. The alliance's strategic evolution culminated in 2016 with the formal recognition of cyberspace as a domain of operations, alongside air, land, and sea. This was not merely a symbolic gesture; it signified that cyber-operations could potentially trigger an Article 5 response and mandated that NATO must be able to defend its networks and missions as effectively in cyberspace as in other domains.

Operationally, this is coordinated through the NATO Cooperative Cyber Defence Centre of Excellence (CCDCOE) in Tallinn, a hub of excellence that conducts research, training, and large-scale exercises like Locked Shields. Perhaps most importantly, NATO provides a platform for capability development, assisting member states in enhancing their national cyber-defenses and ensuring a degree of interoperability among allies. This military-focused, deterrence-based model is predicated on building a high level of trust and integration among its members, aiming to deny potential adversaries the opportunity to exploit divisions within the alliance through cyber means.

5.2.2 OSCE: Building Confidence and Preventing Conflict through Dialogue

In stark contrast to NATO's military alliance structure, the OSCE operates as a inclusive security community encompassing 57 participating States from North America, Europe, and Asia, including historical adversaries like the United

States and Russia. This diverse membership makes its approach to cyber security fundamentally different. The OSCE's primary value lies not in collective defense or military integration, but in its role as a permanent diplomatic forum dedicated to conflict prevention, crisis management, and the building of confidence- and security-building measures (CSBMs).

Its work in cyberspace is a direct extension of this mandate. The OSCE has focused on reducing the risks of conflict stemming from miscommunication, miscalculation, or escalation in cyberspace. Through a series of landmark decisions, participating States have agreed to a set of voluntary CSBMs, including the exchange of national points of contact for urgent communication, the sharing of views on national cyber-security strategies, and the facilitation of cooperation between states in investigating cyber-incidents. The OSCE process provides a rare channel for dialogue between geopolitical blocs, aiming to foster predictability and transparency even amidst profound political disagreements.

5.2.3 Complementary Roles: Deterrence and Dialogue in Tandem

While their methods differ, the roles of NATO and the OSCE are not contradictory but deeply complementary. They represent two essential pillars of a comprehensive regional security architecture: deterrence and dialogue. NATO's function is to strengthen the defensive and deterrence capabilities of its members, ensuring that aggression in cyberspace carries a credible risk of consequence. This hard-power posture is essential for protecting the alliance's critical infrastructure and military assets.

Conversely, the OSCE provides the essential diplomatic channels for de-escalation and communication, especially during periods of heightened tension. It offers a neutral table where states can discuss contentious issues, clarify ambiguous activities, and manage incidents before they spiral out of control. A cyber incident involving a NATO member and a non-NATO OSCE state, for instance, could be addressed through both frameworks: NATO would assure its member and consider a collective response, while the OSCE could provide the communication channel for dialogue and clarification to prevent unintended escalation. This tandem operation allows for a nuanced response that combines strength with diplomacy.

5.2.4 Challenges and Frictions in Regional Cooperation

Despite their importance, both organizations face significant challenges in their cyber-defense endeavors. Within NATO, the primary challenge is maintaining cohesion and ensuring equitable burden-sharing. Members possess vastly different cyber capabilities, leading to concerns about a two-tiered alliance where a handful of states provide security for the rest. Furthermore, the precise threshold for triggering Article 5 in response to a cyber attack remains deliberately ambiguous, a strategic necessity that also introduces an element of uncertainty. For the OSCE, the challenges are even more profound. Its consensus-based model is both its greatest strength and its most crippling weakness. Deep-seated political divisions, particularly between Western states and Russia, have often stalled progress and prevented the adoption of more substantive and binding agreements. The very same inclusivity that makes the OSCE's dialogue valuable also makes it vulnerable to deadlock, as states with opposing visions for internet governance and state behavior in cyberspace can block consensus.

5.3 ASEAN, AU, AND OAS CYBER-DIPLOMACY EFFORTS

ASEAN, the AU, and the OAS have made significant strides in advancing cyber-diplomacy, recognizing that regional cooperation is essential for addressing transnational cyber-threats. Through capacity building, norm development, and public-private partnerships, these organizations have strengthened the cyber-security resilience of their member states while contributing to global cyber-security governance.

However, challenges such as resource constraints, geopolitical tensions, and evolving cyber-threats require sustained effort and adaptation. By continuing to invest in regional cooperation, technical assistance, and policy alignment, these organizations can ensure that their cyber-diplomacy efforts remain effective in safeguarding the digital future of their respective regions. The path forward demands not only collaboration but also a shared commitment to building a secure, stable, and inclusive cyber-security environment.

As cyber-threats continue to evolve, ASEAN, the AU, and the OAS must adapt their cyber-diplomacy strategies to address emerging challenges. The rise of artificial intelligence, quantum computing, and the Internet of Things (IoT) will introduce new vulnerabilities that require innovative defense strategies and updated policy frameworks. Regional organizations will need to enhance their capacity-building programs, deepen public-private partnerships, and strengthen international cooperation to keep pace with these developments. Additionally, there will be a growing need for standardized metrics to measure the effectiveness of regional cyber-security initiatives, ensuring that resources are allocated efficiently and progress is tracked transparently. By continuing to foster collaboration, innovation, and shared responsibility, these organizations can play a leading role in shaping a secure and resilient digital future for their regions.

5.3.1 ASEAN's Approach to Cyber-diplomacy and Security

ASEAN has emerged as a key player in shaping cyber-security norms and cooperation in Southeast Asia. The organization's cyber-diplomacy efforts are centered around the ASEAN Regional Forum (ARF) and the ASEAN Ministerial

Conference on Cyber-security (AMCC), which provide platforms for dialogue on cyber-security challenges. A landmark development was the adoption of the ASEAN Cyber-security Cooperation Strategy in 2017, which outlines a framework for enhancing cyber resilience, promoting information sharing, and fostering public-private partnerships. Additionally, ASEAN has established the ASEAN-Singapore Cyber-security Centre of Excellence, which serves as a hub for training and capacity-building initiatives. These efforts aim to strengthen the cyber-security posture of member states while ensuring that regional cooperation aligns with broader international cyber-security norms.

5.3.2 African Union's Cyber-security and Digital Governance Initiatives

The African Union has made significant strides in advancing cyber-diplomacy through its African Union Convention on Cyber Security and Personal Data Protection, adopted in 2014. This convention provides a legal framework for member states to address cybercrime, data protection, and electronic transactions, fostering a harmonized approach to cyber-security across the continent.

The AU has also established the African Union Cyber-security Expert Group, which works to develop policies, enhance incident response capabilities, and promote cyber-security awareness. Furthermore, the AU's Digital Transformation Strategy emphasizes the importance of secure digital infrastructure as a foundation for economic growth and regional integration. Through these initiatives, the AU seeks to bridge the digital divide while ensuring that African nations can collectively defend against cyber-threats that exploit vulnerabilities in their emerging digital economies.

5.3.3 OAS Cyber-security Strategy and Hemispheric Cooperation

The Organization of American States has been at the forefront of cyber-diplomacy in the Western Hemisphere, with a strong focus on building trust and cooperation among its member states. The OAS adopted the Comprehensive Inter-American Cyber-security Strategy in 2004, which was later updated to address evolving threats. This strategy emphasizes the importance of national cyber-security policies, critical infrastructure protection, and international cooperation in cyber incident response.

The OAS also established the Inter-American Committee against Terrorism (CICTE), which includes a cyber-security program that facilitates training, policy development, and information sharing. Additionally, the OAS has promoted the use of the Inter-American Cyber-security Framework, which provides guidelines for member states to enhance their cyber-security governance. These efforts reflect the OAS's commitment to fostering a secure and resilient digital environment across the Americas.

5.3.4 Comparative Analysis of Regional Cyber-diplomacy Approaches

While ASEAN, the AU, and the OAS share the common goal of enhancing regional cyber-security, their approaches differ based on their unique geopolitical and economic contexts. ASEAN's cyber-diplomacy is characterized by its emphasis on consensus-building and non-binding norms, reflecting the organization's tradition of informal diplomacy.

The AU, on the other hand, has taken a more formalized approach through legally binding conventions and structured expert groups, recognizing the need for strong legal frameworks to govern cyber-security in a rapidly digitizing continent. The OAS, with its focus on technical assistance and capacity-building, has prioritized practical cooperation and policy alignment, leveraging its long-standing experience in hemispheric security collaboration. Despite these differences, all three organizations recognize the importance of information sharing, joint exercises, and public-private partnerships in strengthening regional cyber-security.

5.3.5 Capacity Building and Technical Cooperation in Regional Cyber-diplomacy

A central pillar of ASEAN, AU, and OAS cyber-diplomacy efforts is capacity building, which aims to enhance the cyber-security capabilities of member states. ASEAN has focused on establishing regional training centers and promoting best practices through workshops and simulations. The AU has prioritized the development of national Computer Emergency Response Teams (CERTs) and the creation of cyber-security awareness programs to address the skills gap in Africa. The OAS, through its Cyber-security Program, provides technical assistance, policy guidance, and incident response training to help member states build resilient cyber-security frameworks. These capacity-building initiatives are essential for ensuring that all member states, regardless of their current cyber-security maturity, can contribute to and benefit from regional cyber-security cooperation.

5.3.6 Norm Development and International Alignment

Regional organizations play a crucial role in shaping cyber-security norms that align with global standards while addressing local priorities. ASEAN has contributed to international cyber-security discussions through its participation in the United Nations Open-Ended Working Group (OEWG) and other multilateral forums, advocating for norms that respect sovereignty and non-interference. The AU has worked to align its cyber-security conventions with international legal frameworks, ensuring that African perspectives are represented in global cyber-governance. The OAS has similarly engaged in international cyber-diplomacy, promoting the adoption of the Budapest Convention on Cybercrime and other global cyber-security instruments. By participating in these international discussions, regional organizations help bridge the gap between global cyber-security norms and regional implementation.

5.3.7 Challenges in Regional Cyber-diplomacy

Despite their progress, ASEAN, the AU, and the OAS face significant challenges in their cyber-diplomacy efforts. One major obstacle is the varying levels of cyber-security maturity among member states, which can create disparities in regional resilience. Additionally, geopolitical tensions and differing national interests can hinder consensus on cyber-security policies and cooperation frameworks. Resource constraints also pose a challenge, as many member states lack the financial and technical capacity to fully implement regional cyber-security strategies. Furthermore, the rapid evolution of cyber-threats requires continuous adaptation of policies and defenses, demanding sustained investment in training, technology, and international collaboration. Addressing these challenges will require enhanced coordination, increased funding, and a commitment to long-term capacity building.

5.3.8 Role of Public-Private Partnerships in Regional Cyber-security

Public-private partnerships have become an essential component of regional cyber-diplomacy, as governments increasingly recognize the need to collaborate with the private sector to address cyber-threats. ASEAN has encouraged partnerships between its member states and technology companies to enhance threat intelligence sharing and incident response capabilities. The AU has worked with telecommunications providers and cyber-security firms to strengthen Africa's digital infrastructure and improve cyber resilience. The OAS has similarly engaged with private sector stakeholders to develop cyber-security standards and best practices for critical infrastructure protection. These partnerships are vital for leveraging private sector innovation and expertise while ensuring that regional cyber-security efforts are aligned with national and international security objectives.

5.4 EU'S CYBER-DIPLOMACY TOOLBOX AND STRATEGIC AUTONOMY

The EU's cyber-diplomacy toolbox and its pursuit of strategic autonomy reflect a comprehensive strategy to address the challenges of the digital era. The toolbox provides a framework for collective and coordinated responses to cyber-incidents, strengthening deterrence and accountability. Strategic autonomy ensures that the Union can act independently and protect its values in a competitive technological environment. Together, these initiatives highlight Europe's determination to shape the norms, rules, and practices of cyberspace rather than remain a passive actor. Although challenges remain in terms of unity, capability, and credibility, the EU's approach offers a model of how regional organizations can address the complex interplay between cyber-security, diplomacy, and sovereignty in the twenty-first century.

Looking ahead, the EU's cyber-diplomacy toolbox and strategic autonomy will likely evolve in response to both internal and external pressures. Strengthening unity among member states will be critical, requiring greater coordination, information-sharing, and joint exercises. Expanding partnerships with like-minded countries and international organizations will also be important for reinforcing the EU's global influence in cyber-governance. Strategic autonomy will increasingly depend on investments in digital infrastructure, innovation, and supply chain security.

Initiatives such as the European Cyber-security Competence Centre and funding for digital transformation under the EU's budget highlight the Union's recognition of these priorities. As emerging technologies such as quantum computing and artificial intelligence reshape the cyber landscape, the EU's ability to integrate these into its strategies will determine its resilience and influence. Ultimately, the future of EU cyber-diplomacy lies in balancing pragmatism with principle. By combining its cyber-diplomacy toolbox with the pursuit of strategic autonomy, the Union can reinforce its identity as a global actor committed to security, sovereignty, and digital rights.

5.4.1 Origins of the Cyber-diplomacy Toolbox

The cyber-diplomacy toolbox was formally introduced in 2017 in the aftermath of increasing concern about cyber-attacks targeting EU institutions, member states, and critical infrastructure. Events such as the WannaCry and NotPetya attacks highlighted the vulnerabilities of Europe's digital infrastructure and underscored the cross-border nature of cyber-threats. The toolbox was conceived as part of the EU's cyber-diplomacy framework, a broader effort to integrate cyber-issues into its foreign and security policy. By creating a collective mechanism for responding to cyber-incidents, the EU aimed to send a clear message that malicious cyber behavior would not be tolerated and that the Union was capable of coordinated action.

5.4.2 Objectives and Functions of the Toolbox

The central objective of the cyber-diplomacy toolbox is deterrence. By providing a range of diplomatic, restrictive, and coercive measures, the EU intends to dissuade state and non-state actors from engaging in malicious cyber-activities. The toolbox also aims to enhance resilience by ensuring that member states can respond collectively and coherently to threats, thereby reducing the risk of fragmentation in Europe's digital security landscape. Functionally, the toolbox operates through a layered approach. It begins with preventive measures such as diplomatic engagement, dialogue, and information-sharing with partner countries and international organizations. When preventive measures are insufficient, the toolbox allows for diplomatic demarches, public statements, and the use of attribution to hold perpetrators accountable. The most coercive instruments include restrictive measures, such as travel bans and asset freezes, which the EU has applied in cases of severe cyber-attacks. These steps demonstrate the Union's willingness to escalate responses in proportion to the severity of threats.

5.4.3 Attribution and Collective Response

A critical element of the cyber-diplomacy toolbox is the question of attribution, which remains one of the most complex challenges in cyberspace. Attribution involves identifying the actor behind a cyber-attack and publicly or privately acknowledging their responsibility. The EU has sought to establish mechanisms for joint attribution, enabling member states to collectively attribute cyber-incidents and respond in a unified manner. This collective approach enhances the credibility of EU responses, as it prevents individual member states from being isolated or vulnerable when accusing powerful adversaries.

Notable examples of attribution under the toolbox include the EU's coordinated responses to cyber-incidents linked to Russia, China, and North Korea. For instance, in 2020 the EU imposed sanctions on individuals and entities associated with the 2017 WannaCry, 2018 NotPetya, and 2015 Bundestag hack incidents. These actions marked the first use of EU sanctions in response to cyber-attacks, setting a precedent for integrating cyber-issues into the Union's broader foreign policy toolkit.

5.4.4 Strategic Autonomy in the Digital Domain

Parallel to the cyber-diplomacy toolbox, the EU has emphasized the concept of strategic autonomy, particularly in the digital domain. Strategic autonomy refers to the Union's capacity to make decisions and take actions independently, without undue reliance on external powers. This principle has gained urgency in the context of cyber-governance, as Europe has historically depended on technologies, infrastructure, and security assurances from external actors, especially the United States.

In the digital realm, strategic autonomy encompasses reducing dependence on foreign technology providers, enhancing the security of supply chains, and developing indigenous capabilities in critical areas such as cloud computing, artificial intelligence, and 5G networks. The EU's General Data Protection Regulation (GDPR) exemplifies this pursuit by asserting European values and rules over global digital practices, thereby reinforcing the idea that the Union can shape standards independently. Strategic autonomy is not about isolationism but about ensuring that Europe can defend its interests and values in a competitive digital environment.

5.4.5 Link between the Toolbox and Strategic Autonomy

The cyber-diplomacy toolbox and strategic autonomy are deeply interconnected. The effectiveness of the toolbox depends on the EU's ability to act as a cohesive and credible actor on the international stage, which in turn requires reducing dependency on external powers for critical technologies and intelligence. Without strategic autonomy, the EU's cyber-diplomacy efforts risk being undermined by external pressures or technological vulnerabilities. Conversely, the toolbox strengthens the EU's strategic autonomy by giving it instruments to defend its digital space and assert its role in global cyber-governance.

By combining deterrence mechanisms with a commitment to independence, the EU seeks to position itself as a normative power in cyberspace. This dual approach enables the Union to both protect itself against cyber-threats and promote its vision of an open, secure, and rights-respecting digital environment.

5.4.6 Challenges to Implementation

Despite its achievements, the EU faces several challenges in implementing the cyber-diplomacy toolbox and achieving strategic autonomy. One of the most significant obstacles is internal fragmentation among member states. Differences in national cyber capabilities, strategic cultures, and foreign policy orientations can complicate efforts to achieve unity in responses to cyber-incidents. Some member states may be more cautious about attributing attacks or imposing sanctions, while others may advocate for stronger measures.

Another challenge is the rapidly evolving nature of cyber-threats. As adversaries develop more sophisticated techniques, the EU must constantly adapt its tools and strategies. This requires investment in research, innovation, and capacity-building, as well as stronger public-private cooperation. Furthermore, the geopolitical environment adds complexity, as the EU must balance its relations with major powers like the United States, China, and Russia while asserting its autonomy in cyberspace.

A final challenge is the perception of the EU's deterrence credibility. While the imposition of cyber sanctions is a step forward, questions remain about whether such measures are sufficient to change adversaries' behavior. Critics argue that without stronger enforcement mechanisms or the capacity for offensive cyber-operations, the EU's deterrence may be limited.

5.5 CHALLENGES IN ACHIEVING GLOBAL CONSENSUS

The most profound obstacle to global consensus on cyberspace lies in a fundamental and seemingly irreconcilable divergence in philosophy over the very nature of the internet and state authority within it. On one side, a coalition led primarily by Western nations advocates for a multi-stakeholder model of internet governance. This vision promotes a open, interoperable, and secure internet, managed through a decentralized process involving governments, the private sector, technical communities, and civil society.

It emphasizes the free flow of information and views the internet as a global public good that should transcend tight national control. Directly opposing this is the concept of cyber sovereignty, championed by states including China and Russia. This model asserts the primacy of state control over the internet within national borders. It advocates for a state-led multilateral approach to governance, where governments have the authority to regulate content, manage data flows, and protect national security interests as they see fit, often through extensive censorship and surveillance apparatuses. This ideological schism is not merely academic; it represents a battle over the future of the digital world, making consensus on universal rules of the road virtually impossible as any agreement would inherently favor one model over the other, threatening the core strategic interests of the losing side.

5.5.1 Attribution Dilemma: Secrecy, Mistrust, and the Barrier to Accountability

The technical architecture of cyberspace, designed for anonymity and redundancy, creates a pervasive environment of mistrust that fundamentally undermines the prospect of global cooperation. The core challenge of attribution—reliably identifying the perpetrator of a malicious cyber-operation—is weaponized by adversaries and politicized by all parties.

Sophisticated state actors invest significant resources in developing false-flag operations, routing attacks through compromised infrastructure in third countries, and mimicking the tactics of other groups to sow confusion and create plausible deniability. This deliberate obfuscation means that public evidence of wrongdoing is often circumstantial and requires intelligence sources and methods that states are unwilling to reveal.

Consequently, when a victim state publicly attributes an attack, the accused state can easily dismiss the claims as politically motivated fabrication without a transparent, internationally accepted evidentiary standard. This erodes the very foundation of accountability. Without a trusted, neutral technical body to adjudicate claims—a prospect most states reject as an infringement on their sovereignty—the international community is left with a cacophony of accusations and denials. This environment of perpetual mistrust prevents the establishment of a shared reality upon which consensus and collective action could be built.

5.5.2 Legal Labyrinth: Applying Analog Law to a Digital World

The project of applying existing international law to cyberspace, while essential, is itself a source of contention and a significant challenge to consensus. Initiatives like the Tallinn Manual represent meticulous efforts by scholars to interpret how laws governing the use of force and armed conflict translate into the cyber domain. However, this process is fraught with disagreement even among allies. States diverge sharply on critical issues such as the precise threshold at which a cyber-operation constitutes a prohibited use of force or an armed attack triggering the right to self-defense.

They disagree on how core principles like proportionality and distinction can be practically implemented in a domain where effects can be delayed, indirect, and widespread. Furthermore, many nations in the Global South, while not necessarily rejecting the application of international law, express concerns that these frameworks were developed without their input and may not adequately address their specific security concerns. They argue that the focus on jus ad bellum and international humanitarian law overlooks the day-to-day threats they face, such as cybercrime and economic espionage. This legal labyrinth means that instead of a clear, universally accepted set of rules, there is a fragmented and contested landscape where states can selectively interpret legal principles to justify their own actions while condemning those of their adversaries.

5.5.3 Asymmetry of Power and Capacity: Dividing the Global North and South

The vast disparity in cyber capabilities and resources between states creates a misalignment of priorities that stifles global agreement. A small number of technologically advanced states possess offensive cyber commands, advanced persistent threat groups, and the resources to invest in resilient critical infrastructure. Their primary security concerns often revolve around high-end state-sponsored espionage, pre-positioning in critical networks, and the potential for disruptive attacks on national infrastructure. In contrast, many developing nations are focused on more immediate and pervasive threats: crippling cybercrime, ransomware attacks targeting public services, and the challenges of building basic digital literacy and foundational cyber-security institutions. For these states, discussions about the laws of cyber-warfare can seem esoteric and disconnected from their reality. This capacity gap leads to a divergence in strategic interests. Developing nations may prioritize capacity building and international cooperation against cybercrime above all else, while advanced cyber powers focus on norms against targeting critical infrastructure. This asymmetry makes it difficult to forge a single, comprehensive consensus, as a framework that addresses the concerns of one group may seem irrelevant or even detrimental to the interests of the other.

5.5.4 Strategic Imperative of Ambiguity: Why States Resist Clarity

Paradoxically, a significant barrier to consensus is that major cyber powers often perceive a strategic advantage in maintaining ambiguity rather than pursuing clarity. For nations with advanced offensive capabilities, clearly defined red lines and rigid rules of engagement could serve as a constraint on their own freedom of action. Strategic ambiguity allows them to engage in espionage, covert action, and grey-zone coercion below the threshold of war without fear of automatic and severe retaliation. It provides a veil behind which they can operate with a measure of deniability. Agreeing to specific, binding prohibitions could undermine their strategic options and cede a advantage to competitors.

Similarly, even for defensive purposes, states may be reluctant to explicitly define what they consider a red line for fear of inviting adversaries to probe right up to that very edge, or worse, providing them with a blueprint for how to launch an attack that is deliberately designed to stay just below the response threshold. This creates a perverse incentive where the states with the greatest capacity to shape the rules have the least interest in doing so in a concrete and limiting way, preferring a environment of flexible and subjective interpretation that they can navigate to their own benefit.

5.5.5 Faint Path Forward: Incrementalism and Coalition-Building

Given these monumental challenges, the pursuit of a single, comprehensive global treaty akin to the Geneva Conventions for cyberspace is a quixotic endeavor for the foreseeable future. The more pragmatic, though painstakingly slow, path forward lies in incrementalism and coalition-building. Consensus may be achievable not globally, but within smaller groups of like-minded states that share a common vision, such as the G7 or within regional bodies like the OECD or the European Union. These groups can develop detailed frameworks for responsible state behavior, coordinate on attribution, and impose collective costs on malign actors.

Their actions can establish state practice that may eventually crystallize into customary international law. Simultaneously, the focus in broader forums like the United Nations should be on practical confidence-building measures, such as maintaining communication channels during crises, and on combating the lowest common denominator threats, such as cybercrime, where interests are more likely to align. While this fragmented approach falls short of a universal consensus, it represents the only viable strategy for slowly building islands of stability and cooperation in a digital landscape otherwise defined by discord and competition.

CHAPTER 6

Bilateral and Multistakeholder Cyber Engagements

6.1 DIPLOMATIC DIALOGUES BETWEEN STATES

Diplomatic dialogues between states in cyberspace represent one of the most significant developments in contemporary international relations. Bilateral engagements provide targeted and confidential platforms for managing crises, building trust, and reducing tensions, even among adversaries. Multistakeholder and multilateral engagements broaden the scope of cyber-diplomacy, incorporating governments, the private sector, civil society, and international organizations in shaping the rules of the digital age. The interplay between these approaches highlights the complexity of cyber-governance and the necessity of cooperation across levels and actors. As states and societies navigate the risks and opportunities of the digital revolution, diplomatic dialogues will remain central to ensuring stability, security, and the protection of fundamental rights in cyberspace.

As cyber-threats continue to evolve, diplomatic dialogues will play an even greater role in global security. The future of bilateral dialogues may involve more structured agreements on incident response, attribution, and red lines in cyberspace. The deepening of cyber confidence-building measures between rival powers will be essential to prevent escalation in an environment of geopolitical competition.

For multistakeholder engagements, the challenge will be to balance inclusivity with effectiveness. Expanding participation while ensuring that dialogues produce actionable outcomes will require innovation in governance structures. The integration of emerging technologies such as artificial intelligence, quantum computing, and 5G into cyber-diplomacy will also demand new frameworks for dialogue. As cyberspace becomes increasingly central to every aspect of global life, the fusion of bilateral and multistakeholder approaches will define the future of international relations.

- Significance of Bilateral Cyber Dialogues:
  - Bilateral dialogues are among the most direct and practical tools for states to address cyber-security concerns. They create structured platforms where governments can raise issues of national security, share perspectives on threats, and negotiate mechanisms to manage tensions. Bilateral

engagements often emerge between states that are either strategic partners or geopolitical competitors, underscoring the dual role of cyber-diplomacy as both a cooperative and competitive enterprise.

- Bilateral dialogues allow states to address specific incidents of cyber-intrusions, discuss attribution of attacks, and establish communication channels for crisis prevention. For instance, agreements between the United States and Russia have included cyber hotlines designed to reduce the risk of escalation from misinterpreted cyber-activities. Similarly, dialogues between the United States and China have emphasized the need to reduce intellectual property theft and to promote norms of state responsibility in cyberspace. These examples highlight how bilateral cyber-diplomacy can serve as a stabilizing mechanism even among rivals.

- **Trust-Building and Transparency in Bilateral Engagements:**
  - Beyond crisis management, bilateral dialogues play an important role in building trust and promoting transparency between states. Cyber-security is an area often characterized by secrecy and suspicion, as states are reluctant to reveal their cyber capabilities or vulnerabilities. Bilateral frameworks provide a confidential space where states can exchange information about national policies, clarify red lines, and even share technical expertise.
  - Trust-building measures such as establishing direct communication channels, exchanging information on national doctrines, and conducting joint exercises enhance mutual understanding. Although these initiatives rarely eliminate mistrust entirely, they can prevent misperceptions that might otherwise escalate into conflict. The effectiveness of such engagements depends on political will, the broader state of bilateral relations, and the recognition of shared interests in preventing cyber crises.
- **Challenges of Bilateral Cyber-diplomacy:**
  - Despite their importance, bilateral dialogues face significant limitations. One challenge lies in the asymmetry of capabilities between states. Cyber powers like the United States, Russia, and China may dominate the agenda, while smaller or less technologically advanced states may lack leverage. Another challenge is the difficulty of attribution in cyberspace, which often hinders constructive dialogue by creating disagreements over responsibility for malicious activities. Furthermore, geopolitical tensions can undermine trust, making it difficult for dialogues to progress beyond rhetoric.
  - In addition, bilateral dialogues risk creating fragmented governance structures, as agreements between pairs of states may not be compatible with broader international norms. While bilateralism can address immediate concerns, it cannot by itself resolve the global challenges of cyberspace, which require inclusive and multilateral solutions. This is where multi-stakeholder and multilateral cyber engagements become essential.

- Emergence of Multistakeholder Cyber Engagements:
  - Unlike traditional diplomacy, which is conducted solely between governments, cyber-governance requires the participation of a wide range of actors. The private sector owns and operates much of the world's digital infrastructure, while civil society organizations advocate for human rights, digital freedoms, and accountability. International organizations provide platforms for collective action, while academic and technical communities contribute expertise. Multistakeholder cyber engagements bring these diverse actors together, creating a more inclusive and representative approach to managing cyberspace.
  - Such engagements have gained traction in forums like the Internet Governance Forum (IGF), which was established under the auspices of the United Nations to facilitate dialogue on internet policy. The IGF allows governments, companies, non-governmental organizations, and individuals to exchange perspectives on issues ranging from cyber-security to data protection and digital inclusion. By incorporating multiple voices, multistakeholder dialogues recognize that cyberspace is not controlled by states alone but is a shared domain requiring shared responsibility.
- Multilateral Institutions and Regional Frameworks:
  - Alongside multistakeholder efforts, intergovernmental organizations play an important role in cyber-diplomacy. The United Nations has established both the Group of Governmental Experts (GGE) and the Open-Ended Working Group (OEWG) as forums for discussing how international law applies to cyberspace and for promoting norms of responsible state behavior. These UN initiatives provide legitimacy and inclusivity, ensuring that all states, regardless of capacity, can participate in shaping global cyber norms.
  - Regional organizations also contribute to cyber-diplomacy. The Organization for Security and Co-operation in Europe (OSCE) has pioneered confidence-building measures in cyberspace, focusing on transparency and communication among member states. The European Union has advanced cyber-diplomacy through its cyber-diplomacy toolbox, which provides mechanisms for collective responses to malicious activities. The African Union and ASEAN have also developed regional frameworks to address cyber-security challenges, reflecting the diverse and global nature of cyber-governance.
- Role of the Private Sector and Civil Society:
  - The private sector plays an indispensable role in multistakeholder engagements. Technology companies like Microsoft, Google, and Cisco are not only service providers but also powerful political actors shaping cyber-security norms. Initiatives such as Microsoft's call for a Digital Geneva Convention reflect the private sector's attempt to influence the direction of glob-

al cyber-governance. At the same time, industry-led efforts to share threat intelligence, such as the Cyber Threat Alliance, demonstrate the practical importance of private-sector cooperation in strengthening resilience.

  - Civil society organizations contribute by emphasizing the importance of human rights and digital freedoms in cyber-governance. Groups such as Access Now and the Electronic Frontier Foundation highlight issues of surveillance, censorship, and digital exclusion, ensuring that the development of cyber norms does not compromise fundamental rights. Their participation in multistakeholder engagements ensures that cyber-security is not framed solely as a security issue but as one intertwined with democracy, development, and ethics.

- Balancing Bilateral and Multistakeholder Approaches:
  - The interplay between bilateral and multistakeholder cyber engagements illustrates the layered nature of cyber-diplomacy. Bilateral dialogues provide targeted mechanisms for crisis prevention and trust-building between specific states, particularly those with adversarial relationships. They are essential for managing incidents that cannot be resolved in broader forums. However, bilateralism alone cannot create a stable global framework for cyberspace.
  - Multistakeholder engagements fill this gap by incorporating diverse voices and perspectives, ensuring that global governance reflects the realities of cyberspace. Multilateral forums provide legitimacy and inclusivity, while private-sector and civil society involvement bring expertise and values to the table. The combination of bilateral and multistakeholder approaches therefore reflects a pragmatic recognition that no single format can address the multifaceted challenges of cyber-security.

6.1.1 Cyber Hotlines and Memorandums of Understanding

The inherent opacity of cyber-operations creates a uniquely perilous environment for international relations, where a state-sponsored malware implant could be interpreted as preparation for war, a disruptive attack on a financial system could be misconstrued as an act of aggression, and a simple software vulnerability could trigger a catastrophic miscalculation. This digital fog of war, compounded by the lightning speed at which events can unfold, necessitates mechanisms to prevent escalation and manage crises.

Unlike during the Cold War, where physical movements of troops and missiles provided some measurable indicators of intent, cyber-activities are clandestine and easily disguised. In this context, traditional diplomatic channels are often too slow or ill-equipped to address rapidly evolving cyber-incidents. The establishment of dedicated cyber hotlines and Memoranda of Understanding (MoUs) represents a critical adaptation of statecraft, offering a structured pathway for dialogue, clarification, and de-escalation. These instruments are not about building alliances or achieving grand consensus; they are pragmatic tools for risk reduction, designed to prevent a cyber incident from spiraling into a full-blown political or military confrontation.

Modern Red Phone: Anatomy and Function of Cyber Hotlines

The concept of a crisis hotline is famously symbolized by the Cold War-era Moscow-Washington Direct Communications Link, known as the "red telephone." Its cyber equivalent serves a similar purpose but is tailored to the specific challenges of the digital domain. A cyber hotline is not necessarily a physical telephone but rather a secure, reliable, and available communications channel, often involving multiple points of contact within respective governments, including national security councils, foreign ministries, and computer emergency response teams (CERTs). The primary function is to provide immediate clarification during a crisis.

For instance, if State A detects a sophisticated cyber-operation emanating from State B's territory targeting its power grid, it can use the hotline to demand an explanation. State B can then clarify whether this is a sanctioned state action, a rogue actor operating from its soil, or a false-flag operation by a third party. This simple act of communication can dispel dangerous assumptions and provide decision-makers with precious time and information before considering retaliatory measures. Beyond crisis management, hotlines can also be used for routine communication, such as notifying a counterpart of a ongoing cybercrime investigation that may involve their infrastructure or sharing best practices on critical infrastructure protection.

Framing the Dialogue: The Role of Memoranda of Understanding

While a hotline provides the channel for communication, a Memorandum of Understanding provides the content and the framework for the dialogue. An MoU is a non-binding agreement that outlines areas of mutual interest and establishes a structure for bilateral cyber engagement. It serves as a diplomatic script, creating predictability and setting expectations between often-adversarial states.

A typical cyber MoU might include provisions for regular diplomatic consultations on cyber-issues, commitments to share information on cyber-threats and vulnerabilities, and agreements to cooperate on combating cybercrime. Crucially, many MoUs explicitly affirm that the parties will not conduct cyber attacks against each other's critical infrastructure, a foundational norm that, even if non-binding, creates a political benchmark for responsible behavior. The non-binding nature of an MoU is its greatest strength and weakness. It allows states to engage in cooperation without the political difficulty of ratifying a formal treaty, making it a flexible tool for building trust incrementally. However, this also means compliance is voluntary and unenforceable, dependent entirely on the political will of the signatories.

Bilateral Pathway: Tailored Engagement between Specific States

The most common form for these agreements is bilateral, reflecting the pragmatic recognition that cyber tensions are often most acute between specific pairs of states. The 2015 U.S.-China cyber agreement stands as a prominent example. Following years of acrimony over Chinese state-sponsored economic espionage, the agreement saw China commit to not conducting cyber-enabled intellectual property theft for commercial gain. While violations have certainly occurred, the agreement established a clear diplomatic framework for the U.S. to hold China accountable and is credited with reducing the volume of such activity.

Similarly, bilateral cyber dialogues and MoUs between states like the U.S. and Russia, or within regional contexts like India and Pakistan, aim to create islands of stability in otherwise fraught relationships. These bilateral engagements are tailored to the specific grievances and risk profiles of the two parties involved. They allow for direct and focused discussion on the most pressing issues, whether they be intellectual property theft, election interference, or attacks on financial systems, without the complications of achieving multilateral consensus.

Multistakeholder Dimension: Beyond State-to-State Dialogue

While often focused on state-to-state relations, the concept of diplomatic dialogue in cyberspace is expanding to include a multistakeholder approach. This recognizes that governments do not have a monopoly on relevant information or capabilities; the private sector owns and operates most of the world's critical digital infrastructure and possesses unparalleled technical expertise. Consequently, new forms of engagement are emerging. Governments are establishing formal and informal channels with major technology companies and cyber-security firms to share threat intelligence at speed and scale. Forums like the Microsoft Digital Security Unit engage directly with nation-states to warn them of impending threats, as seen when it notified governments in advance of ransomware attacks.

These public-private hotlines are becoming essential components of national cyber-defense. Furthermore, multilateral MoUs between CERTs from different countries facilitate real-time technical cooperation that often bypasses slower political diplomacy, enabling experts to collaborate directly on mitigating attacks and sharing vulnerability information. This multistakeholder model enriches the diplomatic landscape, creating a more resilient and responsive network for managing cyber-incidents.

Limits of Diplomacy: Challenges and Criticisms

Despite their value, cyber hotlines and MoUs face significant limitations and skepticism. Their effectiveness is entirely contingent on the goodwill of the participants. A hotline is useless if the other party refuses to answer, and an MoU is merely a piece of paper if a state decides to violate it for strategic gain. Critics argue that such agreements can create a false sense of security or even provide cover for malicious actors to continue operations while paying lip service to diplomacy. The technical challenge of reliable attribution also looms large; a state may genuinely not know the origin of an attack and thus be unable to provide a meaningful response via a hotline. Furthermore, these agreements often struggle to keep pace with the rapidly evolving nature of cyber-threats and technology. The most profound challenge, however, is that they often paper over deep-seated geopolitical rivalries. While they can manage the symptoms of cyber conflict, they do not resolve the underlying political disputes that drive state-sponsored malicious activity in the first place.

6.2 TECH GIANTS AND PLATFORM DIPLOMACY

6.2.1 Google, Meta, Microsoft, and Their Global Roles

Google, Meta, and Microsoft represent a new category of actors in international relations: technology giants that function simultaneously as corporations, infrastructure providers, and diplomatic entities. Google governs information, Meta shapes communication and social discourse, and Microsoft secures digital infrastructure, collectively demonstrating the multifaceted nature of platform diplomacy. Their roles extend far beyond markets, influencing the norms of international law, the balance of power between states, and the protection of fundamental rights.

As states grapple with the challenges of cyber-security, disinformation, and digital governance, the influence of these firms will only grow. Platform diplomacy raises difficult questions about accountability, sovereignty, and ethics, but it also provides opportunities for innovation in global governance. By engaging with governments, international institutions, and civil society, Google, Meta, and Microsoft have become indispensable players in shaping the future of cyberspace. Their global roles illustrate the profound transformation of diplomacy in the digital era, where the power of platforms rivals the authority of states and redefines the contours of international order.

Google and the Governance of Information

Google's central role in the information ecosystem makes it one of the most influential actors in global affairs. Its search engine organizes the world's knowledge, and its platforms like YouTube and Android reach billions of people daily. This control over information access gives Google significant sway over public discourse, cultural exchange, and even democratic processes. What individuals see when they search, the recommendations they encounter on YouTube, and the accessibility of digital services through Android all influence how societies form opinions and make decisions. Governments recognize Google's enormous influence and attempt to regulate its activities in areas such as privacy, competition, and misinformation. The company has often found itself at the center of debates about censorship, whether in its limited operations in China or in its negotiations with the European Union over the right to be forgotten. At the same time, Google's investments in artificial intelligence and cloud infrastructure highlight its role as a builder of global technological standards. By influencing how societies search, learn, and innovate, Google has become a non-state actor with direct impact on diplomacy, security, and international governance.

Meta and the Diplomacy of Social Networks

Meta, formerly Facebook, controls some of the most widely used social media platforms, including Facebook, Instagram, and WhatsApp. Its platforms have connected billions of people, making it the largest social networking company in the world. With this reach, Meta not only enables social interaction but also serves as a key arena for political communication, activism, and public opinion formation. Governments, civil society, and even insurgent groups have used Meta's platforms to mobilize, persuade, and influence populations. This immense power has also exposed Meta to controversies over disinformation, election interference, and online extremism. From the Cambridge Analytica scandal to the company's role in spreading hate speech in Myanmar, Meta has repeatedly faced scrutiny for failing to prevent harmful outcomes. Yet, the same platforms have facilitated global movements for justice, democratization, and humanitarian response, demonstrating the double-edged nature of its influence. Meta's creation of an Oversight Board to review content moderation decisions represents an attempt to institutionalize accountability, yet it also reflects the extraordinary power of a private company to set rules that affect political communication worldwide. In this sense, Meta practices its own form of diplomacy, mediating between the demands of states, the rights of users, and the imperatives of global stability.

Microsoft and the Security of Digital Infrastructure

While Google and Meta dominate the realms of information and communication, Microsoft has become indispensable to global digital infrastructure and security. With its Windows operating system, Azure cloud platform, and productivity software, Microsoft underpins the daily operations of governments, corporations, and individuals across the globe. This ubiquity makes it a crucial player in ensuring the resilience and security of cyberspace. Microsoft has positioned itself as a leader in cyber-security diplomacy. It has uncovered and publicized state-sponsored hacking campaigns, attributing cyber-attacks to actors from countries such as Russia, China, and North Korea. These disclosures have elevated Microsoft's role as a defender of global networks and as a trusted partner for governments. The company's proposal for a Digital Geneva Convention, which would create rules to protect civilians from cyberwarfare, highlights its efforts to influence international law and norms in cyberspace. Unlike Google and Meta, whose roles revolve around shaping information and communication, Microsoft's global role centers on infrastructure resilience, trust, and the protection of critical systems, placing it at the heart of international security debates.

Platform Diplomacy as a Global Phenomenon

The activities of Google, Meta, and Microsoft illustrate the concept of platform diplomacy, in which technology companies act as diplomatic actors in global politics. Unlike traditional corporations, these companies operate in a domain where their decisions about algorithms, security, and user policies directly affect sovereignty, human rights, and international peace. They negotiate with states over access to data, compliance with local laws, and cooperation in surveillance or censorship. They also participate in international forums, such as United Nations cyber discussions or the Paris Call for Trust and Security in Cyberspace, where they are treated as stakeholders alongside governments. Platform diplomacy reflects the reality that cyberspace is not governed solely by states. Technology giants control critical aspects of the digital world, from undersea cables and data centers to search engines, app stores, and social platforms. This gives them leverage to act as mediators between competing state interests, to promote global standards, and to set their own codes of conduct. Their influence blurs the line between public authority and private power, raising profound questions about accountability and legitimacy in global governance.

Ethical Responsibilities and Human Rights in the Digital Age

The global roles of these tech giants carry significant ethical responsibilities, particularly in relation to human rights. Their platforms influence freedom of expression, access to information, privacy, and digital inclusion. At the same time, their business models often rely on data collection and targeted advertising, raising concerns about surveillance and exploitation of personal information. Governments frequently pressure them to restrict content, monitor communications, or provide backdoor access to data, creating tensions between compliance with state laws and the protection of universal rights. Google's transparency reports, Meta's Oversight Board, and Microsoft's human rights frameworks illustrate attempts to balance these pressures. Yet, each has faced criticism for inconsistency, lack of accountability, or prioritizing profit over principles. The ethical dimension of platform diplomacy highlights that these firms are not neutral intermediaries but actors whose decisions shape the contours of global society. Ensuring that they uphold human rights while responding to security challenges remains one of the greatest dilemmas of the digital age.

Interaction with States and International Institutions

The power of Google, Meta, and Microsoft lies not only in their control over digital platforms but also in their ability to shape relationships with states and international institutions. They negotiate directly with governments on issues such as data localization, taxation, and regulatory compliance. In some cases, such as Google's disputes with the European Union, these negotiations resemble high-level diplomatic confrontations. In others, such as Microsoft's collaboration with NATO or Meta's partnerships with humanitarian organizations, they resemble alliances aimed at addressing shared challenges. International institutions have increasingly recognized the centrality of technology companies in global governance. Initiatives such as the Internet Governance Forum and the UN's Open-Ended Working Group on cyber-security include private sector actors as participants. This reflects the acknowledgment that no state can govern cyberspace alone. By engaging in these multilateral settings, technology giants strengthen their legitimacy as diplomatic actors while also shaping the rules that will govern their own future.

6.3 CIVIL SOCIETY AND NON-STATE ACTORS IN CYBER-GOVERNANCE

Civil society and non-state actors have become indispensable to the governance of cyberspace. From safeguarding digital rights to securing critical infrastructure, from setting technical standards to amplifying marginalized voices, they perform functions that states alone cannot manage. Their inclusion in governance frameworks challenges traditional notions of sovereignty and power, reflecting the unique characteristics of cyberspace as a global, decentralized, and shared domain. The rise of civil society and non-state actors in cyber-governance underscores the importance of collaboration, transparency, and inclusivity in shaping the digital future. While challenges of inequality, representation, and accountability persist, their contributions remain essential to ensuring that cyberspace is governed not merely for the benefit of states or corporations but for the collective good of humanity. The evolution of cyber-governance will depend on how effectively these actors continue to participate, influence, and balance the interests of diverse stakeholders in a rapidly changing world.

The future of cyber-governance depends on deepening collaboration between states, civil society, and other non-state actors. The multistakeholder model, though imperfect, represents the most inclusive approach to managing cyberspace. Strengthening the participation of civil society requires addressing resource disparities, promoting capacity building in developing regions, and safeguarding the independence of NGOs from political pressures. Technology companies must also take greater responsibility for transparency and accountability, ensuring that their global influence is exercised in ways that respect human rights and democratic principles. Technical communities must continue to uphold the open and interoperable nature of the internet, while states must accept that governance cannot be monopolized by governments alone. By building on the strengths of each actor, multistakeholder cyber-governance can provide a balanced framework that addresses the complexities of the digital age.

6.3.1 Concept of Cyber-Governance Beyond States

Cyber-governance refers to the collective management of digital resources, networks, and behaviors to ensure stability, security, and fairness in cyberspace. Unlike conventional governance, where states establish and enforce rules, cyber-governance involves a distributed model that includes non-state actors with unique capabilities and responsibilities. The architecture of the internet itself was not created by governments but by technical communities, academic institutions, and private companies. Civil society groups have long advocated for digital rights, transparency, and inclusivity, ensuring that governance frameworks reflect societal values rather than only state or corporate interests.

Non-state actors occupy positions of influence in areas such as internet standards, cyber-security policy, data protection, and human rights. Their participation challenges the traditional Westphalian notion of state sovereignty, replacing it with multistakeholder governance models that combine states, companies, technical experts, and civil society. This inclusion ensures that governance frameworks are responsive to the realities of a globally interconnected digital world.

6.3.2 Civil Society as a Guardian of Digital Rights

Civil society organizations are among the most visible non-state actors in cyber-governance. Their primary role lies in safeguarding human rights in the digital environment, particularly freedom of expression, privacy, and access to information. In a world where digital platforms and surveillance systems shape political and social life, civil society groups act as watchdogs against abuses of power by both states and corporations.

Organizations such as Access Now, the Electronic Frontier Foundation, and Human Rights Watch have consistently advocated for protecting users against mass surveillance, censorship, and unjustified data collection. They provide expertise in policy forums, participate in multistakeholder initiatives, and campaign for greater transparency from governments and private companies. Civil society also plays a role in amplifying marginalized voices, ensuring that debates on digital governance reflect global diversity rather than only the priorities of powerful states or corporations. By framing cyberspace as a domain of human rights, civil society organizations contribute moral authority and normative legitimacy to cyber-governance.

6.3.3 Private Sector as a Central Non-State Actor

While civil society emphasizes rights and inclusivity, the private sector controls much of the infrastructure and services that enable the digital world. Companies such as Google, Microsoft, Amazon, and Meta operate global networks, data centers, and platforms that connect billions of people. Their decisions about security, content moderation, and data policies directly affect the stability and fairness of cyberspace.

These corporations have emerged as geopolitical actors in their own right. They engage with governments, participate in international forums, and advocate for cyber norms that protect their infrastructure and users. For example, Microsoft's proposal for a Digital Geneva Convention reflects its recognition of the need for global rules to regulate state behavior in cyberspace. Similarly, Google's transparency reports and Meta's Oversight Board are corporate mechanisms that address governance issues traditionally associated with states or international organizations. The centrality of private companies in cyber-governance illustrates how power has shifted from governments to platforms, forcing states to negotiate with non-state actors as equal partners.

6.3.4 Technical Communities and Standards Organizations

Beyond corporations and advocacy groups, technical communities play an essential role in cyber-governance. Bodies such as the Internet Corporation for Assigned Names and Numbers (ICANN), the Internet Engineering Task Force (IETF), and the World Wide Web Consortium (W3C) develop and maintain the technical standards that make the internet function. These organizations operate through consensus-driven processes that emphasize expertise and collaboration rather than geopolitical power.

Their role demonstrates that cyber-governance is not merely about political negotiation but also about technical coordination. The allocation of domain names, the design of protocols, and the maintenance of interoperability are foundational elements of digital governance. Technical communities ensure that the internet remains open, secure, and scalable, balancing the interests of multiple stakeholders. Their independence from direct state control allows them to preserve the global and borderless character of cyberspace.

6.3.5 Non-Governmental Organizations in Multilateral Forums

Civil society and non-governmental organizations have increasingly been included in multilateral forums addressing cyber-governance. The United Nations Internet Governance Forum (IGF) represents one such platform where governments, civil society, private sector actors, and technical experts come together to discuss issues ranging from cyber-security to digital inclusion. Unlike traditional UN negotiations, the IGF emphasizes open dialogue and multistakeholder participation, allowing non-state actors to influence global debates. Civil society participation in such forums has helped highlight issues that might otherwise be marginalized, such as the digital divide, online gender-based violence, and the rights of indigenous peoples in cyberspace. By contributing diverse perspectives, NGOs ensure that governance frameworks are not dominated by the interests of powerful states but instead reflect a broader understanding of justice, equity, and human rights.

6.3.6 Non-State Actors in Cyber-security and Crisis Response

Non-state actors also play a critical role in cyber-security and incident response. Cyber-security companies, for instance, are often the first to detect and analyze cyber-attacks, providing governments and organizations with the technical knowledge needed to respond. Civil society groups also contribute by raising awareness of threats and advocating for stronger protections for vulnerable communities. Multistakeholder collaborations, such as the Cyber Threat Alliance, demonstrate how companies and organizations share threat intelligence to enhance global resilience. These roles highlight the fact that states are no longer the sole guarantors of security. In the digital domain, resilience and defense depend on partnerships between governments, companies, and civil society. This shared responsibility reflects the interconnected nature of cyberspace, where no single actor can defend itself in isolation.

6.3.7 Challenges of Civil Society and Non-State Participation

Despite their contributions, civil society and non-state actors face significant challenges in cyber-governance. Power imbalances between states, corporations, and smaller organizations can marginalize civil society voices. Governments sometimes restrict NGO participation in international forums or impose legal barriers that limit advocacy work. Similarly, corporations may dominate decision-making processes due to their resources and control over infrastructure, raising concerns about corporate capture of governance. Another challenge lies in the global digital divide, which limits the ability of civil society groups from developing countries to participate effectively. Resource constraints, limited access to technical expertise, and lack of representation in international forums hinder the inclusivity of cyber-governance. Addressing these disparities is crucial for ensuring that cyber-governance reflects global needs rather than only those of technologically advanced regions.

6.4 SCIENCE AND TECH DIPLOMACY IN CYBER RELATIONS

In the 21st century, the traditional levers of diplomatic power—military might and economic influence—are increasingly underpinned by a third, crucial element: scientific and technological prowess. This reality has given rise to the practice of science and technology diplomacy (S&T diplomacy), a foreign policy instrument that leverages a nation's knowledge base and innovation ecosystem to advance its strategic interests and build international partnerships. In the realm of cyber relations, S&T diplomacy takes on a critical and dualistic character.

It is simultaneously a tool for cooperation and a arena for intense competition. It involves the collaborative development of secure technologies and the establishment of shared technical standards, but it also encompasses the use of technological assistance as a means of securing influence and shaping the global digital order in a nation's image. This form of diplomacy moves beyond discussions of norms and law to focus on the very architecture of cyberspace itself, recognizing that technological superiority and interdependence are fundamental to determining which nations will write the rules of the digital future.

6.4.1 Building Bridges: S&T Diplomacy as a Tool for Collaboration and Capacity Building

One face of S&T diplomacy in cyber relations is constructive and collaborative, focused on building trust and shared resilience through technical assistance and joint innovation. For developed nations, investing in the cyber capacity of allies and partners is a strategic imperative. A cyber vulnerability in one country can be exploited to launch attacks on others, making collective security dependent on the strength of the weakest link.

Through S&T diplomatic channels, states can share expertise, fund joint research and development (R&D) projects on cyber-security, and help partners establish and train their national computer emergency response teams (CERTs). Initiatives might include collaborative research between universities on secure coding practices, workshops for foreign judges and legislators on cybercrime law, or assistance in deploying secure digital infrastructure. This form of technical assistance strengthens the global network against common threats like transnational cybercrime and ransomware, while simultaneously fostering goodwill and creating lasting professional networks between technical communities. It builds a foundation of trust upon which more difficult political conversations about state behavior can later be built, grounding diplomacy in practical problem-solving rather than abstract principle.

6.4.2 Standards Battlefield: Diplomatic Engagement in Technical Standard-Setting

A less visible but profoundly important arena for S&T diplomacy is the highly technical world of international standard-setting bodies. Organizations like the International Telecommunication Union (ITU), the Institute of Electrical and Electronics Engineers (IEEE), and the Internet Engineering Task Force (IETF) are where the fundamental protocols and specifications that govern the internet are developed. The standards agreed upon in these forums determine the interoperability, security, and very functionality of global networks. Consequently, influencing these standards is a paramount diplomatic objective.

Nations engage in intense diplomatic efforts to ensure their technologies and preferences are embedded in international standards, which can provide their companies with a significant competitive advantage and shape the global technological landscape for decades. This "standards war" is particularly acute in fields like 5G and next-generation wireless networks, where technical choices have deep implications for national security. A nation that successfully promotes its encryption standards or network architecture internationally effectively exports its security model, enhancing its own economic and strategic position while limiting the influence of geopolitical rivals.

6.4.3 Dual-Use Dilemma: Navigating the Fine Line between Cooperation and Restriction

S&T diplomacy in the cyber domain is perpetually complicated by the dual-use nature of nearly all advanced technology. A tool developed for defensive cyber-security can easily be repurposed for offensive operations; artificial intelligence algorithms designed to detect network anomalies can be used to power surveillance systems; and robust encryption protects both the privacy of citizens and the communications of malicious actors. This creates a constant tension within diplomatic circles between the desire to foster open scientific collaboration and the need to protect national security by controlling the export of sensitive technologies.

Wassenaar Arrangement participants, for instance, struggle to update control lists to cover emerging cyber surveillance tools without stifling legitimate security research. This dual-use dilemma forces S&T diplomats to walk a fine line. They must cultivate international research partnerships to maintain their nation's innovative edge while simultaneously constructing complex legal and regulatory frameworks to prevent sensitive knowledge and technology from falling into the hands of adversaries. This balancing act requires deep technical knowledge and close coordination between the diplomatic, scientific, and intelligence communities.

6.4.4 Digital Development and Influence: Tech Assistance as Soft Power

Beyond immediate security concerns, S&T diplomacy is a powerful instrument of soft power and influence, particularly in the developing world. The digital infrastructure being built today in nations across Africa, Southeast Asia, and Latin America will define their economic and political relationships for a generation.

Major powers are engaged in a fierce diplomatic competition to provide this technology. Through development aid, concessional loans, and technical training programs, countries like China offer integrated packages of hardware, software, and expertise to build out a nation's digital ecosystem—from its telecom networks and data centers to its smart city platforms and digital payment systems. This model of "digital development diplomacy" creates profound long-term dependencies, locking countries into a specific technological sphere of influence. It shapes which platforms citizens use, how their data is governed, and which cyber-security standards are implemented. In response, Western nations are crafting their own initiatives to offer "trusted" alternatives, promoting a vision of digital development that is open, transparent, and based on respect for human rights. This battle for digital hearts and minds is a central front in modern S&T diplomacy.

6.4.5 Integrating Expertise: The Imperative for a New Diplomatic Corps

The effective execution of S&T diplomacy requires a fundamental evolution of the diplomatic profession itself. Traditional diplomats, trained in history, law, and political science, often lack the technical literacy required to engage on complex issues like quantum key distribution or algorithmic bias. To bridge this gap, foreign ministries are increasingly integrating scientists, engineers, and technology policy experts into their ranks. They are creating new roles like Science and Technology Advisors, establishing dedicated cyber-diplomacy departments, and providing technical training for career diplomats. Furthermore, they are building new bridges to the academic and private sector communities, recognizing that innovation happens far outside government walls. This fusion of technical expertise with diplomatic skill is essential for negotiating effective agreements, accurately assessing foreign technological capabilities, and crafting policies that promote innovation while mitigating risk. In the final analysis, success in cyber relations will belong to those nations that can most effectively weave scientific insight into the fabric of their foreign policy, using knowledge not just as power, but as a tool for building a stable and secure digital future.

6.5 INTERNET GOVERNANCE AND MULTISTAKEHOLDERISM

6.5.1 ICANN

The Internet Corporation for Assigned Names and Numbers (ICANN) is a global multistakeholder group and nonprofit organization headquartered in the United States. Responsible for coordinating the maintenance and procedures of several databases related to the namespaces and numerical spaces of the Internet while also ensuring the Internet's (smoothly) securely stable operation, ICANN performs the actual technical maintenance (work) of the Central Internet Address pools and DNS root zone registries pursuant to the Internet Assigned Numbers Authority (IANA) function contract. The contract regarding the IANA stewardship functions between ICANN and the National Telecommunications and Information Administration (NTIA) of the United States Department of Commerce ended on October 1, 2016, formally transitioning the functions to the global multistakeholder community.

Much of its work has concerned the Internet's global Domain Name System (DNS), including policy development for internationalization of the DNS, introduction of new generic top-level domains (TLDs), and the operation of root name servers; the numbering facilities ICANN manages include the Internet Protocol (IP) address spaces for IPv4 and v6 in addition to the assignment of address blocks to regional Internet registries (RIRs).

ICANN's primary principles of operation have been described as helping preserve the operational stability of the Internet; promoting competition; achieving broad representation of the global Internet community, and developing policies appropriate to its mission through bottom-up, consensus-based processes. The organization has often included a motto of "One World. One Internet." on annual reports beginning in 2010, on less formal publications, as well as their official website.

ICANN was officially incorporated in the state of California on September 30, 1998, with entrepreneur and philanthropist Esther Dyson as founding chairwoman. Originally headquartered in Marina del Rey in the same building as the University of Southern California's Information Sciences Institute (ISI), its offices are now in the Playa Vista neighbourhood of Los Angeles.

History

Before the establishment of ICANN, the IANA function of administering RIRs (including the distributing top-level domains and IP addresses) was performed by Jon Postel, a computer science researcher who had been involved in the creation of ARPANET, first at UCLA and then at USC-ISI. In 1997 Postel testified before Congress that this had come about as a "side task" to this research work. The Information Sciences Institute was funded by the U.S. Department of Defense, as was SRI International's Network Information Center, which also performed some assigned name functions.

As the Internet grew and expanded globally, the U.S. Department of Commerce initiated a process to establish a new organization to perform the IANA functions. On January 30, 1998, the National Telecommunications and Information Administration (NTIA), an agency of the U.S. Department of Commerce, issued for comment, "A Proposal to Improve the Technical Management of Internet Names and Addresses." The proposed rule making, or "Green Paper", was published in the

Federal Register on February 20, 1998, providing opportunity for public comment. NTIA received more than 650 comments as of March 23, 1998, when the comment period closed.

The Green Paper proposed certain actions designed to privatize the management of Internet names and addresses in a manner that allows for the development of competition and facilitates global participation in Internet management. The Green Paper proposed for discussion a variety of issues relating to DNS management including private sector creation of a new not-for-profit corporation (the "new corporation") managed by a globally and functionally representative board of directors. ICANN was formed in response to this policy. ICANN managed the Internet Assigned Numbers Authority (IANA) under contract to the United States Department of Commerce (DOC) and pursuant to an agreement with the IETF.

ICANN is a public-benefit nonprofit corporation "organized under the California Nonprofit Public Benefit Corporation Law for charitable and public purposes." ICANN was established in California due to the presence of Postel, who was a founder of ICANN and was set to be its first Chief Technology Officer prior to his unexpected death. ICANN formerly operated from the same Marina del Rey building where Postel formerly worked, which is home to an office of the Information Sciences Institute at the University of Southern California. However, ICANN's headquarters is now located in the nearby Playa Vista neighborhood of Los Angeles.

Per its original by-laws, primary responsibility for policy formation in ICANN was to be delegated to three supporting organizations (Address Supporting Organization, Domain Name Supporting Organization, and Protocol Supporting Organization), each of which was to develop and recommend substantive policies and procedures for the management of the addresses within their respective scope. They were also required to be financially independent from ICANN. As expected, the RIRs and IETF agreed to serve as the Address Supporting Organization and Protocol Supporting Organization respectively, and ICANN issued a call for interested parties to propose the structure and composition of the Domain Name Supporting Organization. In March 1999, the ICANN Board, based in part on the DNSO proposals received, decided instead on an alternate construction for the DNSO which delineated specific constituencies bodies within ICANN itself, thus adding primary responsibility for DNS policy development to ICANN's existing duties of oversight and coordination.

On July 26, 2006, the United States government renewed the contract with ICANN for performance of the IANA function for an additional one to five years. The context of ICANN's relationship with the U.S. government was clarified on September 29, 2006, when ICANN signed a new memorandum of understanding with the United States Department of Commerce (DOC). This document gave the DOC oversight over some of the ICANN operations.

In July 2008, the DOC reiterated an earlier statement that it has "no plans to transition management of the authoritative root zone file to ICANN". The letter also stresses the separate roles of the IANA and VeriSign.

On September 30, 2009, ICANN signed an agreement with the DOC (known as the "Affirmation of Commitments") that confirmed ICANN's commitment to a multistakeholder governance model, but did not remove it from DOC oversight and control. The Affirmation of Commitments, which aimed to create international oversight, ran into criticism.

On March 10, 2016, ICANN and the DOC signed a historic, culminating agreement to finally remove ICANN and IANA from the control and oversight of the DOC. On October 1, 2016, ICANN was freed from U.S. government oversight.

Since its creation, ICANN has been the subject of criticism and controversy. In 2000, professor Michael Froomkin of the University of Miami School of Law argued that ICANN's relationship with the U.S. Department of Commerce is illegal, in violation of either the Constitution or federal statutes. On June 10, 2024, it was announced that Kurt Erik Lindqvist, who has been CEO of the London Internet Exchange since 2019, was to become the new president and CEO of ICANN on December 5, 2024.

Notable Events

- On March 18, 2002, publicly elected At-Large Representative for North America board member Karl Auerbach sued ICANN in the Superior Court of Los Angeles County, California, to gain access to ICANN's accounting records without restriction. Judge Dzintra Janavs ruled in Auerbach's favor on July 29, 2002.
- During September and October 2003, ICANN played a crucial role in the conflict over VeriSign's "wild card" DNS service Site Finder. After an open letter from ICANN issuing an ultimatum to VeriSign, later endorsed by the Internet Architecture Board, the company voluntarily ended the service on October 4, 2003. After this action, VeriSign filed a lawsuit against ICANN on February 27, 2004, claiming that ICANN had exceeded its authority. By this lawsuit, VeriSign sought to reduce ambiguity about ICANN's authority. The antitrust component of VeriSign's claim was dismissed during August 2004. VeriSign's challenge that ICANN overstepped its contractual rights is currently outstanding. A proposed settlement already approved by ICANN's board would resolve VeriSign's challenge to ICANN in exchange for the right to increase pricing on .com domains. At the meeting of ICANN in Rome, which took place from March 2 to 6, 2004, ICANN agreed to ask approval of the U.S. Department of Commerce for the Waiting List Service of VeriSign.

- On May 17, 2004, ICANN published a proposed budget for the year 2004–05. It included proposals to increase the openness and professionalism of its operations, and increased its proposed spending from US$8.27 million to $15.83 million. The increase was to be funded by the introduction of new top-level domains, charges to domain registries, and a fee for some domain name registrations, renewals and transfers (initially US$0.20 for all domains within a country-code top-level domain, and US$0.25 for all others).
- The Council of European National Top Level Domain Registries (CENTR), which represents the RIRs of 39 countries, rejected the increase, accusing ICANN of a lack of financial prudence and criticizing what it describes as ICANN's "unrealistic political and operational targets". Despite the criticism, the registry agreement for the top-level domains jobs and travel includes a US$2 fee on every domain the licensed companies sell or renew.
- After a second round of negotiations during 2004, the TLDs eu, asia, travel, jobs, mobi, and cat were introduced during 2005.
- On February 28, 2006, ICANN's board approved a settlement with VeriSign in the lawsuit resulting from SiteFinder that involved allowing VeriSign (the registry) to raise its registration fees by up to 7% a year. This was criticised by a few members of the U.S. House of Representatives' Small Business Committee.
- During February 2007, ICANN began procedures to end accreditation of one of their registrars, RegisterFly amid charges and lawsuits involving fraud, and criticism of ICANN's management of the situation. ICANN has been the subject of criticism as a result of its handling of RegisterFly, and the harm caused to thousands of clients as a result of what has been termed ICANN's "laissez faire attitude toward customer allegations of fraud".
- On May 23, 2008, ICANN issued enforcement notices against ten accredited registrars and announced this through a press release entitled "'Worst Spam Offenders' Notified by ICANN, Compliance system working to correct Whois and other issues." This was largely in response to a report issued by KnujOn, called "The 10 Worst Registrars" in terms of spam advertised junk product sites and compliance failure. The mention of the word "spam" in the title of the ICANN memo is somewhat misleading since ICANN does not address issues of spam or email abuse. Website content and usage are not within ICANN's mandate. However, the KnujOn report details how various registrars

have not complied with their contractual obligations under the Registrar Accreditation Agreement (RAA). The main point of the KnujOn research was to demonstrate the relationships between compliance failure, illicit product traffic, and spam. The report demonstrated that out of 900 ICANN accredited registrars, fewer than 20 held 90% of the web domains advertised in spam. These same registrars were also most frequently cited by KnujOn as failing to resolve complaints made through the Whois Data Problem Reporting System (WDPRS).

- On June 26, 2008, the ICANN Board started a new process of TLD naming policy to take a "significant step forward on the introduction of new generic top-level domains." This program envisioned the availability of many new or already proposed domains, as well a new application and implementation process.
- On October 1, 2008, ICANN issued breach notices against Joker and Beijing Innovative Linkage Technology Ltd. after further researching reports and complaints issued by KnujOn. These notices gave the registrars 15 days to fix their Whois investigation efforts.
- In 2010, ICANN approved a major review of its policies with respect to accountability, transparency, and public participation by the Berkman Center for Internet and Society at Harvard University. This external review was an assistance of the work of ICANN's Accountability and Transparency Review team.
- On February 3, 2011, ICANN announced that it had distributed the last batch of its remaining IPv4 addresses to the world's five RIRs (the organizations that manage IP addresses in different regions); these registries began assigning the final IPv4 addresses within their regions until they completely ran out.
- On June 20, 2011, the ICANN board voted to end most restrictions on the names of generic top-level domains (gTLD). Companies and organizations became able to choose essentially arbitrary top-level Internet domain names. The use of non-Latin characters (such as Cyrillic, Arabic, Chinese, etc.) is also allowed in gTLDs. ICANN began accepting applications for new gTLDS on January 12, 2012. The initial price to apply for a new gTLD was set at $185,000 and the annual renewal fee is $25,000.
- During December 2011, the Federal Trade Commission stated ICANN had long failed to provide safeguards that protect consumers from online swindlers.

- Following the 2013 NSA spying scandal, ICANN endorsed the Montevideo Statement, although no direct connection between these could be proven.
- On October 1, 2016, ICANN ended its contract with the United States Department of Commerce National Telecommunications and Information Administration (NTIA) and entered the private sector.
- The European Union's General Data Protection Regulation (active since May 25, 2018) has had an impact on ICANN's operations, which had to be fixed via some last minute changes.[clarification needed]

Structure

From its founding to the present, ICANN has been formally organized as a nonprofit corporation "for charitable and public purposes" under the California Nonprofit Public Benefit Corporation Law. It is managed by a 16-member board of directors composed of eight members selected by a nominating committee on which all the constituencies of ICANN are represented; six representatives of its Supporting Organizations, sub-groups that deal with specific sections of the policies under ICANN's purview; an at-large seat filled by an at-large organization; and the president / CEO, appointed by the board. There are currently three supporting organizations: the Generic Names Supporting Organization (GNSO) which deals with policy making on generic top-level domains (gTLDs); the Country Code Names Supporting Organization (ccNSO) deals with policy making on country-code top-level domains (ccTLDs); the Address Supporting Organization (ASO) deals with policy making on IP addresses.

ICANN also relies on some advisory committees and other advisory mechanisms to receive advice on the interests and needs of stakeholders that do not directly participate in the Supporting Organizations. These include the Governmental Advisory Committee (GAC), which is composed of representatives of a large number of national governments from all over the world; the At-Large Advisory Committee (ALAC), which is composed of individual Internet users from around the world selected by each of the Regional At-Large Organizations (RALO) and Nominating Committee; the Root Server System Advisory Committee (RSSAC), which provides advice on the operation of the DNS root server system; the Security and Stability Advisory Committee (SSAC), which is composed of Internet experts who study security issues pertaining to ICANN's mandate; and the Technical Liaison Group (TLG), which is composed of representatives of other international technical organizations that focus, at least in part, on the Internet.

Trusted Community Representatives

As the operator of the IANA domain name functions, ICANN is responsible for the

DNSSEC management of the root zone. While day-to-day operations are managed by ICANN and Verisign, the trust is rooted in a group of Trusted Community Representatives. The members of this group must not be affiliated with ICANN, but are instead members of the broader DNS community, volunteering to become a Trusted Community Representative. The role of the representatives are primarily to take part in regular key ceremonies at a physical location, organized by ICANN, and to safeguard the key materials in between.

Democratic Input

In the memorandum of understanding that set up the relationship between ICANN and the U.S. government, ICANN was given a mandate requiring that it operate "in a bottom-up, consensus-driven, democratic manner." However, the attempts that ICANN has made to establish an organizational structure that would allow wide input from the global Internet community did not produce results amenable to the current Board.

As a result, the At-Large constituency and direct election of board members by the global Internet community were soon abandoned. ICANN holds periodic public meetings rotated between continents for the purpose of encouraging global participation in its processes. Resolutions of the ICANN Board, preliminary reports, and minutes of the meetings are published on the ICANN website, sometimes in real-time. However, there are criticisms from ICANN constituencies including the Noncommercial Users Constituency (NCUC) and the At-Large Advisory Committee (ALAC) that there is not enough public disclosure and that too many discussions and decisions take place out of sight of the public.

During the early 2000s, there had been speculation that the United Nations might assume control of ICANN, followed by a negative reaction from the U.S. government and worries about a division of the Internet. At UN's World Summit on the Information Society in Tunisia in November 2005, the world's governments agreed not to get involved in the day-to-day and technical operations of ICANN.

However they also agreed to establish an international Internet Governance Forum, with a consultative role on the future governance of the Internet. ICANN's Government Advisory Committee is currently established to provide advice to ICANN regarding public policy issues and has participation by many of the world's governments. Some have attempted to argue that ICANN was never given the authority to decide policy, e.g., choose new TLDs or exclude other interested parties who refuse to pay ICANN's US$185,000 fee but was to be a technical caretaker. Critics[who?] suggest that ICANN should not be allowed to impose business rules on market participants and that all TLDs should be added on a first-come, first-served basis and the market should be the arbiter of who succeeds and who does not.

Activities

Uniform Domain-Name Dispute Resolution Policy (UDRP)

One task that ICANN was asked to do was to address the issue of domain name ownership resolution for generic top-level domains (gTLDs). ICANN's attempt at such a policy was drafted in close cooperation with the World Intellectual Property Organization (WIPO), and the result has now become known as the Uniform Dispute Resolution Policy (UDRP).

This policy essentially attempts to provide a mechanism for rapid, cheap and reasonable resolution of domain name conflicts, avoiding the traditional court system for disputes by allowing cases to be brought to one of a set of bodies that arbitrate domain name disputes. According to ICANN policy, domain registrants must agree to be bound by the UDRP—they cannot get a domain name without agreeing to this. Examination of the UDRP decision patterns has caused some to conclude that compulsory domain name arbitration is less likely to give a fair hearing to domain name owners asserting defenses under the First Amendment and other laws, compared to the federal courts of appeal in particular.

Proposed Elimination of Public DNS Whois

In 2013, the initial report of ICANN's Expert Working Group has recommended that the present form of Whois, a utility that allows anyone to know who has registered a domain name on the Internet, should be "abandoned". It recommends it be replaced with a system that keeps most registration information secret (or "gated") from most Internet users, and only discloses information for "permissible purposes".

ICANN's list of permissible purposes includes domain name research, domain name sale and purchase, regulatory enforcement, personal data protection, legal actions, and abuse mitigation. Whois has been a key tool of investigative journalists interested in determining who was disseminating information on the Internet. The use of whois by journalists is not included in the list of permissible purposes in the initial report.

Proposals for Reform

Proposals have been made to internationalize ICANN's monitoring responsibilities (currently the responsibility of the US), to transform it into an international organization (under international law), and to "establish an intergovernmental mechanism enabling governments, on an equal footing, to carry out their roles and responsibilities in international public policy issues pertaining to the Internet".

IBSA Proposal (2011)

One controversial proposal, resulting from a September 2011 summit between

India, Brazil, and South Africa (IBSA), sought to move Internet governance into a "UN Committee on Internet-Related Policy" (UN-CIRP). The action was a reaction to a perception that the principles of the 2005 Tunis Agenda for the Information Society had not been met; the statement proposed the creation of a new political organization operating as a component of the United Nations to provide policy recommendations for the consideration of technical organizations such as ICANN and international bodies such as the ITU. Subsequent to public criticism, India backed away from the proposal.

Montevideo Statement on the Future of Internet Cooperation (2013)

On October 7, 2013, the Montevideo Statement on the Future of Internet Cooperation was released by the managers of a number of organizations involved in coordinating the Internet's global technical infrastructure, loosely known as the "I*" (or "I-star") group. Among other things, the statement "expressed strong concern over the undermining of the trust and confidence of Internet users globally due to recent revelations of pervasive monitoring and surveillance" and "called for accelerating the globalization of ICANN and IANA functions, towards an environment in which all stakeholders, including all governments, participate on an equal footing". This desire to reduce United States association with the internet is considered a reaction to the ongoing NSA surveillance scandal. The statement was signed by the managers of the ICANN, the Internet Engineering Task Force, the Internet Architecture Board, the World Wide Web Consortium, the Internet Society, and the five regional Internet address registries (African Network Information Center, American Registry for Internet Numbers, Asia-Pacific Network Information Centre, Latin America and Caribbean Internet Addresses Registry, and Réseaux IP Européens Network Coordination Centre).

Global Multistakeholder Meeting on the Future of Internet Governance (2013)

During October 2013, Fadi Chehadé, former president and CEO of ICANN, met with Brazilian president Dilma Rousseff in Brasilia. Upon Chehadé's invitation, the two announced that Brazil would host an international summit on Internet governance during April 2014. The announcement came after the 2013 disclosures of mass surveillance by the U.S. government, and Rousseff's speech at the opening session of the 2013 United Nations General Assembly, where she strongly criticized the American surveillance program as a "breach of international law". The "Global Multistakeholder Meeting on the Future of Internet Governance (NET mundial)" will include representatives of government, industry, civil society, and academia. At the IGF VIII meeting in Bali in October 2013 a commenter noted that Brazil intends the meeting to be a "summit" in the sense that it will be high level with decision-making authority. The organizers of the "NET mundial" meeting decided that an online forum called "/1net", set up by the I* group, will be a major conduit of non-governmental input into the three committees preparing for the meeting in April. The Obama administration, which had joined critics of ICANN in 2011, announced in March 2014 that they intended to transition away from oversight of the IANA functions contract. The current contract that the United States Department of Commerce has with ICANN expired in 2015, in its place the NTIA will transition oversight of the IANA functions to the 'global multistakeholder community'.

NetMundial Initiative (2014)

The NetMundial Initiative is a plan for international governance of the Internet that was first proposed at the Global Multistakeholder Meeting on the Future of Internet Governance (GMMFIG) conference (April 23–24, 2014) and later developed into the NetMundial Initiative by ICANN CEO Fadi Chehadé along with representatives of the World Economic Forum (WEF) and the Brazilian Internet Steering Committee (Comitê Gestor da Internet no Brasil), commonly referred to as "CGI.br".

The meeting produced a nonbinding statement in favor of consensus-based decision-making. It represented a compromise and did not harshly condemn mass surveillance or support net neutrality, despite initial endorsement for the latter from Brazil; the final resolution states that ICANN should be controlled internationally by September 2015. A minority of governments, including Russia, China, Iran, and India, were unhappy with the final resolution and wanted multilateral management for the Internet (such as a UN-based model), rather than broader multistakeholder management. A month later, the Panel on Global Internet Cooperation and Governance Mechanisms (convened by the ICANN and WEF with assistance from The Annenberg Foundation), endorsed and included the NetMundial statement in its own report. During June 2014, France vehemently lambasted ICANN, saying they are an unfit venue for Internet governance, and that alternatives should be sought.

TLD Expansion and Concerns about Specific Top-Level Domains

During 2011, seventy-nine companies, including The Coca-Cola Company, Hewlett-Packard, Samsung and others, signed a petition against ICANN's new TLD program (sometimes referred to as a "commercial landgrab"), in a group organized by the Association of National Advertisers. As of September 2014, this group, the Coalition for Responsible Internet Domain Oversight, that opposes the rollout of ICANN's TLD expansion program, has been joined by 102 associations and 79 major companies. Partly as a response to this criticism, ICANN initiated an effort to protect trademarks in domain name registrations, which eventually culminated in the establishment of the Trademark Clearinghouse.

.Sucks Domain

ICANN has received more than $60 million from gTLD auctions, and has accepted the controversial domain name ".sucks" (referring to the primarily US slang for being inferior or objectionable). sucks domains are owned and controlled by the Vox Populi Registry which won the rights for .sucks gTLD in November 2014.

The .sucks domain registrar has been described as "predatory, exploitive and coercive" by the Intellectual Property Constituency that advises the ICANN board. When the .sucks registry announced their pricing model, "most brand owners were upset and felt like they were being penalized by having to pay more to protect their brands." Because of the low utility of the ".sucks" domain, most fees come from "Brand Protection" customers registering their trademarks to prevent domains being registered.

Canadian brands had complained that they were being charged "exorbitant" prices to register their trademarks as premium names. FTC chair Edith Ramirez has written to ICANN to say the agency will take action against the .sucks owner if "we have reason to believe an entity has engaged in deceptive or unfair practices in violation of Section 5 of the FTC Act". The Register reported that intellectual property lawyers are infuriated that "the dot-sucks registry was charging trademark holders $2,500 for .sucks domains and everyone else $10."

U.S. Representative Bob Goodlatte has said that trademark holders are "being shaken down" by the registry's fees. Jay Rockefeller says that .sucks is "a predatory shakedown scheme" and "Approving '.sucks', a gTLD with little or no public interest value, will have the effect of undermining the credibility ICANN has slowly been building with skeptical stakeholders."

.Islam, .Halal Top Level Domains

In a long-running dispute, ICANN has so far declined to allow a Turkish company to purchase the .islam and .halal gTLDs, after the Organisation of Islamic Cooperation objected that the gTLDs should be administered by an organization that represents all the world's 1.6 billion Muslims. After a number of attempts to resolve the issue the domains are still held "on hold" as of 2019.

.Org Price Cap Removal

In April 2019, ICANN proposed an end to the price cap of org domains and effectively removed it in July in spite of having received 3,252 opposing comments and only six in favor. A few months later, the owner of the domain, the Public Interest Registry, proposed to sell the domain to investment firm Ethos Capital.

.Amazon gTLD Dispute

In May 2019, ICANN decided in favor of granting exclusive administration rights to amazon.com for the .amazon gTLD after a 7 year long dispute with the Amazon Cooperation Treaty Organization (ACTO).

6.5.2 IGF

The Internet Governance Forum (IGF) is a multistakeholder governance group for policy dialogue on issues of Internet governance. It brings together all stakeholders in the Internet governance debate, whether they represent governments, the private sector or civil society, including the technical and academic community, on an equal basis and through an open and inclusive process. The establishment of the IGF was formally announced by the United Nations Secretary-General in July 2006. It was first convened in October–November 2006 and has held an annual meeting since then.

History and Development of the Internet Governance Forum

WSIS Phase I, WGIG, and WSIS Phase II

The first phase of World Summit on the Information Society (WSIS), held in Geneva in December 2003, failed to agree on the future of Internet governance, but did agree to continue the dialogue and requested the United Nations Secretary-General to establish a multi-stakeholder Working Group on Internet Governance (WGIG).

Following a series of open consultations in 2004 and 2005 and after reaching a clear consensus among its members the WGIG proposed the creation of the IGF as one of four proposals made in its final report. Paragraph 40 of the WGIG report stated:

"(t)he WGIG identified a vacuum within the context of existing structures, since there is no global multi-stakeholder forum to address Internet-related public policy issues. It came to the conclusion that there would be merit in creating such a space for dialogue among all stakeholders. This space could address these issues, as well as emerging issues, that are cross-cutting and multidimensional and that either affect more than one institution, are not dealt with by any institution or are not addressed in a coordinated manner".

The WGIG report was one of the inputs to the second phase of the World Summit on the Information Society held in Tunis in 2005. The idea of the Forum was also proposed by Argentina, as stated in its proposal made during the last Prepcom 3 in Tunis:

"In order to strengthen the global multistakeholder interaction and cooperation on public policy issues and developmental aspects relating to Internet governance we propose a forum. This forum should not replace existing mechanisms or institutions but should build on the existing structures on Internet governance, should contribute to the sustainability, stability and robustness of the Internet by addressing appropriately public policy issues that are not otherwise being adequately addressed excluding any involvement in the day to day operation of the Internet. It should be constituted as a neutral, non-duplicative and non-binding process to facilitate the exchange of information and best practices and to identify issues and make known its findings, to enhance awareness and build consensus and engagement. Recognizing the rapid development of technology and institutions, we propose that the forum mechanism periodically be reviewed to determine the need for its continuation."

The second phase of WSIS, held in Tunis in November 2005, formally called for the creation of the IGF and set out its mandate. Paragraph 72 of the Tunis Agenda called on the UN Secretary-General to convene a meeting with regards to the new multi-stakeholder forum to be known as the IGF. The Tunis WSIS meeting did not reach an agreement on any of the other WGIG proposals that generally focused on new oversight functions for the Internet that would reduce or eliminate the special role that the United States plays with respect to Internet governance through its contractual oversight of ICANN.

The US Government's position during the lead-up to the Tunis WSIS meeting was flexible on the principle of global involvement, very strong on the principle of multi-stakeholder participation, but inflexible on the need for US control to remain for the foreseeable future in order to ensure the "security and stability of the Internet".

2005 Mandate

The mandate for the IGF is contained in the 2005 WSIS Tunis Agenda. The IGF was mandated to be principally a discussion forum for facilitating dialogue between the Forum's participants. The IGF may "identify emerging issues, bring them to the attention of the relevant bodies and the general public, and, where appropriate, make recommendations," but does not have any direct decision-making authority. In this mandate, different stakeholders are encouraged to strengthen engagement, particularly those from developing countries.

In paragraph 72(h), the mandate focused on capacity-building for developing countries and the drawing out of local resources. This particular effort, for instance, has been reinforced through Diplo Foundation's Internet Governance Capacity Building Programme (IGCBP) that allowed participants from different regions to benefit from valuable resources with the help of regional experts in Internet governance.

Formation of the IGF

The United Nations published its endorsement of a five-year mandate for the IGF in April 2006. There were two rounds of consultations with regards to the convening of the first IGF:

- 16 – 17 of February 2006 – The first round of consultations was held in Geneva. The transcripts of the two-day consultations are available in the IGF site.

- 19 May 2006 – The second round of consultations was open to all stakeholders and was coordinated for the preparations of the inaugural IGF meeting. The meeting chairman was Nitin Desai who is the United Nations Secretary-General's Special Adviser for Internet Governance.

The convening of the IGF was announced on 18 July 2006, with the inaugural meeting of the Forum to be held in Athens, Greece from 30 October to 2 November 2006.

2011 Mandate Renewal and Improvements Process

In the lead-up to the completion of the first five-year mandate of the IGF in 2010, the UN initiated a process of evaluating the continuation of the IGF, resulting in a United Nations General Assembly resolution to continue the IGF for a further five years (2011–2015).

In addition to the renewed mandate, another UN body, the Commission on Science and Technology for Development (CSTD), established a Working Group on Improvements to the IGF (CSTDWG), which first met in February 2011, held five working group meetings, completed its work in early 2012, and issued a report to the commission for consideration during its 15th session to be held 21–25 May 2012, in Geneva. The Working Group report made 15 recommendations with regard to five specific areas, namely:

- Shaping of the outcomes of IGF meetings;
- Working modalities of the IGF, including open consultations, the Multi-stakeholder Advisory Group (MAG) and the Secretariat;
- Funding of the IGF;
- Broadening participation and capacity-building; and
- Linking the IGF to other Internet governance-related entities.

At its meeting held from 21 to 25 May 2012 the CSTD made the following recommendations to the Economic and Social Council regarding Internet governance and the Internet Governance Forum, which the Council accepted at its meeting on 24 July 2012:

- 25. Takes note that the CSTD Working Group on improvements to the Internet Governance Forum successfully completed its task;
- 26. Takes note with appreciation of the report of the Working Group on improvements to the Internet Governance Forum and expresses its gratitude to all its members for their time and valuable efforts in this endeavour as well as to all member states and other relevant stakeholders that have submitted inputs to the Working Group consultation process;

- 35. Urges the Secretary-General to ensure the continued functioning of the IGF and its structures in preparation for the seventh meeting of the Internet Governance Forum, to be held from 6 to 9 November 2012 in Baku, Azerbaijan and future meetings of the Internet Governance Forum;
- 36. Notes the necessity to appoint the Special Advisor to the Secretary-General on Internet Governance and the Executive Coordinator to the IGF.

2015 Mandate Renewal

The second five-year mandate of the IGF ended in 2015. On 16 December 2015 the United Nations General Assembly adopted the outcome document on the 10-year review of the implementation of the outcomes of the World Summit on the Information Society. Among other things the outcome document urges the need to promote greater participation and engagement in Internet governance discussions that should involve governments, the private sector, civil society, international organizations, the technical and academic communities, and all other relevant stakeholders. It acknowledges the role the Internet Governance Forum (IGF) has played as a multistakeholder platform for discussion of Internet governance issues. And it extends the existing mandate of the IGF as set out in paragraphs 72 to 78 of the Tunis Agenda for a third period of ten years. During the ten-year period, the IGF should continue to show progress on working modalities, and participation of relevant stakeholders from developing countries.

IGF Retreat, July 2016

After the UN General Assembly extended the IGF's mandate for ten additional years in December 2015, but before the December 2016 IGF meeting in Mexico, an IGF Retreat was held on 14–16 July 2016 in Glen Cove, New York to focus on "Advancing the 10-Year Mandate of the Internet Governance Forum".

At the time that the IGF mandate was extended, the UN General Assembly called for "progress on working modalities and the participation of relevant stakeholders from developing countries" and "accelerated implementation of recommendations in the report of the UN Commission on Science and Technology for Development (CSTD) Working Group on Improvements to the IGF."

Thus the retreat was framed by the mandates of the Tunis Agenda and WSIS+10 review. It also aimed to build on the report of the CSTD Working Group on improvements to the IGF and the many years of reflection of the MAG and the IGF community on improving the working methods of the IGF. The retreat was to focus on "how" the IGF could best work to deliver its role and how it could be best supported. As it focused on the "how", it would not try to carry out the substantive discussions that are to happen in the IGF itself. The retreat reached the following understandings:

- In addition to its renewal of the IGF's mandate in December 2015, the UN General Assembly expressed expectations, specifically the need to show progress on working modalities and the participation of relevant stakeholders from developing countries, as well as for the accelerated implementation of the recommendations of the CSTD Working Group on improvements to the IGF.
- There was also recognition that improvements have been and continue to be made on an ongoing basis.
- The relevance of the IGF in the future is not assured, being dependent inter alia on increased voluntary funding to the multi-donor extra-budgetary IGF Trust Fund Project of the UN that funds the IGF Secretariat and on increased participation from a balanced and diverse set of stakeholders.
- Other fora are emerging for those wishing to engage in discussions about Internet governance. This suggested that the IGF's distinctiveness and value within this range of alternatives would need to remain sufficient to maintain participation levels from governments and the private sector in particular.
- A few participants felt that the MAG does not engage all parts of the community who want to take part in the discussion on Internet governance, and the IGF itself as well as the various intersessional activities could address this.
- The IGF has evolved over the years and is now seen by many as much more than an annual forum. Increasingly, it is seen as an ecosystem including national and regional IGFs, intersessional work, best practice fora, dynamic coalitions and other activities.
- More could be done to take a strategic, long-term view of the role and activities of the IGF, such as through a predictable multi-year programme of work. Even if not undertaken generally, it might be possible to reinvigorate the IGF by taking a longer-term view of particular issues, dedicating time and resources to progressing discussions and achieving concrete outcomes on these over time. it might be possible to move towards a continuous, predictable process for programming the work of the IGF.
- The IGF's innovative and unconventional multistakeholder structure and culture, compared with other UN processes, is generally felt to be

one of its strengths. However, it also made it more difficult to integrate it with other UN processes. The same is true with respect to integrating the IGF and its institutional arrangements comfortably into expectations of multistakeholder processes. One of the challenges therefore is how to reconcile its bottom-up approach and stakeholder expectations with other multilateral processes within the UN system.

- The role of the MAG, in particular whether the MAG is expected or authorized to take on responsibilities beyond the programming of the annual IGF meetings, needs to be clarified in order to pursue significant innovations in the IGF.
- It was generally felt that the IGF Secretariat is under-resourced and hence lacks capacities for its current responsibilities, let alone additional activities.

Organizational Structure

Multistakeholder Advisory Group (MAG)

The Advisory Group, now known as the Multistakeholder Advisory Group (MAG), was established by the then UN Secretary-General, Kofi Annan on 17 May 2006, to assist in convening the first IGF, held in Athens, Greece. The MAG's mandate has been renewed or extended each year to provide assistance in the preparations for each upcoming IGF meeting. The MAG meets for two days three times each year – in February, May and September. All three meetings take place in Geneva and are preceded by a one-day Open Consultations meeting. The details on the MAG's operating principles and selection criteria are contained in the summary reports of its meetings.

The MAG was originally made up of 46 members, but membership grew first to 47, then 50, and eventually 56. Members are from international governments, the commercial private sector and public civil society, including academic and technical communities. The MAG tries to renew roughly one third of the members within each stakeholder group each year.

In 2011, because there were only three new MAG members in 2010, it was suggested that two thirds of each group's membership be renewed in 2012 and in fact 33 new members were appointed to the 56 member group. The first MAG chairman was Nitin Desai, an Indian economist and former UN Under-Secretary-General for Economic and Social Affairs from 1992 to 2003. He also served as the Secretary-General's Special Adviser for the World Summit on the Information Society, later Special Advisor for Internet Governance.

- In 2007 Nitin Desai and Brazilian diplomat Hadil da Rocha Vianna served as co-chairs of the MAG.

- In 2008, 2009 and 2010 Nitin Desai served as MAG chair.
- In 2011 Alice Munyua, the Chair of the Kenyan IGF Steering Committee, was MAG chair.
- In 2012 Elmir Valizada, Deputy Minister of Communications and Information Technology, Azerbaijan was MAG chair.
- In 2013 Ashwin Sasongko, Director General of ICT Application, Ministry of Communication and Information Technology (CIT), Indonesia served as Honorary Chair with Markus Kummer, vice-president for Public Policy of the Internet Society as interim chair of the MAG.
- In 2014 and 2015 Janis Karkliņš, Ambassador-at-Large for the Government of Latvia, former Assistant Director-General of Communication and Information of UNESCO, Latvian Ambassador to France, Andorra, Monaco and UNESCO and participant in the World Summit on Information Society, serves as MAG chair.
- In 2016 United Nations Secretary-General Ban Ki-moon appointed Lynn St. Amour of the United States as the new MAG chair. Amour served from 2001 to 2014 as president and CEO of the Internet Society.
- In 2019 United Nations Secretary-General António Guterres appointed Anriette Esterhuysen of the Republic of South Africa as the new MAG chair. Before the appointment Esterhuysen was the executive director of the Association for Progressive Communications.

Secretariat

The Secretariat, based in the United Nations Office in Geneva, assists and coordinates the work of the Multistakeholder Advisory Group (MAG). The Secretariat also hosts internships and fellowships. Chengetai Masango is the Secretariat's Head of Office. Until 31 January 2011 the IGF Secretariat was headed by Executive Coordinator Markus Kummer. Kummer was also Executive Coordinator of the Secretariat of the UN Working Group on Internet Governance (WGIG). On 1 February 2011 he joined the Internet Society as its vice president for Public Policy.

Activities at the IGF

The following activities take place during IGF meetings: Main or focus sessions, Workshops, Dynamic Coalition meetings, Best Practice Forums, Side meetings, Host Country Sessions, 'Flash' Sessions, Open Forums, Inter-regional dialogue sessions, Newcomers track sessions, Lightning sessions, Unconference sessions, Pre-events, and the IGF Village.

Main or Focus Sessions

The first IGF meeting in Greece in 2006 was organized around the main themes of: openness, security, diversity, and access. For IGF Brazil in 2007 a new theme, critical Internet resources, was introduced.

- For 2009 through 2012 there were six standard themes:
  - Internet governance for development,
  - Emerging issues,
  - Managing critical Internet resources,
  - Security, openness, and privacy,
  - Access and diversity, and
  - Taking stock and the way forward.
- For IGF Indonesia in 2013 the six main themes were:
  - Access and Diversity-Internet as an engine for growth and sustainable development;
  - Openness - Human rights, freedom of expression and free flow of information on the Internet;
  - Security - Legal and other frameworks: spam, hacking and cyber-crime;
  - Enhanced cooperation;
  - Principles of multi-stakeholder cooperation;
  - Internet governance principles.
- For IGF Turkey in 2014 the eight main themes were:
  - Policies Enabling Access;
  - Content Creation, Dissemination and Use;
  - Internet as an Engine for Growth and Development;
  - IGF and The Future of the Internet Ecosystem;
  - Enhancing Digital Trust;
  - Internet and Human Rights;
  - Critical Internet Resources; and
  - Emerging issues.
- For IGF Brazil in 2015 the eight main themes were:
  - Cyber-security and Trust;
  - Internet Economy;
  - Inclusiveness and Diversity;
  - Openness;
  - Enhancing Multistakeholder Cooperation;
  - Internet and Human Rights;
  - Critical Internet Resources; and
  - Emerging issues.
- For IGF Mexico in 2016 a less formal and more bottom up approach was used to develop the meeting's main themes. The nine themes that emerged were:

- Sustainable Development and the Internet Economy;
- Access and Diversity;
- Gender and Youth Issues;
- Human Rights Online;
- Cyber-security;
- Multistakeholder Cooperation;
- Critical Internet Resources;
- Internet governance capacity building; and
- Emerging Issues that may affect the future of the open Internet.

Workshops

Each year starting in 2007, the IGF has hosted a number of workshops (workshop with panel, roundtable, capacity building session). Examples of workshops held at IGF meetings include:

- Universalization of the Internet - How to reach the next billion (Expanding the Internet).
- Low cost sustainable access.
- Multilingualization.
- Implications for development policy.
- Managing the Internet (Using the Internet).
- Critical Internet resources.
- Arrangements for Internet governance.
- Global cooperation for Internet security and stability.
- Taking stock and the way forward.
- Emerging issues.
- Internet Governance and RPKI.
- Spectrum for Democracy and Development.
- Internet Regulation for Improved Access in Emerging Markets.
- Understanding Internet Infrastructure: an Overview of Technology and Terminology.
- Freedom of expression and freedom from hate on-line (Young People Combating Hate Speech On-line).
- Protecting the rule of law in the online environment.
- Evaluating Internet Freedom Initiatives: What works?
- DNSSEC for ccTLDs: Securing National Domains.

- Media pluralism and freedom of expression in the Internet age.
- An industry lead approach for making internet a better place for kids.
- Best Common Practices for Building Internet Capacity.
- Law Enforcement via Domain Names: Caveats to DNS Neutrality.
- Defining the Successful Factors of Different Models for Youth Participation in Internet Governance.
- How to engage users on Internet Policies?
- New gTLDs: Implications and Potential for Community Engagement, advocacy and Development.
- Human Rights, Internet Policy and the Public Policy Role of ICANN.
- Innovative application of ICTs to facilitate child protection online.
- EURid/UNESCO World Report on IDN Deployment 2012 – opportunities and challenges associated with IDNs and online multilingualism.
- The Benefits of Using Advanced Mobile Technologies and Global Spectrum Harmonization.
- Empowering Internet Users – which tools?

Dynamic Coalitions

Active Dynamic Coalitions:	Inactive Dynamic Coalitions:
• Accessibility and Disability. • Child Online Safety. • Core Internet Values. • Freedom of Expression and Freedom of the Media on the Internet (FOEonline). • Gender and Internet Governance. • Internet and Climate Change. • Internet of Things. • Internet Rights and Principles/Internet Bill of Rights. • Network Neutrality. • Platform Responsibility. • Public Access in Libraries. • Sustainability of Journalism and News Media (DC-Sustainability). • Youth Coalition on Internet Governance.	• Access and Connectivity for Remote, Rural and Dispersed Communities. • Access 2 Knowledge (A2K@IGF). • Framework of Principles for the Internet. • Global Localization Platform. • Linguistic Diversity. • Online Collaboration. • Online Education. • Open Standards. • Privacy. • Social Media and Legal Issues. • Stop Spam Alliance.

The most tangible result of the first IGF in Athens was the establishment of a number of so-called Dynamic Coalitions. These coalitions are relatively informal, issue-specific groups consisting of stakeholders that are interested in the particular issue. Most coalitions allow participation of anyone interested in contributing. Thus, these groups gather not only academics and representatives of governments, but also members of the civil society interested in participating on the debates and engaged in the coalition's works.

Best Practice Forums

Starting in 2014 these sessions demonstrate some of the best practices that have been adapted with regard to the key IGF themes and the development and deployment of the Internet. The sessions provide an opportunity to discuss what constitutes a "best practice", to share relevant information and experiences and build consensus around best practices that can then be transferred to other situations, and strengthen capacity building activities.

The five Best Practice Forums held during IGF 2014 were:

- Developing Meaningful Multistakeholder Mechanisms;
- Regulation and Mitigation of Unwanted Communications (Spam);
- Establishing and Supporting CERTs for Internet Security;
- Creating an Enabling Environment for the Development of Local Content; and
- Online Child Safety and Protection.

'Flash' Sessions

A flash session provides an opportunity for presenters/organisers to evoke/sparkle interest of the participants in specific reports, case studies, best practices, methodologies, tools, etc. that have already been implemented or are in the process of implementation. Participants have an opportunity to ask very specific questions. Flash Sessions will generally be shorter than other types of sessions.

Flash sessions held at IGF 2014 were:

- Internet and Jurisdiction Project; and
- Crowd Sourced Solutions to Bridge the Gender Digital Divide.

Open Forums

All major organizations dealing with Internet governance related issues are given a 90-minute time slot, at their request, to hold an Open Forum in order to present and discuss their activities during the past year and allow for questions and discussions. Examples of recent Open fora include:

- Consultation on ten-year review of WSIS (CSTD).
- The Economics of an Open Internet (OECD).

- Governmental Advisory Committee (GAC) Open Forum (ICANN).
- ICANN Open Forum.
- Internet & Jurisdiction Policy Network Open Forum.
- ISOC@IGF: Dedicated to an open accessible Internet (Internet Society).
- South Korea's effort to advance the Internet environment including IPv6 deployment (MSIP and KISA).
- Launch of Revised Guidelines on for Industry on Child Online Protection (ITU and UNICEF).
- Measuring what and how: Capturing the effects of the Internet we want (World Wide Web Foundation).
- Multi-stakeholder Consultation on UNESCO's Comprehensive Study on the Internet (UNESCO).
- Protecting Human Rights Online (Freedom Online Coalition).
- Your Internet, Our Aim: Guide Internet Users to Their Human Rights (Council of Europe).

Lightning Sessions

At IGF 2016 Lightning sessions were introduced as quicker, more informal versions of full-length workshops or presentations. The 20-minute sessions took place during lunch breaks in a shaded outdoor plaza in front of the venue. A few examples of the 23 Lightning sessions held in 2016 include:

- Are Tribunals re-inventing Global Internet Governance?
- Sharing research on tech-facilitated crimes against children.
- Research and Policy Advocacy Tools for #WomensRightsOnline.
- Internet users' data and their unlawful use.
- Governance of Cyber Identity.
- Unveiling Surveillance Practices in Latin America.
- Redefining Broadband Affordability for a more Inclusive Internet.
- Holding algorithms accountable to protect fundamental rights.
- Human Rights Online: Internet Access and minorities.
- Anonymity vs Hate speech?
- Conflict Management & Human Rights on the Internet.
- Electronic voting: Is not digital the future of democracy?

Unconference Sessions

At IGF 2016 Unconference sessions were introduced. The 20 to 40 minute talks are not pre-scheduled, participants reserve a speaking slot by signing up on a scheduling board on a first-come, first-served basis on the day of the Unconference. Five Unconference talks took place at IGF 2016:

- Freedom of Expression and Religion in Asia: Desecrating Expression – Launch of a Report.
- #africaninternetrights - a best practice policy.
- Derecho de videojuegos (videogames law) y Ciberseguridad: "El Nuevo Internet of Toys" [Super Lawyer Bros.].
- Free Trade Agreements and IG in Latin America.
- Violencia Digital in the World.

Newcomers Track

Introduced at IGF 2016 the Newcomers track helps participants attending the IGF meeting for the first time, to understand the IGF processes, foster the integration of all new-coming stakeholders into the IGF community, and make the meeting participant's first IGF experience as productive and welcoming as possible. Newcomer sessions held in 2016 included:

- What is the IGF?
- Newcomers Mentor Session
- 'Knowledge cafes':
  - Private sector and Technical community at the IGF: What is the role of these stakeholder groups within the IGF and ways for engagement?
  - Governments and IGOs at the IGF: What's the role of these stakeholder groups in the IGF processes and ways for engagement?
  - The role of Civil Society within the IGF: work modalities and ways for engagement.
  - Wrap up: Taking Stock and How to engage in the IGF 2017 community intersessional work.

IGF Meetings

- IGF I — Athens, Greece 2006: The first meeting of the IGF was held in Athens, Greece from 30 October to 2 November 2006. The overall theme for the meeting was: "Internet Governance for Development". The agenda was structured along five broad themes: openness, security, diversity, access and new issues.
- IGF II — Rio de Janeiro, Brazil 2007: The second meeting of the IGF was held in Rio de Janeiro on 12–15 November 2007. The overall theme

for the meeting was: "Internet Governance for Development". The main sessions were organized around five themes: (i) Critical Internet resources; (ii) Access; (iii) Diversity; (iv) Openness, and (v) Security.

- IGF III — Hyderabad, India 2008: The third meeting of the IGF was held in Hyderabad, India between 3–6 December 2008. The overall theme for the meeting was "Internet for All". The meeting was held in the aftermath of terrorist attacks in Mumbai. The participants expressed their sympathies to the families of the victims and the Government and the people of India. The five main sessions were organized around the themes: (i) Reaching the next billion, (ii) Promoting cyber-security and trust, (iii) Managing critical Internet resources, (iv) Emerging issues - the Internet of tomorrow, and (v) Taking stock and the way forward. The meeting was attended by 1280 participants from 94 countries.
- IGF IV — Sharm El Sheikh, Egypt 2009: Egypt hosted the fourth IGF meeting from 15 to 18 November 2009 in Sharm El Sheikh. The overall theme for the meeting was: "Internet Governance – Creating Opportunities for all". IGF IV marked the beginning of a new multi-stakeholder process. The main sessions on the agenda were (i) Managing critical Internet resources; (ii) Security, openness and privacy; (iii) Access and diversity; (iv) Internet governance in light of the WSIS principles; (v) Taking stock and the way forward: the desirability of the continuation of the forum; and (vi) Emerging Issues: impact of social networks. A key focus of IGF 2009 was encouraging youth participation in Internet Governance issues.
- IGF V — Vilnius, Lithuania 2010: The fifth IGF meeting was held in Vilnius, Lithuania on 14–17 September 2010. The overall theme for the meeting was "Developing the future together". The meeting was organized around six themes: (i) Internet governance for development, (ii) Emerging issues: cloud computing, (iii) Managing critical Internet resources, (iv) Security, openness, and privacy, (v) Access and diversity, and (vi) Taking stock and the way forward.
- IGF VI — Nairobi, Kenya 2011: The sixth IGF meeting was held in Nairobi, Kenya on 27–30 September 2011, at the United Nations Office (UNON). The overall theme for the meeting was "Internet as a catalyst for change: access, development, freedoms and innovation". The meeting was organized around the traditional six themes: (i) Internet governance for development, (ii) Emerging issues, (iii) Managing critical Internet resources, (iv) Security, openness, and privacy, (v) Access and diversity, and (vi) Taking stock and the way forward.

- IGF VII — Baku, Azerbaijan 2012: The seventh IGF meeting was held in Baku, Azerbaijan on 6–9 November 2012. The overall theme for the meeting was: "Internet Governance for Sustainable Human, Economic and Social Development", with six themes of "development"; new issues; internet resources; security, openness and privacy; access and diversity; present and future.
- IGF VIII — Bali, Indonesia 2013: The eighth IGF meeting was held in Bali, Indonesia from 22 to 25 October 2013. 135 focus sessions, workshops, open forums, flash sessions, and other meetings took place over the 4 day event. The overarching theme for meeting was: "Building Bridges - Enhancing Multistakeholder Cooperation for Growth and Sustainable Development". The meeting was organized around six sub-themes: (i) Access and Diversity - Internet as an engine for growth and sustainable development; (ii) Openness - Human rights, freedom of expression and free flow of information on the Internet; (iii) Security - Legal and other frameworks: spam, hacking and cyber-crime; (iv) Enhanced cooperation; (v) Principles of multi-stakeholder cooperation; (vi) Internet governance principles. In the context of the recent revelations about government-led Internet surveillance activities, IGF 2013 was marked by many discussions about the need to ensure better protection of all citizens in the online environment and to reach a proper balance between actions driven by national security concerns and the respect for internationally recognized human rights, such as the right to privacy and freedom of expression.
- IGF IX — Istanbul, Turkey 2014: The ninth IGF meeting was held in Istanbul, Turkey from 2 to 5 September 2014. The meeting included 135 sessions and 14 pre-events. The overarching theme for meeting was: "Connecting Continents for Enhanced Multi-stakeholder Internet Governance". The meeting was organized around eight sub-themes: (i) Policies Enabling Access; (ii) Content Creation, Dissemination and Use; (iii) Internet as an Engine for Growth and Development; (iv) IGF and The Future of the Internet Ecosystem; (v) Enhancing Digital Trust; (vi) Internet and Human Rights; (vii) Critical Internet Resources; and (viii) Emerging Issues.
- IGF X — João Pessoa, Brazil 2015: The tenth IGF meeting was held in João Pessoa, Brazil from 10 to 13 November 2015. The meeting included more than 150 sessions and 21 pre-events. The overarching theme for the meeting was: "Evolution of Internet Governance: Empowering Sustainable Development". The meeting was organized

around eight sub-themes: (i) Cyber-security and Trust; (ii) Internet Economy; (iii) Inclusiveness and Diversity; (iv) Openness; (v) Enhancing Multistakeholder Cooperation; (vi) Internet and Human Rights; (vii) Critical Internet Resources and (viii) Emerging Issues.

- IGF XI — Guadalajara, Mexico 2016: The eleventh IGF meeting was held in Guadalajara, Mexico, from 6 to 9 December 2016. The meeting included 205 sessions as well as 24 pre-events (7 host country and ceremonial sessions; 8 main sessions; 96 workshops; 31 open forums; 4 individual Best Practice Forum sessions; 14 individual Dynamic Coalition sessions; 23 lightning sessions; 5 unconference sessions; 17 sessions classified "other"; and 24 pre-events). Experimental Lightning and Unconference sessions were held for the first time. A newcomers track helped participants attending the IGF meeting for the first time, to understand the IGF processes, foster the integration of all new-coming stakeholders into the IGF community, and make the meeting participant's first IGF experience as productive and welcoming as possible. The overarching theme for the meeting was: "Enabling Inclusive and Sustainable Growth". The meeting addressed a broad range of themes and issues including, but not limited to, Sustainable Development and the Internet Economy; Access and Diversity; Gender and Youth Issues; Human Rights Online; Cyber-security; Multistakeholder Cooperation; Critical Internet Resources; Internet governance capacity building; and Emerging Issues that may affect the future of the open Internet.
- IGF XII — Geneva, Switzerland 2017: The twelfth IGF meeting took place in Geneva, Switzerland, from 18 to 21 December 2017. The programme included 4 host country and ceremonial sessions; 8 main/special sessions; 99 workshops; 45 open forums; 4 individual BPF sessions; 15 individual DC sessions; 8 individual NRIs sessions; 13 sessions classified as "other"; 24 lightning sessions; and 40 Day 0 events; for a total of 260 sessions in the overall programme (220 if Day 0 events are not counted). 55 booths were featured in the IGF Village. The overarching meeting theme was "Shape Your Digital Future!". The meeting addressed a broad range of issues including, the future of global cooperation on Digital Governance; the impact of digitization on democracy, public trust and public opinion; Internet and the Sustainable Development Goals; access and diversity; the digital transformation and its socio-economic and labour impacts; youth and gender challenges pertaining to the Internet; the protection and promotion of human rights online; cyber-security; intended and unintended global impacts of local interventions; the need

to enhance multistakeholder cooperation; critical Internet resources; Internet governance capacity-building; and other emerging issues that enhance and affect the future of the open Internet.

- IGF XIII — Paris, France 2018: The thirteenth IGF meeting took place in Paris, from 12 to 14 November 2018. In addition to the Opening and Closing Sessions, the IGF 2018 programme featured 8 main/special sessions; 71 workshops; 27 open forums; 5 individual best practice forum (BPF) sessions; 15 individual dynamic coalition (DC) sessions; 5 individual national, regional, and youth (NRIs) collaborative sessions; 14 sessions classified as "other"; and 24 lightning sessions; for a total of 171 sessions in the overall programme. IGF XIII was held as part of the Paris Digital Week which, in addition to the IGF, featured the inaugural events of the Paris Peace Forum and the Govtech Summit. UN Secretary-General (SG) António Guterres addressed the IGF, marking the first time in Forum's history that a SG has attended in person. French President Macron addressed the IGF at the opening ceremony and launched the "Paris Call for Trust and Security in Cyberspace", a framework for regulating the Internet and fighting back against cyber attacks, hate speech and other cyber-threats. Eight themes formed the backbone of the 2018 agenda: (i) Cyber-security, Trust and Privacy; (ii) Development, Innovation and Economic Issues; (iii) Digital Inclusion and Accessibility; (iv) Human Rights, Gender and Youth; (v) Emerging Technologies; (vi) Evolution of Internet Governance; (vii) Media and Content; and (viii) Technical and Operational Issues.
- IGF XIV — Berlin, Germany 2019: The fourteenth IGF meeting took place in Berlin, from 25 to 29 November 2019.
- IGF XV — Online, 2020: The Fifteenth Annual Meeting of the Internet Governance Forum (IGF) was hosted online by the United Nations under the overarching theme: Internet for human resilience and solidarity. The first phase was hosted on 2–6 November and the second one on 9–17 November 2020.
- IGF XVI — Katowice, Poland 2021: The 16th annual IGF meeting was hosted by the Government of Poland in Katowice during 6–10 December, under the overarching theme.
- IGF XVII — Addis Ababa, Ethiopia 2022: The 17th annual IGF meeting was hosted by the Government of Ethiopia in Addis Ababa from 28 November to 2 December.
- IGF XVIII — Kyoto, Japan 2023: The 18th annual IGF meeting was hosted by the Government of Japan in Kyoto from 8 to 12 October, under the

overarching theme: The Internet We Want - Empowering All People, see https://igf2023.intgovforum.org

- IGF XIX — Riyadh, Saudi Arabia 2024: The 19th annual IGF meeting was hosted by the Government of Saudi Arabia in Riyadh from 15 to 19 December. The location drew strong criticism and calls by Access Now and Article 19 to reverse it due to the situation of human rights in Saudi Arabia.
- IGF XX — Lillestrøm/Oslo, Norway 2025: The 20th annual IGF meeting was hosted by the Government of Norway in Lillestrøm near Oslo from 23 to 27 June. There were two known bidders, Norway and Russia.

6.5.3 WSIS

The World Summit on the Information Society (WSIS) was a two-phase United Nations-sponsored summit on information, communication and, in broad terms, the information society that took place in 2003 in Geneva and in 2005 in Tunis. WSIS Forums have taken place periodically since then. One of the Summit's chief aims is to bridge the global digital divide separating rich countries from poor countries by increasing internet accessibility in the developing world. The conferences established 17 May as World Information Society Day.

The WSIS+10 Process marked the ten-year milestone since the 2005 Summit. In 2015, the stocktaking process culminated with a High-Level meeting of the UN General Assembly on 15 and 16 December in New York. A WSIS+20 review will take place in July 2025 in Geneva.

Background

In the last decades of the 20th century, Information and Communications Technology (ICT) has changed modern society in many ways. This is often referred to as the digital revolution, and along with it have come new opportunities and threats. Many world leaders hope to use ICT to solve societal problems; yet, at the same time, there are concerns about the digital divide, both international level and domestic levels. This trend could lead to shaping new classes of those who have access to ICT and those who do not. Recognizing that these challenges and opportunities require global discussion on the highest level, the government of Tunisia made a proposal at the International Telecommunication Union (ITU) Plenipotentiary Conference in Minneapolis in 1998 to hold a World Summit on the Information Society. This resolution was then put forward it to the United Nations. In 2001, the ITU Council decided to hold the Summit in two phases, the first from 10 to 12 December 2003, in Geneva, and the second from 16 to 18 November 2005 in Tunis. On 21 December 2001, the United Nations General Assembly by approving Resolution 56/183 endorsed the holding of the World Summit on the Information

Society (WSIS) to discuss on information society opportunities and challenges. According to this resolution, the General Assembly related the Summit to the United Nations Millennium Declaration to implement ICT to facilitate achieving Millennium Development Goals. It also emphasized on the multi-stakeholder approach to use all stakeholders including civil society and private sector beside the governments. The resolution gave ITU the leading managerial role to organize the event in cooperation with other UN bodies as well as the other international organizations and the host countries and recommended that preparations for the Summit take place through an open-ended intergovernmental Preparatory Committee - or PrepCom - that would define the agenda of the Summit, decide on the modalities of the participation of other stakeholders, and finalize both the draft Declaration of Principles and the draft Plan of Action.

Stocktaking Process

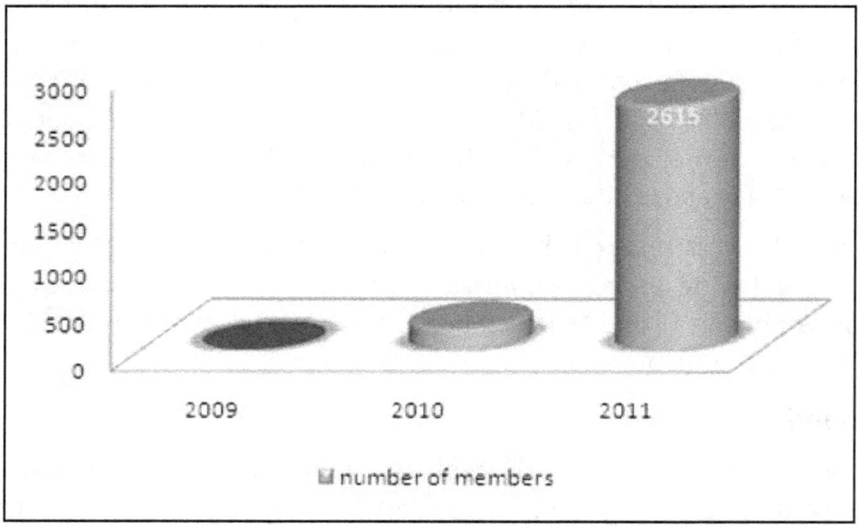

Evolution of the Number of WSIS Stocktaking Members

The WSIS stocktaking process is a follow-up to WSIS. Its purpose is to provide a register of activities carried out by governments, international organizations, the business sector, civil society and other entities, in order to highlight the progress made since the landmark event. Following § 120 of TAIS, ITU has been maintaining the WSIS Stocktaking database as a publicly accessible system providing information on ICT-related initiatives and projects with reference to the 11 WSIS Action Lines. ECOSOC Resolution 2010/12 on "Assessment of the progress made in the implementation of and follow-up to the outcomes of the World Summit on the Information Society" reiterated the importance of maintaining a process for coordinating the multi-stakeholder implementation of WSIS outcomes through effective tools, with the goal of exchanging of information among WSIS Action

Line Facilitators; identification of issues that need improvements; and discussion of the modalities of reporting the overall implementation process. The resolution encourages all WSIS stakeholders to continue to contribute information to the WSIS Stocktaking database (www.wsis.org/stocktaking).

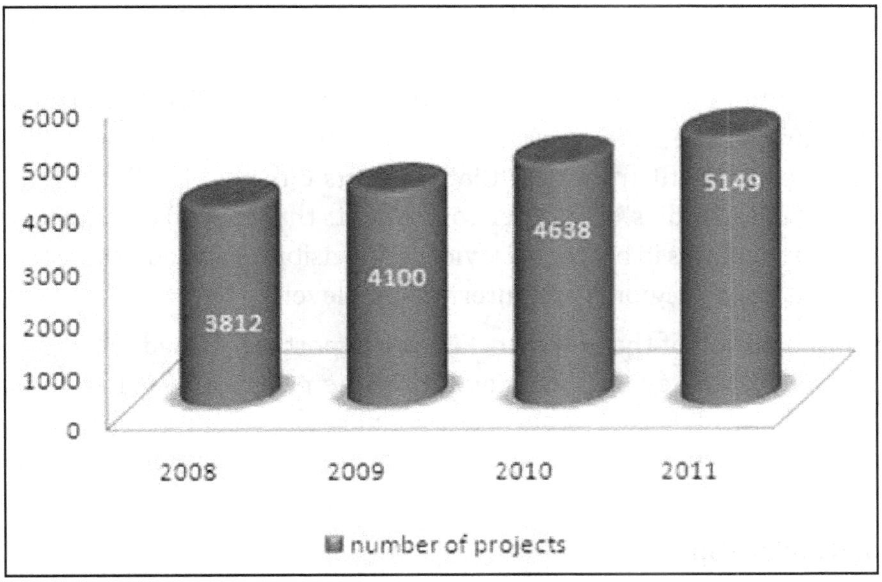

Evolution of the Number of WSIS Stocktaking Projects

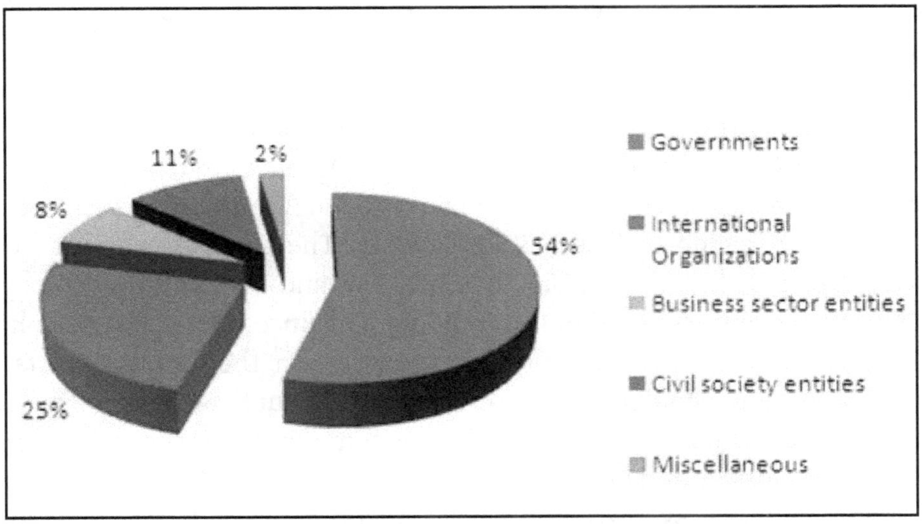

Origin of the WSIS Stocktaking Members

Furthermore, regular reporting on WSIS Stocktaking is the outcome of the Tunis phase of the Summit, which was launched in order to serve as a tool for assisting with the WSIS follow-up. The purpose of the regular reports is to update stakeholders on the various activities related to the 11 Action Lines identified in the Geneva Plan of Action, that was approved during First Phase of the WSIS.

Platform

The WSIS stocktaking platform is the new initiative that was launched by Mr Zhao, ITU Deputy Secretary-General and chair of ITU's WSIS Task Force, in February 2010 to improve existing functionalities and transform the former static database into a portal to highlight ICT-related projects and initiatives in line with WSIS implementation.

The platform offers stakeholders interactive networking opportunities via Web 2.0 applications. In the framework of the WSIS Stocktaking Platform, all types of stakeholders can benefit from the "Global Events Calendar", "Global Publication Repository", "Case Studies" and other components that tend to extend networking and create partnerships in order to provide more visibility and add value to projects at the local, national, regional and international levels.

Since the first edition of the WSIS Stocktaking Report was issued in 2005, biannual reporting has been a key tool for monitoring the progress of ICT initiatives and projects worldwide. The 2012 report reflects more than 1,000 recent WSIS-related activities, undertaken between May 2010 and 2012, each emphasizing the efforts deployed by stakeholders involved in the WSIS process.

Forum and Follow-Up

The WSIS follow-up works towards achieving the indicative targets, set out in the Geneva Plan of Action and serves as a global reference for improving connectivity and universal, ubiquitous, equitable, non-discriminatory and affordable access to, and use of, ICTs, considering different national circumstances, to be achieved by 2015, and to using ICTs, as a tool to achieve the internationally agreed development goals and objectives, including the Millennium Development Goals. Since 2006 the WSIS Forum has been held in Geneva around World Information Society Day (17 May) to implement the WSIS Follow-up. The event is organized by the WSIS facilitators including ITU, UNESCO, UNCTAD and UNDP and hosted by ITU. Until 2010 the Forum was held in ITU building and since then it has been held in International Labour Organization building. Every year the Forum attracts more than 1000 WSIS Stakeholders from more than 140 countries. Several high-level representatives of the wider WSIS Stakeholder community graced the Forum, and more than 20 Ministers and Deputies, several Ambassadors, CEOs, and Civil Society leaders contributed passionately towards the program of the Forum. Remote participation was an integral component of the WSIS Forum over 1000 stakeholders followed and contributed to the outcomes of the event in a remote manner from all parts of the world. Onsite networking was facilitated by the imeetYouatWSIS online community platform. More than 250 on-site participants have actively used the tool before and during the event which facilitated fruitful networking leading to win-win partnerships.

WSIS+10

The WSIS+10 High-Level Event, an extended version of the WSIS Forum, took place 9–13 June 2014 in Geneva, Switzerland. The event reviewed the progress made in the implementation of the WSIS outcomes under the mandates of participating agencies and took stock of developments in the last 10 years based on reports of WSIS stakeholders, including those submitted by countries, action line facilitators, and other stakeholders. The event reviewed the WSIS Outcomes (2003 and 2005) related to the WSIS Action Lines and agreed on a vision of how to proceed beyond 2015.

The WSIS+10 High-Level Event endorsed the "WSIS+10 Statement on Implementation of WSIS Outcomes" and the "WSIS+10 Vision for WSIS Beyond 2015". These outcome documents were developed in an open and inclusive preparatory process, the WSIS+10 Multistakeholder Preparatory Platform (WSIS+10 MPP). "High-Level Track Policy Statements" and a "Forum Track Outcome Document" are also available.

The WSIS+10 open consultation process was an open and inclusive consultation among WSIS stakeholders to prepare for the WSIS + 10 High-Level Event. It focused on developing multistakeholder consensus on two draft outcome documents. Eight open consultation meetings among stakeholders, including governments, the private sector, civil society, international organizations, and relevant regional organizations, were held between July 2013 and June 2014. Two draft outcome documents were developed and submitted for consideration at the WSIS+10 High-Level Event:

- Draft WSIS+10 Statement on the Implementation of WSIS Outcomes.
- Draft WSIS+10 Vision for WSIS Beyond 2015 under mandates of participating agencies.

The final WSIS+10 High-Level Meeting of the General Assembly took place on 15–16 December 2015 in New York, and concluded with the adoption of the Outcome Document of the high-level meeting of the General Assembly on the overall review of the implementation of the outcomes of the World Summit on the Information Society was adopted.

WSIS+20

The WSIS+20 is scheduled to take place on 7-11 July 2025 in Geneva, Switzerland and address key trends, challenges and opportunities since the Geneva Plan of Action in 2003.

Digital Divide and Digital Dilemma

Two main concerns seemed to be the issue and talk of the UN World Summit on the Information Society held in Tunis:

- The digital divide .
- The digital dilemma.

First the digital divide, which was addressed in Archbishop John P. Foley's address before the WSIS and in the Vatican document, Ethics in the Internet. According to Archbishop Foley the digital divide is the current disparity in the access to digital communications between developed and developing countries and it requires the joint effort of the entire international community. The digital divide is considered a form of discrimination dividing the rich and the poor, both within and among nations, on the basis of access, or lack of access, to the new information technology. It is an updated version of an older gap that has always existed between the information rich and the information poor. The term digital divide underlines the reality that not only individuals and groups but also nations must have access to the new technology in order to share in the promised benefits of globalization and not fall behind other nations.

In a statement delivered by Senator Burchell Whiteman from Jamaica he stressed that Jamaica realizes the importance of bridging the digital divide which he sees as promoting social and economic development for 80% of the countries that are still struggling with this gap and the impact that it has on them. In a statement given by Mr. Ignacio Gonzalez Planas, who is the minister of Informatics and Communications of the Republic of Cuba, he also talked about the concern of only a few countries enjoying these privileges. Mentioning that over half of the world population does not have telephone access, which was invented more than a century ago. A statement by Vice Premier Huang Ju, the State Council of the People's Republic of China, said that the information society should be a people centered society in which all peoples and all countries share the benefit to the fullest in greater common development in the information society.

Second the digital dilemma, which the Holy See emphasized as a disadvantage to the information society and urged caution to avoid taking the wrong steps. It is a real and present danger with technology especially the Internet. The Holy See strongly supports freedom of expression and the free exchange of ideas, but argues that the moral order and common good must be respected. One must approach it with sensitivity and respect for other people's values and beliefs and protect the distinctiveness of cultures and the underlying unity of the human family.

Whiteman from Jamaica agreed on the issue of facing digital dilemmas as well. He stated that information resources combined with technology resources are available to the world and they have the power to transform the world for good or ill. In a statement made by Mr. Stjepan Mesic, President of Croatia, it was stated that we are flooded with data and we think that we know and can find everything about everyone but we also must remember that we don't know what so easily accessible is like. He states that although the information society is a blessing one should not ignore the potentiality of it turning into a nightmare.

The Holy See's caution of the information society is being heard and echoed by other countries especially those that were present at the WSIS in Tunis.[who?] Echoing the statement made in Ethics in the Internet, "The internet can make an enormously valuable contribution to human life. It can foster prosperity and peace, intellectual and aesthetic growth, mutual understanding among peoples and nations on a global scale."

In a press statement released 14 November 2003 the Civil Society group warned about a deadlock, already setting in on the very first article of the declaration, where governments are not able to agree on the Universal Declaration of Human Rights as the common foundation of the summit declaration. It identified two main problems:

- On the issue of correcting imbalances in riches, rights and power, governments do not agree on even the principle of a financial effort to overcome the so-called "digital divide", which was precisely the objective when the summit process was started in 2001.
- In its view, not even the basis of human life in dignity and equality, the Universal Declaration of Human Rights, finds support as the basis for the Information Society. Governments are not able to agree on a commitment to basic human right standards as the basis for the Information Society, most prominent in this case being the freedom of expression.

Internet Governance

The Summit's first phase took place in December 2003 in Geneva. The summit process began with the first "Prepcom" in July 2002. The last Prepcom, held from 19 to 30 September 2005 in Geneva, ended without securing final agreement on Internet governance, with the U.S. rejecting a European Union proposal to relinquish control of ICANN.

An issue that emerged was Internet governance and the dominant role that the USA plays in policy making. The most radical ideas about devolving this authority were those supporting a civil society approach to Internet governance.

In a document released on 3 December 2003 the United States delegation to the WSIS advocated a strong private sector and rule of law as the critical foundations for development of national information and communication technologies (ICT). Ambassador David Gross, the US coordinator for international communications and information policy, outlined what he called "the three pillars" of the US position in a briefing to reporters 3 December.

- As nations attempt to build a sustainable ICT sector, commitment to the private sector and rule of law must be emphasized, Gross said, "so that countries can attract the necessary private investment to create the infrastructure."
- A second important pillar of the US position was the need for content creation and intellectual property rights protection in order to inspire ongoing content development.
- Ensuring security on the internet, in electronic communications and in electronic commerce was the third major priority for the US. "All of this works and is exciting for people as long as people feel that the networks are secure from cyber attacks, secure in terms of their privacy," Gross said.

As the Geneva phase of the meeting drew closer, one proposal that was gaining attention was to create an international fund to provide increased financial resources to help lesser-developed nations expand their ICT sectors. The "voluntary digital solidarity fund" was a proposal put forth by the president of Senegal, but it was not one that the United States could currently endorse, Gross said. Gross said the United States was also achieving broad consensus on the principle that a "culture of cyber-security" must develop in national ICT policies to continue growth and expansion in this area. He said the last few years had been marked by considerable progress as nations update their laws to address the galloping criminal threats in cyberspace. "There's capacity-building for countries to be able to criminalize those activities that occur within their borders...and similarly to work internationally to communicate between administrations of law enforcement to track down people who are acting in ways that are unlawful," Gross said.

Many governments are very concerned that various groups use U.S.-based servers to spread anti-semitic, nationalist, or regime critical messages. This controversy is a consequence of the American position on free speech which does not consider speech as criminal without direct appeals to violence. The United States argues that giving the control of Internet domain names to international bureaucrats and governments may lead to massive censorship that could destroy the freedom of the Internet as a public space. Ultimately, the US Department of Commerce made it clear it intends to retain control of the Internet's root servers indefinitely. The main UN level body in this field is the Internet Governance Forum, which was established in 2006.

CHAPTER 7

Digital Trade, Sanctions, and Economic Diplomacy

7.1 CYBER-SECURITY AND CROSS-BORDER DIGITAL TRADE

Cyber-security is an essential pillar of cross-border digital trade, linking the safety of digital networks to economic growth, international competitiveness, and global trust. The interdependence between secure networks and digital commerce requires the integration of cyber-security into national policies, trade agreements, and multistakeholder initiatives. While challenges such as disparities in capabilities, attribution difficulties, and supply chain vulnerabilities persist, proactive measures and cooperation among governments, companies, and civil society offer pathways to resilience.

Emerging technologies present both opportunities and risks, reinforcing the need for adaptive and forward-looking governance. By prioritizing cyber-security, nations can create an environment in which digital trade flourishes, consumer confidence is maintained, and economic relationships across borders are strengthened. The future of global commerce depends not only on innovation and market access but also on the collective ability to secure the digital foundations upon which trade increasingly relies. Cyber-security and cross-border digital trade are, therefore, inseparable pillars of the twenty-first-century global economy.

Emerging technologies such as artificial intelligence, blockchain, and quantum computing are reshaping both digital trade and cyber-security. AI-driven platforms improve logistics, fraud detection, and predictive analytics, while also presenting new risks related to algorithmic manipulation, adversarial attacks, and data privacy. Blockchain offers secure and transparent methods for cross-border transactions but requires careful attention to cryptographic vulnerabilities and regulatory harmonization.

Quantum computing poses potential threats to current encryption standards, highlighting the need for proactive measures to safeguard trade systems. The rapid evolution of these technologies necessitates adaptive governance and continuous collaboration. Countries and companies must remain vigilant, investing in research, cyber-security capacity-building, and regulatory frameworks that can respond to emerging threats. Ensuring that digital trade remains secure while taking advantage of technological innovation is a defining challenge for policymakers, businesses, and civil society alike.

7.1.1 Interdependence of Cyber-security and Digital Trade

Cross-border digital trade depends on a robust and secure cyber environment. E-commerce platforms, online financial services, cloud computing, and digital supply chains all require networks that are resilient to cyber-attacks. If a major breach occurs, it can disrupt trade flows, damage reputations, and lead to economic losses. For instance, ransomware attacks on shipping or logistics companies can halt deliveries, affect international supply chains, and trigger contractual disputes between businesses in different countries. Similarly, cyber-attacks on financial institutions can compromise payment systems and undermine consumer confidence in cross-border transactions.

This interdependence creates a direct link between cyber-security and economic growth. Countries with strong cyber-defenses attract more digital investment and trade, while those with weak security frameworks face barriers to participation in global markets. Consequently, cyber-security is increasingly treated as a component of trade policy, rather than merely a domestic technical concern. Governments are recognizing that the ability to secure digital trade infrastructure is essential to maintaining competitiveness in the global economy.

7.1.2 International Regulatory Frameworks

The governance of cyber-security in the context of cross-border trade is guided by a combination of domestic regulations, regional frameworks, and international agreements. Domestic laws such as data protection regulations and cyber-security standards play a central role in ensuring that companies adhere to security practices. The European Union's General Data Protection Regulation (GDPR) exemplifies how national or regional rules can affect cross-border data flows by imposing strict requirements for the handling and transfer of personal data. Companies engaged in international trade must comply with such regulations, integrating cyber-security measures into their operational and compliance frameworks.

Regional agreements and multilateral treaties further shape the landscape of digital trade. Trade agreements increasingly include chapters on digital trade, cyber-security, and data protection, reflecting the recognition that secure networks are fundamental to facilitating commerce. For example, provisions in agreements like the Comprehensive and Progressive Agreement for Trans-Pacific Partnership (CPTPP) and the US-Mexico-Canada Agreement (USMCA) highlight the importance of protecting information, safeguarding payment systems, and ensuring cooperation in cyber-security incident response. These frameworks illustrate that cyber-security is no longer a siloed concern; it is central to trade diplomacy and international cooperation.

Fig: Cyber-security be a Unifying Factor in Digital Trade Negotiations

7.1.3 Challenges in Securing Cross-Border Digital Trade

Despite efforts to harmonize regulations and improve security, multiple challenges complicate the protection of cross-border digital trade. One major challenge is the variation in cyber-security capabilities across countries. While advanced economies may possess sophisticated defense mechanisms, developing countries often lack the resources, expertise, and infrastructure to defend against cyber-threats effectively. This disparity creates vulnerabilities in global supply chains and can disrupt trade even when only one link in the chain is compromised.

Another challenge is the attribution problem in cyber-attacks. Identifying the source of a cyber incident is often difficult due to the anonymity afforded by digital networks. When attacks cross international borders, it becomes even more complex, as legal jurisdictions and enforcement mechanisms differ. Without reliable attribution, countries may struggle to respond effectively, undermining trust in the digital trade ecosystem.

Furthermore, the reliance on multinational technology providers introduces supply chain risks. Software vulnerabilities, hardware backdoors, and third-party dependencies can expose critical trade infrastructure to cyber-threats. Attackers can exploit these vulnerabilities to disrupt commerce, steal sensitive information, or manipulate market operations, posing risks to both private companies and national economies.

7.1.4 Cyber-security as a Facilitator of Trade Trust

Trust is the cornerstone of cross-border digital trade. Consumers and businesses must have confidence that their data, transactions, and communications are secure. Cyber-security measures, therefore, serve not only as protection but also as enablers of trust in international commerce. Secure payment systems, encrypted communications, authentication protocols, and resilient cloud infrastructures provide the assurance that transactions can be conducted safely across borders.

The establishment of trust extends to governments and regulatory bodies. Countries that demonstrate strong cyber-security practices are more likely to attract international business, investment, and partnerships. Conversely, nations with weak cyber-defenses may face economic isolation or reduced participation in digital markets. This dynamic has incentivized governments to prioritize cyber-security in national trade strategies, recognizing that a robust digital economy is inseparable from strong cyber-governance.

7.1.5 Role of Multistakeholder Cooperation

The complexity of cross-border digital trade and cyber-security necessitates cooperation among multiple stakeholders. Governments, private sector actors, technical communities, and civil society organizations all contribute to creating secure trade environments. Public-private partnerships are particularly vital, as many of the networks and platforms facilitating international commerce are privately owned. Collaboration allows for threat intelligence sharing, coordinated incident response, and the establishment of best practices that enhance global resilience.

International institutions and forums also play a significant role in promoting cyber-security norms for digital trade. The World Trade Organization (WTO) addresses e-commerce and digital trade rules, while initiatives such as the United Nations' Group of Governmental Experts on Cyber-security facilitate dialogue on cross-border norms. These multistakeholder approaches ensure that cyber-security considerations are integrated into the broader architecture of global commerce, balancing economic growth, security, and human rights.

7.2 EXPORT CONTROLS AND DUAL-USE TECHNOLOGIES

In the intricate landscape of international security and trade, few issues are as complex and fraught with tension as the management of dual-use technologies. These are items, software, and technologies—often cutting-edge and fundamental to modern industry—that have legitimate civilian applications but can also be repurposed for military use or to fuel weapons of mass destruction (WMD) programs. This category encompasses a vast array of goods, from high-performance computers and advanced materials to unmanned aerial vehicles and certain chemicals. Perhaps the most relevant category in the digital age is cyber-security tools, including intrusion software, surveillance systems, and vulnerability exploitation platforms. These tools are vital for national security agencies and cyber-security professionals to test network defenses and protect critical infrastructure. However, in the hands of authoritarian regimes, the very same technologies can be wielded as instruments of internal repression, used to monitor dissidents, suppress free speech, and violate human rights on a massive scale. Export controls are the regulatory mechanisms designed to navigate this dilemma. They are a set of laws and policies that governments use to restrict the export of sensitive dual-use items to specific end-users or destinations where there is a risk they could be diverted to harmful ends. The primary objective is to safeguard national and international security without unduly hampering legitimate trade, scientific collaboration, and economic competitiveness.

The future effectiveness of export controls depends on their ability to adapt to several disruptive trends. First, the global nature of innovation means that sensitive technologies are increasingly developed in countries outside traditional control regimes, creating new hubs for proliferation that are beyond the reach of Wassenaar. Second, the rise of open-source software, cloud computing, and additive manufacturing (3D printing) further erodes the efficacy of traditional border-centric controls. You cannot control the export of a digital blueprint that can be emailed and printed anywhere. Finally, the emergence of foundational technologies like artificial intelligence and quantum computing presents a new category of threat. These are general-purpose technologies with ubiquitous civilian applications that also hold the potential to revolutionize warfare and break existing encryption. Controlling them without stifling entire industries is an unprecedented challenge. The response will likely require a shift in strategy: from controlling specific end-items to controlling key enabling components and know-how; from a purely multilateral approach to building coalitions of like-minded states; and from a reactive posture to a more proactive one that anticipates technological breakthroughs. The delicate balance between security and prosperity has never been more difficult to maintain, nor more critical to the stability of the international order.

7.2.1 Wassenaar Arrangement: The Multilateral Foundation of Control Lists

The most significant international effort to harmonize export controls on dual-use technologies is the Wassenaar Arrangement on Export Controls for Conventional Arms and Dual-Use Goods and Technologies. Established in 1996, it is a voluntary export control regime with 42 participating states, including most major industrial and technological powers. The Arrangement is not a treaty and has no legally binding authority; instead, it functions as a forum for transparency and consensus-building. Its core achievement is the creation and maintenance of two detailed control lists: one for munitions and another for dual-use goods and technologies. Participating states agree to implement national policies to control the export of items on these lists, with the goal of preventing destabilizing accumulations of arms and sensitive technologies. The Wassenaar Arrangement's dual-use list is particularly dynamic, as members must constantly debate and update it to keep pace with rapid technological innovation. For instance, in 2013, the list was amended to include "intrusion software" and "internet surveillance systems," a direct response to the growing market for sophisticated cyber surveillance tools. However, the consensus-based nature of Wassenaar means that updating these lists is a slow and politically charged process, often lagging behind the breakneck speed of technological development and leaving dangerous gaps in control coverage.

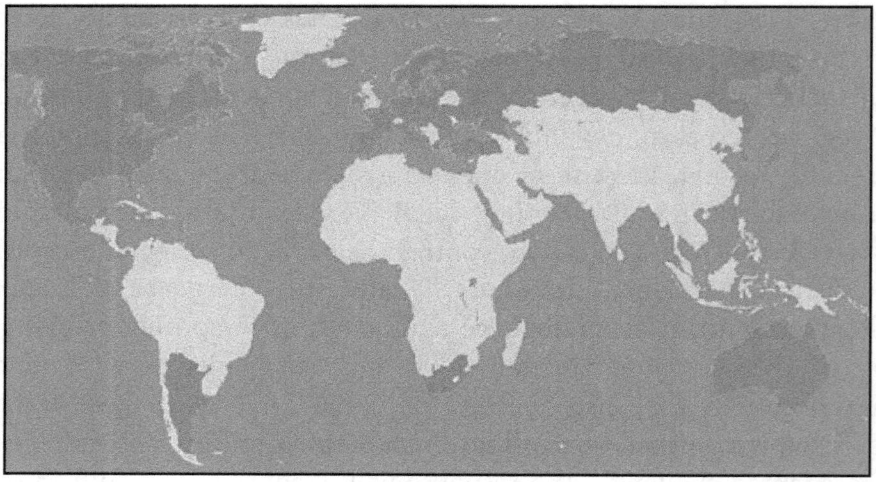

Wassenaar Arrangement

7.2.2 Implementation Challenge: National Enforcement and Divergent Interests

While the Wassenaar Arrangement provides a common framework, the actual implementation of export controls is a matter of national sovereignty. Each participating state translates the agreed-upon control lists into its own legal and regulatory system, leading to significant variations in enforcement rigor, licensing procedures, and penalties for non-compliance. In the United States, the Export Administration Regulations (EAR) administered by the Bureau of Industry and Security (BIS) govern dual-use exports, while in the European Union, the Dual-Use Regulation provides a common legal basis for all member states, albeit one that allows for national additions. This decentralized system creates inherent challenges. A technology might be approved for export from one country but denied by another, creating loopholes that can be exploited by determined proliferators. Furthermore, national economic interests can clash with non-proliferation goals. Governments face intense pressure from domestic industries that argue stringent controls put them at a competitive disadvantage against rivals in countries with weaker export regimes. This tension between security and commerce is a constant feature of the export control landscape, forcing governments to perform a delicate balancing act on a case-by-case basis for every sensitive export license application.

7.2.3 Cyber-security Conundrum: Controlling the Intangible

The digital nature of many modern dual-use technologies presents a unique and formidable challenge for traditional export control paradigms. Classical controls were designed for tangible goods—physical items that could be inspected at a border. How does one control the export of a software vulnerability, a line of malicious code, or an encryption algorithm that can be transmitted across the globe instantaneously via the internet? The attempt to control "intrusion software" under the Wassenaar Arrangement sparked fierce backlash from the cyber-security research community.

Experts argued that controlling the export of hacking tools would cripple vital security research, hinder international collaboration on vulnerability disclosure, and ultimately make the digital ecosystem less secure for everyone. They pointed out that the boundaries are incredibly blurry; a tool used to test a network's defenses is functionally identical to one used to attack it. The distinction often lies solely in the intent of the user, which is impossible for a developer or exporter to reliably ascertain. This episode highlighted a critical weakness in the existing system: its 20th-century tools are ill-equipped to manage the intangible, easily reproducible, and globally distributed nature of 21st-century digital technology.

7.2.4 Human Rights Imperative: Preventing Digital Repression

Beyond the concerns of military proliferation, export controls on dual-use technologies have become a frontline tool in the effort to prevent digital repression. There is a well-documented global trade in sophisticated cyber surveillance technologies sold by private companies in democratic states to security services in authoritarian regimes.

Technologies like facial recognition systems, network monitoring tools, and mobile device forensics kits have been used to identify, track, and silence journalists, human rights defenders, and political opponents. Controlling the export of these technologies is a profound moral and ethical issue. It requires governments to conduct enhanced due diligence, not just on the item itself, but on the human rights record of the end-user. This involves assessing whether a piece of software destined for a foreign ministry of interior could be used for internal surveillance. Several jurisdictions, including the EU with its recent modernization of the Dual-Use Regulation, are moving to include explicit human rights considerations as a criterion for denying an export license. This represents an evolution of export controls from a purely non-proliferation tool into an instrument of human rights foreign policy, though enforcement remains inconsistent and often secondary to strategic and economic partnerships.

7.3 TECHNOLOGY SANCTIONS AND GEOPOLITICAL RESPONSES

Technology sanctions have become a defining feature of modern geopolitics, reflecting the strategic importance of technological dominance in global power dynamics. While these measures are intended to protect national security and curb adversarial advancements, they also provoke complex geopolitical responses that reshape supply chains, accelerate indigenous innovation, and escalate cyber competition.

The challenge for policymakers lies in balancing the imperative of technological containment with the risks of fragmentation, economic disruption, and unintended escalation. As nations navigate this digital battlefield, the future of technology sanctions will hinge on their ability to adapt to evolving technological landscapes while maintaining a rules-based international order. The path forward demands not only strategic foresight but also a commitment to fostering innovation within ethical and legal boundaries, ensuring that technological progress remains a force for stability rather than conflict.

As technology continues to drive economic and military power, the use of sanctions as a geopolitical tool is likely to expand. Emerging technologies such as quantum computing, biotechnology, and advanced AI will become new battlegrounds for technological containment, with states imposing restrictions to maintain strategic advantages. The effectiveness of these sanctions will depend on the ability of imposing nations to sustain global coalitions, as unilateral measures are increasingly vulnerable to circumvention. Meanwhile, targeted nations will continue to pursue strategies of indigenous innovation, supply chain diversification, and retaliatory measures to counter technological isolation. The future of technology sanctions will also be shaped by the evolution of international norms, where debates over digital sovereignty, data governance, and technological ethics will influence how sanctions are designed and enforced. In this environment, the interplay between technological advancement and geopolitical strategy will define the contours of global power competition for decades to come.

7.3.1 Strategic Rationale behind Technology Sanctions

Technology sanctions are typically imposed to achieve multiple strategic objectives. First, they aim to curb the military and intelligence capabilities of adversarial states by restricting access to critical technologies such as advanced semiconductors, quantum computing, and cyber-security tools. Second, they seek to protect domestic industries by preventing the transfer of sensitive intellectual property and proprietary technologies to competitors. Third, sanctions are used as a coercive tool to influence state behavior, particularly in cases of cyber espionage, human rights violations, or aggressive military posturing. The United States, European Union, and other Western nations have frequently employed technology sanctions against states like China, Russia, and Iran, targeting entities involved in cyber-warfare, surveillance, and military modernization. These measures reflect a broader strategy of technological containment, where leading powers attempt to maintain their edge in innovation while limiting the rise of strategic competitors.

7.3.2 Mechanics of Technology Sanctions

Technology sanctions operate through a combination of export controls, investment restrictions, and supply chain disruptions. Export controls, such as those enforced by the U.S. Bureau of Industry and Security (BIS), restrict the sale of advanced technologies to designated entities or countries. Investment restrictions limit foreign direct investment in sensitive sectors, preventing adversaries from acquiring cutting-edge capabilities through financial means.

Supply chain disruptions, meanwhile, involve pressuring multinational corporations to cease business with sanctioned entities, effectively isolating them from global markets. For instance, the U.S. restrictions on semiconductor exports to China have forced companies like ASML and NVIDIA to limit sales of high-end chipmaking equipment, significantly impacting China's ability to advance its domestic semiconductor industry. These mechanisms are designed to create technological bottlenecks, forcing targeted nations to either comply with geopolitical demands or invest heavily in indigenous alternatives.

7.3.3 Geopolitical Responses to Technology Sanctions

The imposition of technology sanctions rarely goes unanswered, as affected states deploy a range of countermeasures to mitigate their impact. One common response is the acceleration of domestic innovation, where sanctioned nations invest in research and development to reduce dependence on foreign technology. China's push for semiconductor self-sufficiency through massive state-backed initiatives exemplifies this strategy. Another response involves supply chain diversification, where targeted countries seek alternative suppliers or develop parallel trade networks to circumvent restrictions. Russia, for instance, has turned to countries like China and Iran to acquire restricted technologies following Western sanctions. Additionally, retaliatory sanctions and diplomatic escalation are often employed, with nations imposing reciprocal restrictions on foreign firms or expelling diplomatic personnel in protest. These geopolitical maneuvers reflect the broader struggle for technological sovereignty, where states seek to maintain strategic autonomy in the face of external pressures.

7.3.4 Role of Economic and Industrial Espionage

In response to technology sanctions, some nations have resorted to economic and industrial espionage to acquire restricted technologies. Cyber espionage campaigns targeting defense contractors, semiconductor firms, and research institutions have become a common tactic for circumventing export controls. State-sponsored hacking groups, such as those linked to China's Ministry of State Security or Russia's intelligence services, have been implicated in numerous high-profile breaches aimed at stealing proprietary technology. These operations are often justified as necessary countermeasures to level the playing field in an era of technological containment. However, they also escalate tensions, leading to further sanctions, diplomatic expulsions, and heightened cyber-security defenses. The cycle of sanctions and espionage underscores the increasingly adversarial nature of global technology competition, where economic and military security are deeply intertwined.

7.3.5 Impact on Global Supply Chains and Technological Fragmentation

Technology sanctions have profound implications for global supply chains, often leading to fragmentation and the emergence of parallel technological ecosystems. The U.S.-China tech war, for example, has resulted in the bifurcation of supply chains, with Western firms reducing reliance on Chinese components and China fostering domestic alternatives. This decoupling extends beyond hardware to software, cloud computing, and artificial intelligence, where competing standards and platforms are emerging.

The semiconductor industry, in particular, has become a focal point of this fragmentation, with nations like the U.S., China, and the EU investing heavily in domestic chip production to reduce vulnerabilities. While this trend may enhance national security, it also risks increasing costs, reducing efficiencies, and stifling innovation through reduced global collaboration. The long-term consequences of technological fragmentation remain uncertain, but they are likely to reshape the geopolitical landscape in ways that favor states with the resources to sustain independent innovation ecosystems.

7.3.6 Legal and Ethical Dimensions of Technology Sanctions

The use of technology sanctions raises significant legal and ethical questions, particularly regarding their compliance with international trade laws and human rights standards. Critics argue that broad sanctions can have unintended humanitarian consequences, such as limiting access to medical technologies or disrupting civilian communications infrastructure. Additionally, the extra-territorial application of sanctions—where one nation's restrictions affect global firms operating in third countries—has sparked legal disputes and diplomatic tensions. The World Trade Organization (WTO) and other international bodies have seen challenges to technology sanctions, with some states arguing that they violate free trade principles. Ethically, the weaponization of technology through sanctions blurs the line between national security and economic warfare, prompting debates over the legitimacy of using technological dominance as a tool of coercion. These legal and ethical dilemmas complicate the geopolitical calculus of sanctions, requiring careful balancing of security imperatives with international legal obligations.

7.3.7 Case Studies

Several high-profile cases illustrate the dynamics of technology sanctions and their geopolitical repercussions. The U.S. sanctions on Huawei, which restricted the company's access to American semiconductor technology, forced the Chinese telecom giant to develop its own chip designs and seek alternative suppliers. Similarly, the U.S. restrictions on advanced AI and supercomputing exports to China have spurred Beijing to accelerate its domestic AI industry, with significant state investment in research and development.

In another example, Russia's exclusion from global semiconductor markets following its invasion of Ukraine has led to a surge in smuggling and black-market procurement of restricted technologies. These cases demonstrate how technology sanctions can both hinder and inadvertently stimulate technological advancement in targeted nations, reshaping global innovation landscapes in unpredictable ways.

7.4 DATA LOCALIZATION AND FREE FLOW OF INFORMATION

Data localization and the free flow of information represent two competing paradigms in the governance of cyberspace. While localization emphasizes state control, privacy, and national security, free flow focuses on efficiency, innovation, and global connectivity. The balance between these approaches has implications for economic growth, cyber-security, trade, and human rights. Both strategies present benefits and risks, and neither alone can address the complex realities of the digital economy. Multistakeholder cooperation, international frameworks, and adaptive policies are essential to reconciling these priorities.

By establishing harmonized standards for data protection, cyber-security, and cross-border trade, countries can enable secure and efficient data flows while safeguarding privacy and national interests. Emerging technologies will continue to shape this debate, requiring flexible, forward-looking policies that support innovation and global economic integration. Ultimately, the future of cyberspace governance will depend on the ability of states, companies, and civil society to work together, balancing the imperatives of sovereignty, security, and the free flow of information in a rapidly evolving digital world.

Emerging technologies such as artificial intelligence, blockchain, and cloud computing further complicate the debate over data localization and free flow. AI systems require access to large datasets for training, often sourced from multiple countries. Blockchain networks may operate across borders, challenging traditional jurisdictional frameworks. Cloud-based services rely on global infrastructure to deliver scalable and efficient solutions. These technologies underscore the need for flexible and adaptive policies that can accommodate evolving business models, technological advancements, and international trade requirements. Policymakers must anticipate future developments and foster cooperation that ensures data mobility, innovation, and security coexist. Otherwise, rigid localization requirements may hinder the adoption of transformative technologies and reduce competitiveness in the global economy.

7.4.1 Data Localization

Data localization refers to laws, regulations, or policies requiring that data collected within a country's borders be stored and processed locally. Governments adopt data localization measures for multiple reasons, including national security, privacy protection, law enforcement, and economic development. By keeping data within national jurisdictions, states aim to ensure that it is subject to domestic legal frameworks, protecting citizens from foreign surveillance and cyber-threats.

Beyond security, data localization is often framed as a tool to strengthen domestic digital economies. By mandating local storage, governments hope to encourage the growth of local data centers, cloud services, and technology companies, generating employment and fostering innovation. Countries such as Russia, China, and India have enacted stringent data localization policies, reflecting both geopolitical considerations and domestic regulatory ambitions. These measures are often justified as safeguards against foreign access to sensitive data, especially in sectors such as finance, healthcare, and public administration.

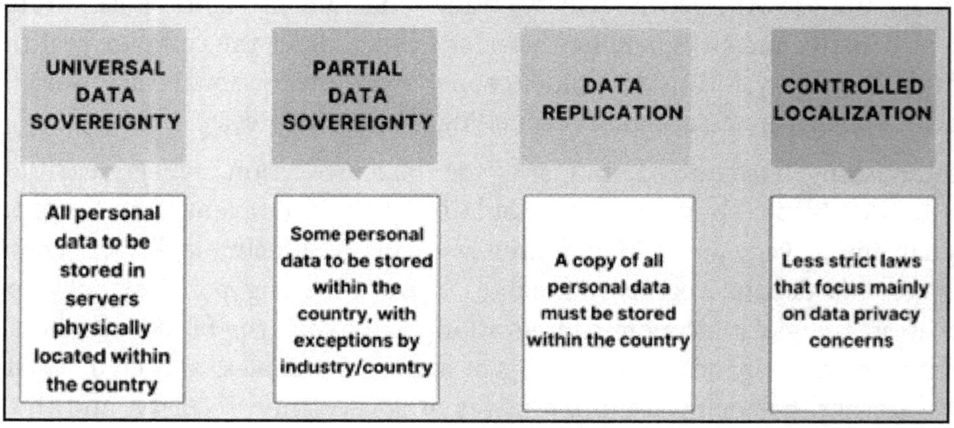

Fig: Data Localization

7.4.2 Free Flow of Information and Global Connectivity

In contrast, the principle of free flow of information emphasizes the unrestricted movement of data across borders. Advocates argue that open data flows are essential for global commerce, innovation, cloud computing, and collaborative research. The ability to transmit, store, and process data in any jurisdiction enables multinational corporations, small businesses, and startups to access advanced infrastructure, reduce costs, and deliver services efficiently.

Free flow of information is also critical for international trade. Modern economies increasingly rely on digital services, e-commerce, and cloud-based platforms that require seamless cross-border data transfers. Trade agreements such as the Comprehensive and Progressive Agreement for Trans-Pacific Partnership (CPTPP) and the US-Mexico-Canada Agreement (USMCA) explicitly recognize the importance of cross-border data flows for economic growth. Restrictions on such flows can disrupt supply chains, increase operational costs, and hinder technological advancement.

7.4.3 Tensions between Localization and Free Flow

The tension between data localization and the free flow of information reflects a broader struggle between national sovereignty and global connectivity. While data localization prioritizes state control, privacy, and security, free flow policies emphasize efficiency, innovation, and market integration. Countries that adopt strict localization laws risk creating digital borders that fragment the global internet, leading to what scholars refer to as the "splinternet."

This tension also manifests in trade disputes. Localization measures can be perceived as barriers to trade, potentially conflicting with World Trade Organization (WTO) principles or bilateral trade agreements. Companies operating across borders face increased compliance costs when they must store and process data in multiple jurisdictions. Conversely, unrestricted data flows can expose sensitive information to foreign governments, cyber-attacks, and commercial exploitation, prompting calls for stricter regulations. Policymakers must balance competing interests, ensuring security and sovereignty without stifling innovation and trade.

7.4.4 Security and Privacy Considerations

Data localization is often justified as a means of enhancing security and protecting citizens' privacy. By keeping data within national borders, governments aim to prevent unauthorized access by foreign entities and reduce vulnerabilities associated with cross-border transmission. In theory, local storage allows regulators and law enforcement agencies to monitor data, enforce compliance, and respond rapidly to breaches or cyber-threats. However, localization does not automatically guarantee security. Localized data centers can still be vulnerable to cyber-attacks, insider threats, or natural disasters. Moreover, by limiting the use of international cloud services, countries may forgo advanced security technologies and expertise offered by global providers. Conversely, proponents of free flow argue that robust encryption, secure cloud services, and international cyber-security standards can protect data without restricting its movement. Thus, security considerations must be addressed through a combination of regulatory oversight, technical safeguards, and international cooperation.

7.4.5 Economic and Innovation Impacts

The debate over data localization and free flow also has profound economic implications. Free data flows enable multinational corporations to optimize operations, leverage global talent, and offer services at scale. They allow startups and small businesses to access international markets and cloud infrastructure without heavy investments in local data storage. Conversely, strict localization requirements can increase costs, reduce competitiveness, and limit the availability of advanced technologies. At the same time, data localization can stimulate domestic technology sectors. By requiring local storage, governments incentivize investment in local data centers, cloud providers, and digital infrastructure. This can create jobs, foster innovation, and strengthen technological self-reliance. The challenge for policymakers is to balance these potential domestic benefits with the broader economic advantages of global data mobility, ensuring that localization policies do not isolate their economies from the global digital ecosystem.

7.4.6 Multistakeholder Approaches and International Cooperation

Resolving the tension between data localization and the free flow of information requires multistakeholder engagement. Governments, international organizations, technology companies, civil society, and technical communities must collaborate to establish standards, norms, and best practices that reconcile security, privacy, and trade. Initiatives such as the OECD Guidelines on the Protection of Privacy and Transborder Flows of Personal Data provide frameworks for balancing data mobility with individual rights. Trade agreements increasingly incorporate provisions on cross-border data flows and data protection, emphasizing the importance of harmonization. International cooperation on cyber-security standards, encryption protocols, and privacy safeguards can allow data to move freely while mitigating risks. By involving multiple stakeholders, policymakers can ensure that digital trade and innovation are not hindered by unnecessary restrictions while maintaining security, privacy, and public trust.

7.5 DIPLOMACY OF EMERGING TECH: AI, QUANTUM, AND SEMICONDUCTORS

The landscape of international diplomacy is undergoing a fundamental transformation, driven not by traditional territorial disputes but by the relentless advance of technology. Artificial Intelligence (AI), quantum information sciences, and semiconductor manufacturing have emerged as the critical substrates of future economic and military power, placing them at the very heart of 21st-century statecraft. This triad of technologies represents a new form of geopolitical currency, where dominance in research, development, and deployment translates directly into global influence.

Nations are no longer just vying for resources or strategic allies; they are engaged in a high-stakes competition to control the underlying technologies that will define the next era of human civilization. This competition has given rise to a new form of diplomacy—one that is conducted in research laboratories, at standards-setting bodies, and through complex export control regimes. The diplomacy of emerging tech is characterized by a complex interplay of collaboration and containment, where states must simultaneously partner to advance the frontiers of science while competing to secure a national advantage and prevent rivals from acquiring a decisive edge.

7.5.1 AI Diplomacy: Shaping the Global Normative Framework

Artificial Intelligence, with its vast potential to revolutionize industries and warfare, has become a primary arena for diplomatic maneuvering. The core diplomatic challenge lies in its dual-use nature; the same algorithms that can diagnose diseases and optimize logistics can also power autonomous weapons systems and sophisticated surveillance states. Consequently, a major front in AI diplomacy is the struggle to shape global norms and standards. Different governance models are competing for international acceptance.

Artificial Intelligence in Diplomacy

On one side, a coalition led by the United States and its allies advocates for a principles-based approach that emphasizes innovation, ethical guidelines, and a multi-stakeholder model involving industry and civil society. Conversely, China promotes a state-centric model of AI governance that prioritizes state control and social stability.

This ideological contest is playing out in forums like the United Nations, the Organisation for Economic Co-operation and Development (OECD), and the Global Partnership on Artificial Intelligence (GPAI). Beyond norms, AI diplomacy also involves building strategic coalitions for research and development. Initiatives like the EU-U.S. Trade and Technology Council (TTC) have a significant AI component, aiming to align policies, coordinate investments, and establish common technical standards to ensure interoperability and trust among allies, thereby creating a technological bloc that can exert collective influence on the global stage.

7.5.2 Quantum Imperative: Securing the Next Revolution

Quantum technology, particularly quantum computing and quantum cryptography, represents a future leap in capability so profound that it has sparked a preemptive diplomatic race. The ability of a large-scale quantum computer to break widely used public-key encryption protocols poses an existential threat to global digital security, potentially rendering all current financial, governmental, and military communications vulnerable. This threat, known as Y2Q or "Q-Day," has catalyzed a diplomatic push toward quantum-resistant cryptography. Nations are collaborating through standards bodies like the National Institute of Standards and Technology (NIST) to develop and vet new cryptographic algorithms, a rare example of deep technical cooperation in the face of a common vulnerability.

Simultaneously, the race to achieve quantum advantage—a point where quantum computers outperform classical ones on practical tasks—has intensified competitive diplomacy. States are forming exclusive technological alliances, such as the AUKUS pact's pillar on advanced cyber and quantum technologies, which explicitly aims to share quantum capabilities among the United States, United Kingdom, and Australia. This creates a new technological hierarchy, potentially leaving non-participating nations behind. Quantum sensing and communication technologies also have clear military applications, driving efforts to control the export of sensitive knowledge and components and to establish rudimentary norms around testing and deployment to prevent dangerous escalation.

7.5.3 Semiconductor Siege: Diplomacy of the Supply Chain

Semiconductors are the physical bedrock upon which AI and quantum technologies are built, making their supply chain a paramount concern of national security and a focal point of intense diplomatic activity. The concentration of advanced manufacturing capability in Taiwan and South Korea, and the reliance on specific equipment and design software from a handful of companies in the United States, the Netherlands, and Japan, has created critical chokepoints. The diplomacy of semiconductors is therefore a complex game of economic statecraft, industrial policy, and alliance management.

The United States has employed a strategy of "small yard, high fence," using export controls to strategically deny China access to the most advanced chips and the tools to make them. This policy's effectiveness is wholly dependent on diplomatic coordination to ensure a united front among key suppliers. This has led to intense bilateral negotiations, such as those with the Netherlands regarding ASML's extreme ultraviolet (EUV) lithography machines and with Japan on restricting specialized chemicals and materials. Conversely, China is engaged in its own diplomatic offensive to break this technological containment, seeking alternative suppliers and investing heavily in domestic capabilities. This struggle over semiconductors is more than a trade war; it is a diplomatic battle for control over the foundational technology of the digital age, with every nation seeking to secure its own access to chips while limiting the advancement of strategic competitors.

7.5.4 Integration of Tech Statecraft: Weaving a Coherent Strategic Tapestry

The most significant challenge for nations is to move beyond a siloed approach and develop an integrated tech statecraft that weaves together AI, quantum, and semiconductor strategies into a coherent diplomatic whole. This requires a fundamental reorganization of foreign policy institutions. Traditional foreign ministries, staffed by generalists, are often ill-equipped to engage on deeply technical issues. In response, governments are creating new roles such as Ambassador-at-Large for Technology and establishing dedicated cyber and digital directorates within their diplomatic corps.

The goal is to ensure that technological considerations are embedded into every facet of foreign policy, from trade negotiations and intelligence sharing to development aid and military alliances. This integrated approach also recognizes the interdependence of these technologies. Advances in AI require more powerful semiconductors, which in turn can be designed more efficiently using AI. Quantum computing could revolutionize AI itself. Therefore, a diplomatic win or loss in one area has immediate ripple effects across the others. A nation's ability to articulate a compelling vision for the future of technology, back it with robust investment, and build a coalition of partners around that vision will be the defining factor in its geopolitical standing for decades to come. The diplomacy of emerging tech is not a side event; it is the main arena where the future global order is being constructed, one algorithm, qubit, and transistor at a time.

CHAPTER 8

Attribution, Cybercrime, and Law Enforcement Cooperation

8.1 TECHNICAL AND POLITICAL CHALLENGES IN CYBER ATTRIBUTION

8.1.1 Technical Complexity of Attribution

The technical nature of cyber-attacks inherently complicates attribution. Unlike physical attacks, which leave tangible evidence, cyber-operations are conducted through digital networks that can be easily masked or routed through intermediary systems. Attackers often use techniques such as IP spoofing, proxy servers, virtual private networks, and botnets to conceal their true origin. Malware can be obfuscated, encrypted, or purposefully designed to mimic the coding style of other groups, creating false trails that mislead investigators. Even when digital forensic evidence is available, reconstructing the chain of events to definitively identify the source can require sophisticated tools, deep technical expertise, and extensive resources. Another technical challenge lies in the shared nature of cyber infrastructure. Many attacks pass through cloud services, third-party servers, or compromised devices in multiple countries. Tracing the attack to its true origin often involves differentiating between the location of the infrastructure used and the identity of the actual perpetrator. This creates ambiguity, as an attacker may exploit innocent users' devices or cloud platforms to obscure their identity. Consequently, technical attribution is rarely straightforward and often results in probabilistic conclusions rather than absolute certainty.

8.1.2 False Flags and Deception Techniques

Cyber adversaries increasingly employ deception techniques designed to mislead investigators. False-flag operations, where attackers deliberately mimic the methods, tools, or signatures of another actor, can obscure attribution and provoke political misinterpretation. For example, malware may contain language artifacts, coding conventions, or operational patterns intended to suggest a different nation-state or hacker group as the perpetrator. Such tactics complicate both technical analysis and policy responses, potentially causing misattribution that can escalate geopolitical tensions. Deception is further amplified by the open nature of the internet. Attackers can route operations through multiple countries, leveraging jurisdictions with weak cyber-security regulations or limited international cooperation. The ability to manipulate digital traces and exploit the distributed nature of networks ensures that attribution remains a complex and uncertain endeavor. Cyber-security professionals must therefore exercise caution in drawing conclusions, balancing technical evidence against the possibility of intentional obfuscation.

8.1.3 Political and Diplomatic Dimensions

Beyond technical difficulties, cyber attribution is deeply political. Identifying the perpetrator of a cyber-attack carries significant diplomatic implications, as states may respond with sanctions, retaliatory measures, or public condemnation. The potential for escalation makes governments cautious, particularly when evidence is circumstantial or ambiguous. Policymakers must weigh the risks of accusing another state incorrectly against the need to defend national interests and deter future attacks.

Political considerations also influence how attribution is communicated. Governments may choose to classify intelligence supporting their conclusions, limiting public disclosure to avoid revealing sensitive sources or methods. Conversely, states may publicly attribute attacks selectively, using carefully curated evidence to shape international opinion or justify policy measures. These dynamics illustrate that attribution is not purely a technical exercise; it is entwined with strategic calculation, national security priorities, and international diplomacy.

8.1.4 Challenges in Multilateral Contexts

Attributing cyber-attacks in a multilateral context introduces additional complications. Cyber-incidents often span multiple jurisdictions, requiring cooperation among states, law enforcement agencies, and private sector entities. Differences in legal frameworks, evidentiary standards, and political agendas can hinder information sharing and delay attribution. In some cases, states may withhold cooperation due to conflicting interests, concerns over sovereignty, or distrust of intelligence-sharing mechanisms.

The global nature of cyberspace also raises questions about norms and accountability. Even when technical evidence points to a particular actor, enforcing consequences may require consensus among international actors or alignment with established norms of behavior. The lack of universally accepted rules for state behavior in cyberspace complicates the attribution process and limits the efficacy of responses. Multilateral attribution efforts, while essential for legitimacy, are often slow, politically sensitive, and constrained by differing priorities.

8.1.5 Role of Private Sector and Civil Society

Private companies and civil society actors play an increasingly critical role in attribution. Technology firms, cyber-security companies, and threat intelligence organizations often detect, analyze, and report on attacks faster than government agencies. These actors have access to data, networks, and forensic tools that are not always available to states. Their involvement can enhance the accuracy and timeliness of attribution but also introduces challenges related to credibility, bias, and coordination.

Civil society and independent research groups contribute transparency and accountability to the attribution process. By publicly documenting attacks and sharing technical analyses, they create an independent record that can corroborate or challenge official claims. However, differences in methodology, access to data, and analytical frameworks can lead to varying conclusions, adding another layer of complexity to international discussions and policymaking.

8.1.6 Consequences of Misattribution

Misattribution in cyberspace carries serious consequences. Incorrectly attributing an attack to a state or non-state actor can escalate tensions, provoke retaliatory measures, and undermine trust between nations. For example, if a ransomware attack or critical infrastructure disruption is wrongly attributed, it could trigger sanctions or military responses, potentially escalating into conflict. Misattribution also risks damaging reputations, creating economic losses, and weakening the credibility of governments or institutions responsible for attribution.

Even accurate attribution is challenging to communicate effectively. States must balance transparency with the protection of sources, intelligence methods, and operational security. Public disclosure may be limited to avoid revealing sensitive capabilities, further complicating international understanding and consensus-building. These dynamics underscore the interplay between technical certainty and political prudence in the cyber domain.

8.1.7 Emerging Technologies and Attribution Tools

Advances in artificial intelligence, machine learning, and network forensics have improved the technical capacity for cyber attribution. AI-driven analytics can detect patterns in malware, network traffic, and attack behaviors that may indicate the origin or affiliation of attackers. Enhanced threat intelligence platforms aggregate data across networks and jurisdictions, providing a more comprehensive picture of cyber activity. However, emerging technologies also introduce new challenges. Attackers can leverage AI to automate deception, adapt malware behavior, and obfuscate signatures, making detection and attribution more difficult. The evolving technical landscape ensures that attribution will remain an iterative process, combining traditional forensics, intelligence analysis, and probabilistic reasoning. Policymakers and cyber-security professionals must continuously adapt to these technological developments to maintain credibility and effectiveness in attribution efforts.

8.2 ATTRIBUTION AS A DIPLOMATIC TOOL

8.2.1 Multi-Layered Process: From Technical Forensics to High-Confidence Assessment

Attribution is not a single action but a complex, multi-layered investigative process that synthesizes technical evidence with intelligence and geopolitical analysis. The initial phase involves digital forensics, where analysts from cyber-security firms or national agencies dissect the malware used, examine network logs, and trace the infrastructure employed in the attack. They search for unique code signatures, patterns of behavior, domain registration details, and technical configurations that may be linked to known threat groups. However, sophisticated adversaries are adept at planting false flags—deliberate clues intended to mislead investigators and implicate another party.

Consequently, technical evidence alone is rarely sufficient for a high-confidence assessment, especially when attributing actions to a state. This necessitates a second layer: intelligence gathering. Signals intelligence (SIGINT), human intelligence (HUMINT), and other classified methods provide the crucial context that technical data lacks. Intelligence agencies may intercept communications related to the operation, have sources within foreign institutions, or possess a deep understanding of a specific nation's cyber capabilities and strategic interests. The final, decisive layer is the political and diplomatic assessment, where policymakers weigh the assembled evidence against broader strategic considerations to make a determination of responsibility.

8.2.2 Public Attribution as a Diplomatic Instrument: Naming and Shaming with Strategic Intent

The decision to publicly attribute a cyber incident is a calculated diplomatic act, not merely a statement of fact. Governments employ public attribution as a tool of "naming and shaming," with several strategic objectives in mind. A primary goal is deterrence. By systematically exposing malicious activity and identifying its perpetrators, a state seeks to impose a cost on the aggressor's reputation and undermine its strategy of operating with impunity. The theory is that by removing the shield of anonymity, the action becomes a diplomatic liability, potentially deterring future attacks by raising the calculus of risk for the adversary. Secondly, public attribution serves to enable accountability and facilitate further response. It is the necessary predicate for imposing diplomatic sanctions, economic penalties, or other countermeasures. A public declaration of responsibility provides the legitimacy and justification for these subsequent actions, aligning them with the international law of state responsibility. Furthermore, attribution can be used to rally allies and partners, building a coalition of like-minded states to jointly condemn the action and present a unified front, thereby amplifying the political cost for the offending state and strengthening norms of responsible behavior.

8.2.3 Law Enforcement Dimension: Attribution for Arrests and Prosecutions

While diplomatic attribution focuses on state responsibility, a parallel process operates within the realm of law enforcement to attribute cybercrime to specific individuals for the purpose of arrest and prosecution. This judicial attribution requires an even higher standard of evidence, as it must be admissible in a court of law to secure a conviction. Agencies like the U.S. Federal Bureau of Investigation (FBI) and the U.K.'s National Crime Agency (NCA) conduct lengthy investigations to link online personas and actions to real-world identities.

This involves traditional police work—financial investigations, witness interviews, surveillance, and cooperation with foreign counterparts—alongside technical analysis. Successful law enforcement attribution has led to high-profile arrests and indictments of cybercriminals, such as ransomware operators and state-sponsored hackers. These indictments serve multiple purposes: they bring criminals to justice, disrupt criminal networks, and serve as a powerful form of deterrence by demonstrating that even the most anonymous-seeming actors can be identified. Importantly, they also function as a diplomatic signal, publicly demonstrating a state's capability and resolve to hold individuals accountable, even when they are acting on behalf of or with the protection of a foreign nation.

8.3 CYBERCRIME TREATIES AND INTERNATIONAL AGREEMENTS

8.3.1 Budapest Convention

The Budapest Convention on Cybercrime has played a transformative role in shaping international responses to cyber-threats, providing a legal and cooperative framework that has influenced national laws and global enforcement efforts. Its emphasis on harmonization, mutual legal assistance, and public-private collaboration has made it an indispensable tool in the fight against cybercrime. However, the convention's continued success will depend on its ability to evolve alongside technological advancements, expand its global reach, and address criticisms regarding privacy and sovereignty. As cyber-threats grow in sophistication and scale, the Budapest Convention remains a critical foundation for international cyber-security governance, demonstrating the power of collective action in safeguarding the digital realm. The path forward requires sustained commitment from signatory states, ongoing modernization efforts, and a shared vision of a secure and just cyberspace for all.

As cyber-threats continue to evolve, the Budapest Convention will remain a cornerstone of international cybercrime governance, but its future effectiveness will depend on several factors. First, the treaty must continue to adapt through additional protocols and amendments that address emerging technologies and criminal methodologies. Second, broader global participation, particularly from major cyber powers currently outside the convention's framework, will be crucial for its universal applicability.

Third, the convention must balance enhanced law enforcement capabilities with robust protections for human rights and digital freedoms, ensuring that its measures do not become tools for repression. Finally, the integration of private sector expertise and resources will be essential for maintaining the treaty's relevance in an increasingly digitized world. By addressing these challenges, the Budapest Convention can continue to serve as a vital instrument in the global fight against cybercrime, fostering cooperation and legal alignment in an era of unprecedented digital threats.

Legal Framework of the Budapest Convention

The Budapest Convention establishes a robust legal foundation for addressing cybercrime by defining offenses, procedural measures, and international cooperation mechanisms. It criminalizes a range of cyber-activities, including illegal access to computer systems, data interference, computer-related fraud, and child exploitation offenses. The treaty also mandates that signatory states adopt domestic legislation to prosecute these crimes effectively. Beyond substantive law, the convention outlines procedural powers for law enforcement, such as the authority to conduct searches and seizures of digital evidence, real-time collection of traffic data, and preservation of stored computer data. These provisions ensure that investigations can proceed efficiently while respecting human rights and legal safeguards. The convention's emphasis on international cooperation is particularly notable, as it requires states to assist one another in investigations, extradition proceedings, and mutual legal assistance, thereby closing jurisdictional gaps that cybercriminals often exploit.

Global Adoption and Expansion beyond Europe

Although initially a Council of Europe initiative, the Budapest Convention has gained global traction, with non-European states such as the United States, Japan, and Australia acceding to the treaty. This expansion reflects the convention's adaptability and relevance in addressing cybercrime across diverse legal systems. The convention's open accession policy allows non-member states to join, provided they meet its legal and procedural requirements. This inclusivity has facilitated broader international alignment on cybercrime standards, even as some nations, particularly those with differing legal traditions, have expressed reservations.

For instance, Russia and several other states have criticized the convention for its perceived Western-centric approach, leading to the development of alternative frameworks such as the Shanghai Cooperation Organization's cybercrime initiatives. Despite these tensions, the Budapest Convention remains the most widely endorsed cybercrime treaty, serving as a benchmark for national legislation and international cooperation.

Role of the Convention in Harmonizing National Laws

One of the Budapest Convention's most significant contributions is its role in harmonizing national cybercrime laws, ensuring that legal frameworks across jurisdictions are compatible and mutually reinforcing. Before the convention, many countries lacked comprehensive legislation addressing digital offenses, leading to inconsistencies in prosecution and enforcement.

By providing a model legal framework, the convention has encouraged states to modernize their laws, criminalize cyber offenses, and establish procedures for digital investigations. This harmonization has been particularly valuable in facilitating cross-border cooperation, as law enforcement agencies can rely on consistent legal standards when pursuing cybercriminals operating across multiple jurisdictions. The convention's influence is evident in how many non-signatory states have nonetheless modeled their cybercrime laws on its provisions, demonstrating its de facto role as a global standard-setter.

International Cooperation and Mutual Legal Assistance

A defining feature of the Budapest Convention is its emphasis on international cooperation, recognizing that cybercrime's transnational nature demands coordinated responses. The treaty establishes mechanisms for mutual legal assistance, enabling states to request and provide support in investigations, evidence collection, and extradition proceedings. This framework has proven essential in cases involving cybercriminals who operate from jurisdictions with weak enforcement or those who exploit legal loopholes.

The convention's 24/7 network of contact points further enhances cooperation by ensuring rapid communication between national authorities during cyber-incidents. These provisions have been instrumental in dismantling cybercriminal networks, recovering stolen assets, and prosecuting offenders who might otherwise evade justice by exploiting jurisdictional boundaries. The success of these mechanisms underscores the convention's value in bridging gaps in global cyber-security enforcement.

8.3.2 UN Cybercrime Treaty Debates

The UN Cybercrime Treaty debates represent a critical juncture in international efforts to combat digital threats, offering an opportunity to establish a universal framework for cybercrime governance. The negotiations highlight the complexities of balancing security, sovereignty, and human rights in a rapidly evolving digital landscape.

A successful treaty must be inclusive, adaptable, and grounded in shared principles that respect diverse legal traditions while enabling effective cross-border cooperation. The path forward requires sustained diplomatic engagement, a commitment to addressing legitimate concerns from all stakeholders, and a recognition that cyber-security is a collective responsibility. If these conditions are met, the UN Cybercrime Treaty could mark a significant step toward a more secure and just digital future, reinforcing the rule of law in cyberspace and fostering global collaboration against cyber-threats.

The future of the UN Cybercrime Treaty hinges on the ability of member states to reach consensus on its core provisions while addressing the concerns of diverse stakeholders. A successful treaty would establish a universal framework for cybercrime enforcement, bridging gaps between existing legal systems and fostering international cooperation. However, achieving this will require compromises on contentious issues such as human rights protections, state sovereignty, and the scope of criminalized activities.

The treaty's effectiveness will also depend on its adaptability, as cyber-threats continue to evolve in complexity and scale. Additionally, the treaty must be supported by robust implementation mechanisms, including capacity-building initiatives for developing nations and technical cooperation frameworks. If these challenges are addressed, the UN Cybercrime Treaty could become a landmark agreement in global cyber-security governance, setting a precedent for future international cyber-security collaboration.

Need for a Universal Cybercrime Framework

The proliferation of cybercrime has exposed significant gaps in international legal frameworks, as existing treaties often lack universal adoption or fail to address emerging threats. A UN Cybercrime Treaty seeks to establish a globally accepted standard for defining, prosecuting, and cooperating against cyber offenses.

This is particularly important given the transnational nature of cybercrime, where criminals exploit jurisdictional differences to evade prosecution. A universal treaty would facilitate mutual legal assistance, extradition procedures, and information-sharing mechanisms, ensuring that no nation becomes a safe haven for cybercriminals. Additionally, such a treaty could harmonize national laws, reducing inconsistencies that hinder cross-border investigations. The urgency of this effort is underscored by the increasing sophistication of cyber-threats, which now target critical infrastructure, financial systems, and democratic institutions, necessitating a coordinated global response.

Role of Sovereignty and Jurisdiction in Cybercrime Governance

A central theme in the UN Cybercrime Treaty discussions is the tension between national sovereignty and international cooperation. Many nations, particularly those with authoritarian governance models, emphasize the principle of non-interference, arguing that cybercrime investigations should not infringe on domestic legal systems. Conversely, nations advocating for stronger international cooperation argue that cyber-threats transcend borders, necessitating shared investigative powers and evidence-gathering procedures. This debate is further complicated by differing interpretations of jurisdiction, where some states assert territorial control over digital infrastructure, while others support extraterritorial enforcement in cases of cross-border cybercrime. Resolving these tensions is essential for creating a treaty that respects sovereign rights while enabling effective global cyber-security collaboration.

Human Rights and the Risk of Overreach in Cybercrime Laws

A significant concern in the UN Cybercrime Treaty negotiations is the potential for cybercrime laws to be misused to suppress free expression or justify mass surveillance. Civil society organizations and digital rights advocates have warned that overly broad definitions of cybercrime could enable governments to criminalize legitimate online activities, such as political dissent or investigative journalism. The treaty's provisions on data access and surveillance powers have been particularly contentious, with calls for robust safeguards to prevent abuse. Some nations have proposed including human rights clauses that explicitly protect privacy and free speech, ensuring that cybercrime enforcement does not become a tool for authoritarian control. These discussions reflect a broader struggle to balance security imperatives with fundamental freedoms, a challenge that will define the treaty's legitimacy and effectiveness.

Influence of Existing Cybercrime Treaties and Frameworks

The UN Cybercrime Treaty debates are heavily influenced by existing international agreements, particularly the Budapest Convention, which serves as a benchmark for many nations. Proponents of the Budapest model argue that the UN treaty should align with its principles, ensuring consistency in global cybercrime governance. However, critics contend that the Budapest Convention reflects Western legal traditions and may not be suitable for nations with different judicial systems. Alternative frameworks, such as those proposed by the Shanghai Cooperation

Organization or regional agreements in Africa and Latin America, offer competing visions for cybercrime governance. The UN treaty must navigate these existing structures, either by integrating their strengths or by offering a new paradigm that accommodates diverse legal and political contexts. This balancing act is crucial for securing broad support and avoiding fragmentation in international cyber-security efforts.

8.4 INTERPOL, EUROPOL, AND INTERNATIONAL LAW ENFORCEMENT COLLABORATIONS

The efforts of INTERPOL, Europol, and other international law enforcement collaborations represent a critical front in the global fight against cybercrime. By facilitating information sharing, joint investigations, and capacity-building initiatives, these organizations enhance the ability of nations to respond to digital threats that transcend borders. However, the challenges of legal disparities, jurisdictional conflicts, and resource constraints require sustained attention and investment. The future of cybercrime law enforcement will depend on the ability of international agencies to adapt to technological advancements, deepen public-private partnerships, and foster inclusive global cooperation. Through these efforts, the international community can build a more resilient and secure digital environment, ensuring that cybercriminals are held accountable regardless of where they operate. The path forward demands not only collaboration but also a shared commitment to upholding the rule of law in cyberspace.

Interpol

As cyber-threats continue to evolve, international law enforcement agencies must adapt their strategies to address emerging challenges. The rise of artificial intelligence, quantum computing, and decentralized financial systems will introduce new vulnerabilities and criminal methodologies, requiring innovative investigative techniques and legal frameworks. Future efforts will likely emphasize the development of AI-driven cybercrime analytics, blockchain forensics, and enhanced public-private threat intelligence sharing.

Additionally, the expansion of international law enforcement networks to include more nations, particularly from the Global South, will be essential for ensuring comprehensive cybercrime coverage. Organizations like INTERPOL and Europol will play a central role in these developments, providing the platforms and expertise necessary for global cyber-security collaboration. The path forward demands not only technological adaptation but also a commitment to strengthening legal harmonization, capacity-building, and trust among international law enforcement partners.

8.4.1 INTERPOL's Role in Global Cybercrime Enforcement

INTERPOL, as the world's largest international police organization, plays a pivotal role in coordinating global efforts against cybercrime. Through its Cybercrime Directorate, INTERPOL provides a range of services designed to assist member countries in investigating and prosecuting digital offenses. One of its key functions is the facilitation of information exchange through secure communication channels, enabling law enforcement agencies to share threat intelligence, digital evidence, and investigative leads in real time.

INTERPOL also hosts specialized cybercrime training programs, equipping officers with the technical skills needed to combat evolving threats such as ransomware, phishing, and dark web criminality. Additionally, the organization operates the INTERPOL Global Complex for Innovation (IGCI) in Singapore, which serves as a hub for cybercrime research, digital forensics, and public-private partnerships. By leveraging its global network, INTERPOL enhances the capacity of member states to respond to cyber-threats, regardless of their individual technological capabilities.

8.4.2 Europol's Cybercrime Center and European Law Enforcement Collaboration

Europol, the European Union's law enforcement agency, has established itself as a leader in cybercrime investigations through its European Cybercrime Centre (EC3). EC3 serves as a focal point for cybercrime expertise within the EU, providing operational support to member states in dismantling cybercriminal networks, recovering stolen assets, and mitigating large-scale cyber-attacks. One of Europol's most significant contributions is its role in coordinating joint cybercrime operations, such as the takedown of dark web marketplaces and ransomware gangs. The agency also facilitates the European Cybercrime Task Force, which brings together law enforcement, judicial authorities, and private sector partners to enhance collective cyber-defense capabilities. Europol's analytical capabilities, including its ability to map cybercriminal infrastructures and track illicit financial flows, have proven instrumental in disrupting cybercrime ecosystems. By fostering collaboration among EU member states and international partners, Europol strengthens Europe's resilience against digital threats while contributing to global cyber-security efforts.

8.4.3 Legal and Operational Frameworks Supporting International Collaboration

Effective international law enforcement collaboration against cybercrime relies on robust legal and operational frameworks that enable cross-border investigations. Instruments such as the Budapest Convention on Cybercrime provide a foundational legal structure for harmonizing national laws and facilitating mutual legal assistance. Additionally, bilateral and multilateral agreements on extradition, evidence sharing, and joint investigations ensure that law enforcement agencies can pursue cybercriminals across jurisdictions. Organizations like INTERPOL and Europol operate within these frameworks, providing the technical and procedural mechanisms necessary for seamless cooperation.

For instance, INTERPOL's I-24/7 secure communication network allows police forces to exchange urgent requests for assistance, while Europol's Secure Information Exchange Network Application (SIENNA) enables real-time data sharing among EU member states. These operational tools, combined with standardized legal procedures, create an environment where international law enforcement can act swiftly and decisively against cyber-threats.

8.4.4 Public-Private Partnerships in Cybercrime Investigations

The fight against cybercrime increasingly depends on collaboration between law enforcement agencies and private sector entities, which often possess critical threat intelligence and technical expertise. INTERPOL and Europol have recognized the necessity of these partnerships, establishing formal mechanisms for engaging with technology companies, financial institutions, and cyber-security firms. For example, Europol's European Financial and Economic Crime Centre (EFECC) works closely with banks and fintech companies to trace and intercept illicit financial transactions linked to cybercrime. Similarly, INTERPOL's partnerships with cyber-security firms enable the rapid identification of malware strains, vulnerabilities, and attack vectors, enhancing investigative capabilities. These collaborations are essential, as cybercriminals frequently exploit private sector infrastructure, making industry cooperation a cornerstone of effective cybercrime enforcement. By integrating private sector insights into law enforcement operations, international agencies can enhance their ability to preempt, detect, and respond to cyber-threats.

8.4.5 Case Studies

Several high-profile operations demonstrate the effectiveness of international law enforcement collaboration in combating cybercrime. One notable example is the 2021 takedown of the Emotet malware infrastructure, a global operation coordinated by Europol and involving law enforcement agencies from multiple countries. This operation disrupted one of the most dangerous botnets, which had been used to deliver ransomware and other malicious payloads. Similarly, INTERPOL's Operation HAEAICHI has targeted cyber-enabled financial crimes, leading to the arrest of numerous suspects involved in business email compromise (BEC) scams and online fraud. These cases highlight the importance of coordinated action, where international agencies provide the platforms, intelligence, and operational support necessary for successful cybercrime investigations. The lessons from these operations underscore the value of sustained collaboration, rapid information sharing, and the integration of advanced technical capabilities in law enforcement efforts.

8.5 DIPLOMATIC RESPONSES TO RANSOMWARE AND STATE-SPONSORED ATTACKS

Ransomware and state-sponsored cyber-attacks represent profound challenges to national security, economic stability, and international order. While technical defenses and law enforcement are essential, diplomacy has emerged as a critical tool in responding to these threats. Bilateral engagement, multilateral coordination, norm-building, sanctions, and public-private cooperation all contribute to a comprehensive strategy that addresses both the technical and political dimensions of cybercrime. The effectiveness of diplomatic responses depends on accurate attribution, strategic communication, and multistakeholder collaboration. By integrating these elements, states can deter malicious actors, uphold international norms, and enhance resilience in the face of evolving cyber-threats. As cyber-operations continue to shape the global security landscape, diplomacy will remain indispensable in navigating the intersection of technology, politics, and law in cyberspace.

Looking ahead, effective diplomatic responses to ransomware and state-sponsored cyber-attacks will require integrated, multistakeholder approaches. States must invest in cyber-diplomacy capacity, including specialized teams capable of analyzing incidents, coordinating international responses, and negotiating norms. Public-private partnerships must be strengthened to ensure timely information sharing and coordinated mitigation. Norm development remains critical, emphasizing rules of responsible state behavior, cooperation in cybercrime investigations, and protection of critical infrastructure. International agreements and trade frameworks should incorporate cyber-security obligations, ensuring that states have incentives to act against malicious actors. Finally, diplomatic efforts must adapt to emerging technologies, including artificial intelligence, blockchain, and quantum computing, which introduce both opportunities and new risks for cybercrime.

8.5.1 Global Threat of Ransomware

Ransomware attacks involve malicious software that encrypts data or locks systems until a ransom is paid, often in cryptocurrencies. These attacks have grown in sophistication and scale, targeting healthcare systems, municipal governments, energy grids, and multinational corporations. The global nature of ransomware allows attackers to operate from jurisdictions with limited law enforcement capacity, exploiting differences in legal frameworks and international cooperation. The economic impact is staggering, with estimated losses in the billions annually, in addition to reputational damage and operational disruption. From a diplomatic perspective, ransomware represents a unique challenge because the actors are often transnational criminal groups, yet their operations may be tolerated or indirectly supported by host states. This complicates traditional law enforcement responses, making diplomacy a necessary mechanism for coordinating international action and applying pressure on states to act against malicious actors within their borders.

8.5.2 State-Sponsored Attacks and Geopolitical Tensions

State-sponsored cyber-attacks are distinct from conventional cybercrime due to their political objectives, strategic intent, and advanced capabilities. Nations deploy these attacks to gain intelligence, disrupt adversaries, influence elections, or undermine critical infrastructure. Attribution is often complex, as sophisticated techniques, false flags, and the use of proxies obscure the true source of the attack. Diplomacy plays a central role in responding to state-sponsored attacks, as unilateral retaliation risks escalation and conflict. States employ a range of diplomatic tools, from formal protest notes and bilateral engagement to public attribution statements and multilateral pressure through international organizations. These responses aim to signal disapproval, enforce norms, and deter future attacks while maintaining channels for dialogue to prevent misunderstandings or unintended escalation.

8.5.3 Diplomatic Tools and Strategies

Diplomatic responses to ransomware and state-sponsored attacks encompass both preventive and reactive measures. One key approach is establishing international norms for responsible state behavior in cyberspace. Efforts led by the United Nations Group of Governmental Experts (UN GGE) and regional organizations have sought to articulate principles such as the prohibition of attacks against critical infrastructure, respect for sovereignty, and cooperation in cybercrime investigations. These norms provide a foundation for states to engage diplomatically, even when attribution is uncertain, by framing expectations and establishing standards of conduct.

Bilateral diplomacy is another essential tool. States may engage directly with counterparts to request action against cybercriminals, negotiate joint cyber-security initiatives, or establish communication channels to manage incidents. This form of diplomacy relies on mutual recognition of cyber-threats and the understanding that cooperation benefits all parties.

Public attribution and naming-and-shaming campaigns are increasingly used as diplomatic instruments. By publicly attributing attacks to specific actors or states, governments can generate international pressure, justify sanctions, and influence domestic and global opinion. However, this strategy must be used cautiously, as misattribution or lack of conclusive evidence can exacerbate tensions or damage credibility.

CHAPTER 9

Internet Governance and Digital Sovereignty

9.1 COMPETING VISIONS OF INTERNET GOVERNANCE

9.1.1 Open Internet vs. Sovereign Internet

Concept of an Open Internet

The foundational principle of the Open Internet, often referred to as the concept of network neutrality, is one of universal access and non-discriminatory flow of information. This model envisions a global network where data packets are transmitted from their origin to their destination without being manipulated, prioritized, or blocked based on their content, source, or destination. The internet's original architects designed it as a decentralized and interoperable system, intended to be a borderless realm for the free exchange of ideas, commerce, and innovation. In this ideal, the infrastructure acts as a neutral conduit, treating all bits and bytes equally.

This openness is widely credited as the primary engine behind the internet's explosive growth and its transformative impact on modern society. It has enabled the rise of global tech giants, empowered grassroots movements, and democratized access to information on an unprecedented scale. Proponents argue that an open internet fosters economic growth by creating a level playing field for startups and established companies alike, promotes freedom of expression as a fundamental human right, and facilitates cross-cultural understanding and global collaboration on pressing issues like scientific research and public health.

Rise of the Sovereign Internet

In direct contrast to the open model, the concept of the Sovereign Internet, also known as digital sovereignty or the Balkanization of the internet, has gained significant traction among numerous nation-states. This approach asserts the right of a national government to control, regulate, and govern the internet within its territorial borders, effectively treating cyberspace as an extension of its sovereign territory. The motivations for pursuing digital sovereignty are multifaceted and often presented as matters of national security, social stability, and economic protectionism. Governments argue that such control is necessary to combat cybercrime, prevent the spread of harmful disinformation and extremist content, protect citizens' data from foreign surveillance, and shield domestic industries from the overwhelming dominance of foreign tech conglomerates. This model enables states to enforce local laws regarding content, data storage, and privacy, ensuring that online activities align with national legal frameworks and cultural norms. The technical implementation of a sovereign internet typically involves a combination of legislative measures, sophisticated censorship technologies often called "Great Firewalls," data localization laws requiring citizen data to be stored on domestic servers, and the development of indigenous internet infrastructure and services to reduce reliance on global providers.

Geopolitical and Ideological Divide

The tension between these two models is not merely a technical or regulatory debate; it is a profound reflection of broader geopolitical and ideological struggles in the 21st century. This clash represents a fundamental disagreement over the very nature of the internet: is it a global commons to be managed for the benefit of humanity, or is it a domain subject to the traditional Westphalian principles of state sovereignty? On one side, a coalition primarily led by Western nations, particularly the United States and members of the European Union, advocates for a multi-stakeholder model of internet governance. This model involves cooperation between governments, private industry, technical experts, and civil society to preserve the open and interconnected nature of the network. On the other side, nations like China and Russia champion a multilateral model where nation-states are the primary actors with the authority to regulate the internet within their borders. This divide is often framed as a contest between values. The open internet is associated with ideals of individual liberty and liberal democracy, while the sovereign internet is linked to concepts of collective stability, state authority, and information security as defined by the ruling government. This ideological battleground influences international diplomacy, trade agreements, and global technology standards, creating a splintered and competitive digital landscape.

Implications for Human Rights and Global Discourse

The choice between an open and a sovereign internet has profound implications for human rights, particularly the right to freedom of expression and the right to access information. In an open internet model, individuals generally have a greater capacity to access a wide range of news sources, express dissenting opinions, and organize politically, though this is not without challenges such as online harassment and hate speech. A sovereign internet, when implemented with stringent controls, can be used to systematically suppress political dissent, silence opposition voices, and create a sanitized information ecosystem that exclusively promotes state-approved narratives. This can lead to the creation of extensive digital echo chambers where citizens are exposed only to information that reinforces the government's position, severely limiting their ability to engage in a global discourse or form independent opinions. Furthermore, the fragmentation of the internet into national silos threatens the concept of a global public square. It impedes the free flow of knowledge across borders, potentially hindering academic research, journalistic investigations, and cross-cultural dialogue. The ability for citizens worldwide to share experiences and collaborate on global challenges is significantly diminished when digital borders are heavily fortified.

Economic and Technological Consequences

From an economic perspective, the divergence between these models creates significant friction and uncertainty for the global digital economy. The open internet has been a powerful catalyst for innovation, allowing a startup in one country to instantly reach a global market with minimal barriers. The sovereign internet model, through data localization laws and content restrictions, fragments the global market, forcing multinational corporations to navigate a complex patchwork of national regulations. This increases compliance costs, creates operational inefficiencies, and can stifle innovation, particularly for smaller companies that lack the resources to adapt to numerous jurisdictional demands. Conversely, proponents argue that digital sovereignty can foster local innovation by protecting domestic tech companies from foreign competition, allowing them to grow and flourish in a controlled environment. Technologically, the push for sovereignty is driving the development of parallel internets. Nations are investing in their own root DNS servers, creating national domain name systems, and developing alternative platforms to replace global services like Google, Facebook, and Twitter. This technological decoupling risks undermining the interoperability that is the internet's greatest strength, potentially leading to a future where users in different countries experience entirely different, and mutually inaccessible, online worlds.

Navigating a Fractured Future

The future of the global internet is unlikely to be a wholesale victory for either the open or sovereign model. Instead, the world is moving toward a fragmented and multi-polar digital order, often described as the "splinternet." In this scenario, a fully open global internet will coexist with various nationally controlled segments, creating a spectrum of connectivity and censorship. Navigating this future will require nuanced approaches from policymakers, corporations, and civil society. There may be opportunities for limited interoperability agreements or international frameworks that respect certain fundamental rights while acknowledging legitimate state interests in security and regulation. The European Union's General Data Protection Regulation (GDPR), for instance, represents a regional attempt to assert digital sovereignty in the realm of privacy without completely abandoning the principles of an open internet. Ultimately, the tension between the open internet and the sovereign internet is a defining struggle of our digital age, posing critical questions about the balance between freedom and control, globalization and nationalism, and the individual and the state. The resolution of this tension will shape the evolution of society, politics, and the economy for decades to come.

9.2 ROLE OF ITU AND OTHER STANDARDS-SETTING BODIES

The ITU and other standards-setting bodies occupy a pivotal position in the governance of the internet, shaping the technical, policy, and sovereignty dimensions of the digital world. As nations grapple with the imperatives of digital sovereignty, the ITU provides a platform for negotiating the balance between national control and global connectivity. Its work in cyber-security, critical infrastructure protection, and bridging the digital divide underscores its relevance in an era of technological transformation.

However, the organization's future influence will depend on its ability to adapt to the evolving demands of internet governance, fostering collaboration while respecting diverse national priorities. In a world where digital sovereignty and global interdependence are increasingly intertwined, the ITU's role as a mediator and standard-setter will remain essential in shaping a secure, equitable, and resilient digital future.

The future of internet governance will be shaped by the ongoing interplay between technical standardization, national policy priorities, and geopolitical dynamics. The ITU, alongside other standards-setting bodies, will continue to play a central role in defining the rules and architectures that govern the digital world. However, the organization's influence will depend on its ability to navigate the tensions between multistakeholder collaboration and state sovereignty, ensuring that its standards reflect both technical excellence and policy inclusivity. Emerging technologies such as artificial intelligence, quantum computing, and the Internet of Things (IoT) will introduce new governance challenges, requiring adaptive frameworks that balance innovation with security and sovereignty. The ITU's role in fostering international cooperation on these issues will be critical, as nations seek to assert their digital autonomy while participating in a globally interconnected internet.

9.2.1 ITU's Mandate and Influence in Internet Governance

The ITU, established in 1865, has evolved into a central authority in global telecommunications and internet governance, with a mandate to allocate radio spectrum, develop technical standards, and foster international cooperation in digital policy. Its role in internet governance is particularly significant in areas such as network interoperability, cyber-security, and the deployment of emerging technologies like 5G and artificial intelligence. The ITU's standardization sector (ITU-T) produces recommendations that influence global telecommunications infrastructure, while its development sector (ITU-D) works to bridge the digital divide by promoting equitable access to technology.

The organization's influence is further amplified by its membership structure, which includes governments, private sector entities, and academic institutions, ensuring that its standards reflect a broad consensus among stakeholders. However, the ITU's approach to internet governance has also been a subject of debate, particularly regarding its alignment with state-centric models of digital sovereignty versus the multistakeholder governance favored by many Western nations.

9.2.2 Digital Sovereignty and the ITU's Role in National Policies

Digital sovereignty—the principle that nations should have control over their digital infrastructure, data, and technological development—has become a defining issue in internet governance. The ITU's work intersects with this concept by providing a platform where states can assert their policy preferences in global standards development. For instance, the ITU's support for national internet governance models, such as those advocated by China and Russia, contrasts with the decentralized, multistakeholder approach championed by organizations like ICANN and the IETF.

This tension reflects broader geopolitical dynamics, where nations seek to balance the benefits of global connectivity with the imperative of protecting their digital autonomy. The ITU's role in facilitating discussions on data localization, cyber-security regulations, and critical infrastructure protection underscores its significance in shaping how digital sovereignty is implemented at both national and international levels.

9.2.3 The Role of Other Standards-Setting Bodies in Internet Governance

Beyond the ITU, other standards-setting bodies contribute to the technical and policy frameworks that govern the internet. The Internet Engineering Task Force (IETF), for example, develops the foundational protocols that enable internet communication, such as TCP/IP and DNS standards. Unlike the ITU, the IETF operates on a bottom-up, consensus-driven model, where technical experts rather than governments drive decision-making. This approach has been instrumental in maintaining the internet's open and interoperable architecture, though it has also faced criticism for its perceived lack of accountability to national governments. Similarly, the IEEE and W3C develop standards for hardware, software, and web technologies, influencing how digital systems are designed and deployed. The interplay between these bodies and the ITU highlights the multifaceted nature of internet governance, where technical standardization intersects with policy and sovereignty considerations.

9.2.4 ITU's Approach to Cyber-security and Critical Infrastructure Protection

Cyber-security has become a central focus of the ITU's work, particularly as nations grapple with the threats posed by cyber espionage, ransomware, and attacks on critical infrastructure. The ITU's cyber-security standards and guidelines aim to enhance the resilience of national digital ecosystems, providing frameworks for risk management, incident response, and secure communications. Its Global Cyber-security Index (GCI) measures countries' preparedness against cyber-threats, offering a benchmark for national policies. Additionally, the ITU's collaboration with other UN bodies, such as the United Nations Office on Drugs and Crime (UNODC), reflects its role in addressing cybercrime and digital threats within broader international governance structures. However, the ITU's cyber-security initiatives have also been scrutinized for their potential to enable state surveillance, raising concerns about the balance between security and individual rights in digital governance.

9.2.5 Debate over Multistakeholder vs. State-Centric Governance Models

A fundamental tension in internet governance revolves around the competing visions of multistakeholder and state-centric models. The multistakeholder approach, advocated by organizations like ICANN and the IETF, emphasizes the inclusion of governments, private sector entities, civil society, and technical experts in decision-making processes. This model has been credited with fostering innovation and maintaining the internet's open architecture. In contrast, the state-centric model, often associated with the ITU, prioritizes national sovereignty and government-led regulation, reflecting concerns about security, data control, and geopolitical influence. The debate between these approaches has shaped global internet governance, with nations aligning themselves based on their policy priorities and governance philosophies. The ITU's role in this discourse is particularly significant, as it provides a forum where both models are negotiated, often leading to compromises that influence the future of digital policy.

9.2.6 ITU's Role in Bridging the Digital Divide

Beyond standards and governance, the ITU plays a crucial role in addressing the digital divide—the disparity in access to digital technologies between developed and developing nations. Through initiatives such as the Connect 2030 Agenda, the ITU works to expand broadband connectivity, enhance digital literacy, and promote affordable access to technology. These efforts are essential for ensuring that all nations can participate in the digital economy and benefit from technological advancements. However, the ITU's work in this area also intersects with questions of digital sovereignty, as developing nations seek to build their digital infrastructure without becoming overly dependent on foreign technologies or governance models. The ITU's support for national digital strategies, such as those focused on local content development and data localization, reflects its role in helping countries assert their digital autonomy while advancing global connectivity.

9.3 INTERNET FRAGMENTATION AND SPLINTERNET RISKS

The risks of internet fragmentation and the splinternet are among the most pressing challenges of the digital age. Driven by sovereignty concerns, corporate control, and geopolitical rivalries, fragmentation threatens to erode the universality that made the internet a revolutionary force. The consequences include reduced innovation, weakened cooperation, diminished rights, and deepened inequalities. At the same time, the future is not predetermined. Through inclusive governance, international collaboration, and a commitment to digital equity, it remains possible to safeguard the openness and interoperability of the internet. The struggle against fragmentation is ultimately a struggle over values, determining whether the internet will serve as a platform for global cooperation and empowerment or fracture into competing silos that reflect the divisions of the physical world.

9.3.1 Internet Fragmentation

Internet fragmentation refers to the breaking up of the internet into distinct and often incompatible networks or ecosystems. While the global internet is technically a collection of networks, it has historically operated under common standards that ensure interoperability. Fragmentation occurs when governments, corporations, or other actors create barriers that restrict data flows, limit interoperability, or impose divergent rules that prevent a seamless online experience. This can manifest in several ways, including technical incompatibility of standards, regulatory barriers that limit cross-border access, or deliberate state efforts to isolate domestic users from global platforms. The concept of the splinternet emphasizes that fragmentation is not merely a technical issue but also a political and economic strategy pursued by states and corporations seeking greater control over digital domains.

9.3.2 Drivers of Internet Fragmentation

Several forces are driving the trend toward fragmentation. One of the most significant is the assertion of digital sovereignty by states. Countries such as China and Russia argue that they have the right to regulate the flow of information and data within their borders, leading to national firewalls and censorship systems. Another driver is the rising tide of geopolitical tensions, particularly between the United States and China, which has spilled into the digital domain through restrictions on technology companies, competing 5G infrastructures, and rival visions of governance.

Data protection and privacy regulations also contribute to fragmentation, as seen in the European Union's General Data Protection Regulation, which imposes strict requirements on how companies manage user data. Additionally, corporate dominance of digital ecosystems, such as the creation of proprietary platforms and walled gardens by technology giants, fosters fragmentation by limiting user mobility and interoperability between services. These drivers demonstrate that fragmentation is fueled by a mixture of security concerns, economic interests, and political ideologies.

9.3.3 Role of National Sovereignty

The principle of sovereignty has emerged as a central justification for internet fragmentation. States increasingly argue that controlling digital infrastructure and information flows is a matter of national security and cultural preservation. China's Great Firewall exemplifies this approach, allowing the government to maintain tight control over content and access while fostering the growth of domestic platforms such as WeChat and Baidu.

Similarly, Russia has pursued a sovereign internet strategy designed to isolate its digital infrastructure from the global system during times of crisis. These efforts highlight how governments view the internet not as a neutral, borderless space but as a domain subject to the same principles of control as land, sea, and air. While sovereignty-driven fragmentation may serve national interests, it undermines the universal and open nature of the internet, raising concerns about censorship, reduced innovation, and limited global cooperation.

9.3.4 Corporate Fragmentation and Walled Gardens

Beyond governments, corporations also play a major role in shaping internet fragmentation. Technology giants such as Apple, Google, and Meta build proprietary ecosystems that lock users into specific platforms. For example, app stores operate under tightly controlled rules that determine what services can be accessed and how developers must operate. Social media platforms create enclosed environments where users spend most of their digital time without venturing outside. While these walled gardens offer convenience and security, they fragment the internet by creating closed systems with limited interoperability. The dominance of a few corporations also raises concerns about monopolistic practices, data exploitation, and unequal access to resources. Corporate-driven fragmentation reflects the tension between market efficiency and the public good, with profit motives often leading to practices that undermine the openness and universality of the internet.

9.3.5 Geopolitical Rivalries and the Splinternet

The concept of the splinternet has become most visible in the context of geopolitical rivalry, particularly between the United States and China. The U.S. has traditionally supported an open internet underpinned by the multi-stakeholder model of governance, while China advocates for state sovereignty and centralized control. This clash of visions is increasingly evident in disputes over technology infrastructure, such as the global competition over 5G networks and the regulation of Chinese companies like Huawei and TikTok. As countries align themselves with either the U.S. or Chinese models, the risk of a bifurcated global internet becomes more pronounced. Other powers, including the European Union, pursue their own regulatory paths, adding further complexity. The splinternet thus reflects the broader fragmentation of global politics, where digital infrastructure becomes another arena for strategic competition and ideological conflict.

9.3.6 Risks of Internet Fragmentation

The risks associated with internet fragmentation are profound and multifaceted. One of the most immediate dangers is the loss of interoperability, which threatens the seamless exchange of data and communication that defines the internet. A fragmented internet could undermine innovation by preventing developers from reaching global markets and limiting collaboration across borders. Fragmentation also increases the risk of economic inequality, as wealthier nations and corporations create advanced digital ecosystems while less developed regions are left behind. Furthermore, fragmentation can erode fundamental rights, particularly freedom of expression and access to information, as governments impose stricter controls. Security risks also intensify, as isolated networks may be more vulnerable to cyber-attacks or may foster the development of conflicting standards that complicate global cooperation in addressing threats. Overall, the risks of fragmentation suggest that the splinternet would weaken the internet's role as a universal connector and driver of global progress.

9.3.7 Challenge of Digital Inequality

Internet fragmentation also exacerbates the problem of digital inequality. While some countries develop sophisticated and controlled digital ecosystems, others struggle to provide basic access to affordable and reliable internet. The digital divide between advanced economies and developing nations risks becoming wider as fragmentation makes it harder for marginalized regions to integrate into global digital flows. This inequality is not only technical but also cultural and economic, as citizens of fragmented internets may be exposed to different realities, narratives, and opportunities than those with access to the broader web. In the long term, digital inequality reinforced by fragmentation could entrench existing global divides, limiting the internet's potential as a tool for inclusive development and empowerment.

9.3.8 Preserving a Unified Internet

Despite the risks, efforts are underway to preserve the vision of a unified global internet. The multi-stakeholder model of governance, involving governments, corporations, civil society, and technical experts, continues to promote inclusivity and interoperability. International initiatives encourage cross-border cooperation on issues such as cybercrime, data protection, and technical standards. Regional frameworks like the European Union's regulations, while contributing to some fragmentation, also set global benchmarks that can harmonize practices. Civil society groups advocate for openness, human rights, and digital equity, reminding stakeholders of the internet's original promise as a global commons. These efforts highlight the possibility of balancing national and corporate interests with the need to maintain a shared and interconnected digital infrastructure.

9.4 DIPLOMATIC NEGOTIATIONS OVER DNS, IP, AND GLOBAL STANDARDS

Diplomatic negotiations over DNS, IP, and global standards reveal that internet governance is not simply a technical matter but a reflection of power, values, and visions of the future. The debates over who controls critical resources and how global standards are set underscore the tension between national sovereignty and global cooperation. While the multi-stakeholder model has enabled significant progress, pressures for multilateral oversight and competing visions of technological control continue to shape discussions.

The risks of fragmentation and splintering highlight the stakes of these negotiations, as the internet's universality is at risk. Ultimately, the outcome of diplomatic efforts will determine whether the internet remains a shared, interoperable infrastructure that supports innovation and rights, or fractures into divided networks reflecting geopolitical rivalries and national boundaries.

The future of negotiations over DNS, IP, and global standards will be shaped by technological evolution and geopolitical change. Emerging technologies such as artificial intelligence, quantum computing, and blockchain raise new questions about governance and security. At the same time, rising tensions between major powers suggest that consensus will be increasingly difficult to achieve. Yet, the importance of preserving a unified and interoperable internet may provide incentives for cooperation. Adaptive governance frameworks that combine multi-stakeholder inclusivity with intergovernmental accountability could offer a path forward. Diplomatic negotiations will need to balance the competing imperatives of sovereignty, openness, security, and innovation. The challenge lies in creating arrangements that are both technically effective and politically legitimate.

9.4.1 Importance

The Domain Name System is often described as the internet's phonebook, translating human-readable web addresses into numerical IP addresses that machines can understand. Without DNS, navigating the internet would be cumbersome and inaccessible to most users. Similarly, the allocation of IP addresses ensures that devices are uniquely identifiable and able to communicate across networks. Global standards, developed by organizations such as the Internet Engineering Task Force (IETF) and the World Wide Web Consortium (W3C), establish the protocols that make the internet interoperable and universal. These technical foundations are not neutral; they distribute authority, economic opportunity, and political influence. As such, negotiations over DNS, IP, and standards become arenas where states, corporations, and civil society actors assert their visions for the internet's future.

9.4.2 Early U.S. Dominance and Calls for Internationalization

In the early decades of the internet, the United States held dominant control over DNS and IP allocations through institutions such as the Internet Assigned Numbers Authority (IANA) and later the Internet Corporation for Assigned Names and Numbers (ICANN). This arrangement reflected the internet's origins as a U.S.-funded project but became increasingly contentious as the internet expanded globally. Many states, particularly in the Global South, questioned why a single nation should wield disproportionate influence over resources essential to global connectivity. The World Summit on the Information Society (WSIS) in 2003 and 2005 highlighted these tensions, with countries such as China, Brazil, and members of the European Union advocating for greater international oversight of DNS and IP management. The U.S. defended the status quo by emphasizing the efficiency and technical expertise of the existing system, while critics framed the issue as one of digital sovereignty and fairness. These early negotiations set the stage for a long-standing debate between U.S.-centric and multilateral models of governance.

9.4.3 Role of ICANN and the Multi-Stakeholder Model

ICANN occupies a central place in diplomatic negotiations over DNS and IP. Established in 1998 as a nonprofit corporation based in California, ICANN is responsible for coordinating domain names, root servers, and IP address allocations. Its structure reflects the multi-stakeholder model, incorporating governments, private companies, technical experts, and civil society in its decision-making processes. Proponents argue that this model prevents domination by any single actor and ensures inclusivity. However, critics note that ICANN's incorporation under U.S. jurisdiction gives Washington undue influence. The diplomatic negotiations surrounding ICANN intensified during discussions over the transition of IANA functions from the U.S. Department of Commerce to a global multi-stakeholder community, completed in 2016. This transition was hailed as a milestone in reducing U.S. control, but debates over ICANN's legitimacy and accountability continue to feature prominently in international forums.

9.4.4 United Nations and Multilateral Proposals

While ICANN represents the multi-stakeholder model, some states favor a multilateral approach that places greater authority in intergovernmental organizations, particularly the United Nations. The International Telecommunication Union (ITU), a UN agency with a long history in managing global telecommunications standards, has been proposed as an alternative venue for DNS and IP governance. Proponents argue that the ITU's structure ensures equal representation of states, addressing concerns of sovereignty and fairness. Countries such as China, Russia, and several developing nations support shifting authority toward intergovernmental frameworks. However, Western democracies and corporations often resist such proposals, fearing that they would lead to excessive state control, restrictions on free expression, and bureaucratic inefficiencies. Diplomatic negotiations between these camps reflect broader ideological divides about whether the internet should be governed as a global commons or as a sovereign resource subject to national control.

9.4.5 Internet Protocols and the Transition to IPv6

Negotiations over IP address allocation have also been contentious. The original system, IPv4, provided a limited pool of addresses, most of which were allocated during the early years of the internet, disproportionately favoring the United States and a handful of developed countries. As internet adoption grew globally, developing nations raised concerns about inequitable distribution. The introduction of IPv6, which vastly expanded the pool of available addresses, was intended to address these imbalances. However, the transition required significant technical investment and has proceeded unevenly across regions. Diplomatic discussions about IP allocation reflect underlying concerns about digital inequality, capacity building, and access to resources. Developed countries and corporations often have the resources to implement IPv6, while developing countries depend on international cooperation and technical assistance. These dynamics make IP governance a critical part of the broader debate on bridging the digital divide.

9.4.6 Competing Visions of Global Standards

The development of global internet standards is another site of diplomatic negotiation. Standards ensure that technologies developed in different contexts can work together seamlessly, but they also shape markets and determine which companies and countries benefit economically. Organizations like the IETF and W3C operate on principles of openness and consensus, with participation from diverse stakeholders. Yet, geopolitical rivalries increasingly influence standard-setting processes.

For instance, China has advanced proposals for new internet architectures, sometimes described as "New IP," which emphasize greater control and centralized oversight. Supporters argue that such proposals enhance security and stability, while critics warn they could institutionalize state surveillance and undermine openness. The competition over standards reflects deeper struggles for technological leadership and influence, with the risk that incompatible standards could accelerate internet fragmentation.

9.4.7 Diplomatic Tensions and the Splinternet Risk

Negotiations over DNS, IP, and standards cannot be separated from the broader risk of internet fragmentation. If states pursue incompatible governance models or standards, the universal internet could splinter into regional or national networks. The so-called "splinternet" scenario undermines the foundational principle of interoperability and raises concerns about economic disruption, reduced innovation, and restricted access to information. Diplomatic negotiations attempt to mitigate these risks by fostering compromise and shared frameworks, but geopolitical rivalries, particularly between the United States and China, complicate consensus. Disputes over issues such as root server locations, cross-border data flows, and platform regulation illustrate how technical governance is entangled with security concerns and ideological divides. The outcome of these negotiations will determine whether the internet remains a global commons or fractures into competing spheres of control.

9.4.8 Civil Society and the Demand for Rights-Based Governance

Civil society actors play a crucial role in shaping diplomatic negotiations by advocating for human rights, transparency, and accountability. Organizations such as the Electronic Frontier Foundation, Article 19, and academic networks argue that technical governance must prioritize freedom of expression, privacy, and equitable access. They criticize state-centric approaches for risking censorship and corporate-driven models for prioritizing profit over public interest. Civil society participation in ICANN and standard-setting bodies ensures that negotiations are not limited to states and corporations, though their influence often depends on resources and access. By framing DNS, IP, and standards as matters of rights rather than merely technical issues, civil society groups expand the scope of diplomatic debates and highlight the internet's social and cultural dimensions.

9.5 TECHNO-NATIONALISM AND INFRASTRUCTURE DIPLOMACY

Techno-nationalism and infrastructure diplomacy represent the new frontiers of geopolitical competition, where technological dominance and control over digital infrastructure have become central to national security and economic power. While these trends reflect legitimate concerns over supply chain vulnerabilities and strategic dependencies, they also pose risks to global innovation and cooperation. The challenge for nations lies in balancing the pursuit of technological sovereignty with the imperatives of international collaboration, ensuring that the benefits of global integration are not sacrificed in the name of security. As the world navigates this complex landscape, the future of technology will be defined by the ability of nations to foster resilience without succumbing to isolation, leveraging alliances and multilateral frameworks to achieve shared strategic objectives. In this era of technological competition, the path forward demands not only innovation but also a commitment to sustaining the open, interconnected digital ecosystems that underpin global progress.

The trajectory of techno-nationalism and infrastructure diplomacy will be shaped by the interplay between technological innovation, geopolitical rivalries, and global governance structures. As emerging technologies such as AI, quantum computing, and biotechnology become increasingly central to national security, nations will continue to prioritize domestic development and control over critical infrastructure. However, the risks of technological fragmentation and reduced global cooperation pose significant challenges, potentially stifling innovation and increasing costs. The future will likely see a balance between techno-nationalist policies and strategic alliances, where nations pursue self-sufficiency while leveraging international partnerships to enhance their technological capabilities. The ability to navigate these dynamics will determine which countries emerge as leaders in the digital age, shaping the rules and architectures of the global technological landscape.

CHAPTER 10

Capacity Building and Cyber-diplomacy Training

10.1 BRIDGING CYBER CAPACITY GAPS IN DEVELOPING NATIONS

Bridging cyber capacity gaps in developing nations is essential for achieving a more inclusive, secure, and equitable digital future. These gaps span infrastructure, human capital, governance, and security, reflecting the multifaceted nature of cyber capacity. Addressing them requires a combination of national commitment, international cooperation, and innovative partnerships that place inclusivity and sustainability at the core. By investing in digital skills, strengthening governance frameworks, and building resilient infrastructure, developing nations can harness the transformative potential of cyberspace. Ultimately, bridging these gaps is not only a matter of national development but also a global imperative, as the security and prosperity of the digital world depend on the participation and resilience of all states, regardless of their level of development.

10.1.1 Nature of Cyber Capacity Gaps

Cyber capacity gaps manifest in multiple forms, from limited internet penetration and inadequate technical infrastructure to shortages of skilled professionals and weak policy frameworks. In many developing nations, basic connectivity remains a challenge, with rural populations lacking affordable and reliable access to the internet. Even where connectivity is available, bandwidth constraints, outdated hardware, and high costs limit widespread usage. Beyond infrastructure, human capital gaps are evident in the scarcity of trained engineers, cyber-security experts, and policymakers equipped to navigate the complexities of digital governance. Furthermore, weak legal frameworks often hinder the ability to address cybercrime, protect data privacy, or regulate digital markets. These gaps collectively impede the ability of developing nations to fully harness the benefits of digital technologies and expose them to heightened risks in an interconnected world.

10.1.2 Infrastructure Challenges

The most visible aspect of the cyber capacity gap is infrastructure. Reliable access to broadband internet, robust data centers, and secure networks form the backbone of digital participation, yet these remain underdeveloped in many regions. In Africa, for example, internet penetration rates remain far below the global average, with many areas relying on limited mobile connectivity.

The cost of building undersea cables, terrestrial fiber networks, and rural connectivity solutions is prohibitive for many developing states, especially when combined with broader challenges of economic development. Without adequate infrastructure, developing nations face barriers to participating in e-commerce, digital education, and remote healthcare, which are increasingly central to modern life. Infrastructure deficits also exacerbate vulnerabilities to cyber-attacks, as outdated systems are often easier to exploit. Addressing these challenges requires international investment, regional cooperation, and innovative solutions tailored to local conditions.

10.1.3 Human Capital and Skills Development

While infrastructure is fundamental, the human dimension of cyber capacity is equally critical. Developing nations often struggle with shortages of skilled professionals who can design, secure, and manage digital systems. Educational systems may not prioritize digital literacy, leaving large segments of the population unable to use basic online tools effectively. At the higher levels, universities and technical institutions may lack the resources to train cyber-security experts, data scientists, or policy analysts.

This skills gap limits not only the ability of governments to regulate and protect cyberspace but also the capacity of local businesses to innovate and compete globally. International initiatives that promote digital education, vocational training, and exchange programs are vital to building sustainable human capital. Bridging the skills gap ensures that developing nations are not dependent solely on external expertise but can cultivate local capacity for long-term resilience.

10.1.4 Policy and Governance Deficits

Cyber capacity gaps also emerge from weak or absent policy and governance frameworks. In many developing countries, laws on data protection, cybercrime, and intellectual property are outdated or nonexistent. This regulatory vacuum leaves individuals vulnerable to exploitation, businesses uncertain about operating environments, and governments unable to enforce accountability in cyberspace. Moreover, fragmented governance structures often lead to duplication of efforts and inefficiency. Effective cyber-governance requires coherent policies, clear institutional responsibilities, and mechanisms for stakeholder engagement, including private companies and civil society. Diplomatic engagement and participation in international forums also allow developing nations to contribute to shaping global norms rather than being passive recipients of rules. Building strong policy and governance frameworks ensures that cyberspace is not only secure but also aligned with democratic values, human rights, and sustainable development goals.

10.1.5 Cyber-security Vulnerabilities

Developing nations face heightened cyber-security risks due to weak infrastructure, limited expertise, and inadequate defenses. Cybercriminals often target such countries precisely because they are less protected, exploiting vulnerabilities for financial gain or political influence. Attacks on financial systems, government databases, and critical infrastructure can have devastating effects, undermining trust in digital systems and stalling development. The rise of ransomware, phishing campaigns, and disinformation operations illustrates the scope of the threat. For countries with limited resources, recovering from such attacks is often costly and disruptive. Building cyber resilience therefore requires both technical defenses and the development of incident response mechanisms, threat intelligence sharing, and regional cooperation. Without addressing vulnerabilities, the benefits of digital transformation risk being overshadowed by growing insecurity.

10.1.6 Role of International Cooperation

Bridging cyber capacity gaps cannot be achieved by developing nations in isolation. International cooperation plays a crucial role in providing resources, expertise, and platforms for knowledge exchange. Organizations such as the International Telecommunication Union (ITU) and the World Bank support capacity-building projects aimed at expanding connectivity, improving governance, and fostering skills development. Partnerships between developed and developing countries allow for technology transfer and mentorship, while regional organizations provide opportunities for collective action. Cyber-security exercises, workshops, and training initiatives enable knowledge sharing and foster trust among states. International cooperation also ensures that developing nations have a voice in global discussions about cyber norms and standards, reducing the risk of digital colonialism where rules are imposed without local participation.

10.1.7 Public-Private Partnerships

Private companies, particularly in the technology sector, play a significant role in bridging cyber capacity gaps. Firms such as Microsoft, Google, and Huawei have invested in expanding connectivity and providing digital literacy training in underserved regions. Public-private partnerships allow governments to leverage corporate expertise and resources while ensuring that projects align with national priorities. For example, technology companies can provide cloud infrastructure, cyber-security tools, and educational resources that would otherwise be unaffordable. However, such partnerships must be carefully managed to prevent overdependence on private actors or the exploitation of local markets. Transparent agreements and accountability mechanisms ensure that partnerships contribute to sustainable capacity building rather than reinforcing inequalities.

10.1.8 Addressing the Digital Divide

Cyber capacity gaps are closely tied to the broader digital divide, which separates those with access to digital technologies from those without. Bridging this divide requires not only technical solutions but also policies that address affordability, inclusivity, and accessibility. For many communities, even when connectivity is available, the cost of devices or data remains prohibitive. Gender disparities also persist, with women in many developing nations less likely to access or benefit from digital tools. Efforts to bridge cyber capacity gaps must therefore adopt an inclusive approach, ensuring that marginalized groups, rural populations, and disadvantaged communities are not left behind. Addressing the digital divide transforms cyber capacity building into a tool for social equity and empowerment.

10.1.9 Toward Sustainable Cyber Capacity

Building cyber capacity is not a one-time effort but a long-term process that requires sustainability. Developing nations must not only adopt technologies but also cultivate the ability to adapt to future changes in the digital landscape. Emerging technologies such as artificial intelligence, blockchain, and quantum computing will create new opportunities and challenges, making it essential for countries to invest in forward-looking strategies.

Sustainability also requires local ownership of capacity-building initiatives, with governments, civil society, and private sectors collaborating to ensure continuity. International donors and partners must focus on building institutions and knowledge rather than short-term projects. A sustainable approach ensures that developing nations can not only bridge current gaps but also remain resilient in the face of evolving cyber challenges.

10.2 EDUCATION AND TRAINING FOR CYBER DIPLOMATS

10.2.1 Core Components of a Cyber-diplomacy Curriculum

A robust curriculum for aspiring cyber diplomats must be fundamentally interdisciplinary, blending technical acuity with deep geopolitical understanding. At its foundation lies a necessary grasp of core technical concepts. Diplomats cannot effectively negotiate on topics they do not understand; therefore, a working knowledge of internet infrastructure, networking principles, cyber-security threats like malware and botnets, and foundational cryptography is essential. This technical education must be presented not for engineering purposes but through a policy lens, focusing on how these technologies enable or complicate issues of privacy, surveillance, and offensive capabilities. Alongside this, a thorough grounding in international law and governance is paramount. Trainees must become fluent in the application of existing international law to cyberspace, study the evolving norms of responsible state behavior, and understand the functions of key multilateral forums such as the United Nations Group of Governmental Experts (UNGGE) and the Open-Ended Working Group (OEWG). This legal and normative framework provides the language and structure for most diplomatic engagements in cyberspace.

Furthermore, the curriculum must integrate the core principles of traditional diplomacy and foreign policy analysis. Skills in negotiation, mediation, and building consensus are timeless and directly transferable to digital negotiations. Cyber diplomats must learn to apply these skills in a context characterized by heightened mistrust, attribution challenges, and the involvement of non-state actors. This includes training in crisis management and escalation control specific to cyber-incidents, where the tempo of action can be vastly different from conventional military or political crises. Finally, a critical and often overlooked component is the study of the socio-political dimensions of the digital world. This encompasses understanding the global digital divide, the impact of disinformation campaigns on democratic processes, the role of major technology corporations as powerful non-state actors, and the varying cultural perspectives on issues like data privacy and internet freedom. A cyber diplomat must appreciate how technology intersects with society to fully comprehend the national interests and red lines of their counterparts.

10.2.2 Innovative Pedagogical Approaches and Training Methodals

The teaching methods for cyber-diplomacy must be as dynamic as the field itself, moving far beyond passive lecture-based learning. Active learning scenarios are crucial for developing practical skills. This includes extensive use of simulated negotiations and crisis exercises. Trainees can be tasked with role-playing a multilateral conference aimed at drafting a cyber arms control agreement or responding in real-time to a simulated major cyber incident against critical infrastructure. These simulations force participants to apply their technical and legal knowledge under pressure, navigate complex national instructions, and develop the soft skills of compromise and coalition-building. Case study analysis of past incidents, such as the Stuxnet attack, the NotPetya malware outbreak, or attempts to interfere in elections, provides critical historical context and allows for deep dives into the diplomatic fallout and response strategies employed by various states.

Given the global nature of the field, training programs should also be inherently international. Bringing together mid-career professionals and aspiring diplomats from different countries for joint workshops and courses breaks down barriers and builds the personal networks that are the lifeblood of effective diplomacy. Fostering these relationships before a crisis occurs can pave the way for more effective back-channel communications during times of tension.

Furthermore, effective training requires a faculty composed of both seasoned practitioners and leading academics. Retired ambassadors, active government cyber policy officials, and legal advisors can provide real-world insight and practical wisdom, while university researchers contribute cutting-edge theoretical knowledge and critical analysis. This combination ensures that the education is both grounded in reality and forward-looking, preparing diplomats for challenges that are just emerging on the horizon.

10.2.3 Path Forward: Building a Sustainable Ecosystem

Educating cyber diplomats is not a one-time event but requires a commitment to continuous learning and career-long development. The field evolves at a breathtaking pace; a technology or threat that is irrelevant today may be central to diplomacy tomorrow. Therefore, foundational courses must be supplemented with ongoing professional development opportunities, such as short executive courses on emerging topics like artificial intelligence governance, quantum computing threats, or the diplomacy of digital currency.

Governments and foreign ministries must create dedicated career tracks and incentives for diplomats to specialize in cyber-issues, ensuring that acquired expertise is retained and valued within the institution. This also involves creating opportunities for rotations in other relevant government departments, such as cyber-security agencies, intelligence communities, and telecommunications regulators, to build a whole-of-government perspective.

Ultimately, the goal of this specialized education is to build a sustainable ecosystem of expertise. This means not only training individual diplomats but also fostering a global community of practice where knowledge, best practices, and lessons learned are shared. International organizations, think tanks, and academic institutions all have a role to play in supporting this ecosystem by hosting conferences, facilitating track II diplomacy dialogues, and publishing research that informs policy.

Investing in the education and training of cyber diplomats is an investment in international stability. By equipping a cadre of professionals with the unique blend of skills required to navigate the digital age, the international community can work toward a future where cyberspace remains secure, stable, and open, and where conflicts are resolved through dialogue and agreed-upon rules rather than through unchecked escalation and potential chaos.

10.3 ROLE OF THINK TANKS, ACADEMIA, AND INTERNATIONAL NGOS

Think tanks, academic institutions, and international NGOs have become indispensable partners in the global effort to govern cyber-security effectively and responsibly. Their contributions—ranging from policy analysis and technical research to advocacy and capacity-building—enrich the cyber-security ecosystem by ensuring that strategies are informed, innovative, and inclusive. As cyber-threats continue to evolve, the role of non-state actors will only grow in importance, demanding structured mechanisms for their integration into policy processes and international negotiations. The path forward requires a commitment to fostering collaboration among these diverse stakeholders, recognizing that the challenges of cyber-security governance are too complex and multifaceted to be addressed by governments alone. By embracing the expertise and perspectives of non-state actors, the global community can build a more resilient, equitable, and secure digital future.

The future of cyber-security governance will increasingly depend on the sustained and expanded engagement of non-state actors, as digital threats grow in complexity and global interconnectedness deepens. Think tanks will continue to provide the analytical rigor necessary for adaptive policy development, while academic institutions will drive the technical innovations that underpin secure digital ecosystems. International NGOs will remain essential for ensuring that cyber-security measures uphold human rights and democratic values. The integration of these perspectives will be critical for addressing emerging challenges such as artificial intelligence-driven cyber-threats, quantum computing risks, and the governance of decentralized digital infrastructures. By fostering collaboration among think tanks, academia, and NGOs, the global community can develop cyber-security policies that are not only effective but also equitable, transparent, and aligned with the broader imperatives of digital governance.

10.3.1 Influence of Think Tanks on Cyber-security Policy

Think tanks have emerged as vital players in cyber-security policy development, offering independent research, strategic analysis, and expert recommendations that guide government decision-making. Organizations such as the Center for Strategic and International Studies (CSIS), the International Institute for Strategic Studies (IISS), and the Atlantic Council produce influential reports on cyber-threats, geopolitical risks, and emerging technologies. These analyses often shape national cyber-security strategies, international negotiations, and private sector practices. Think tanks also serve as conveners of high-level dialogues, bringing together policymakers, industry leaders, and technical experts to discuss pressing cyber-security challenges. Their role is particularly significant in bridging the gap between technical complexity and policy formulation, translating intricate cyber-threats into actionable strategies for governments and international bodies. By providing a neutral platform for debate and collaboration, think tanks contribute to the development of more informed, adaptive, and effective cyber-security policies.

10.3.2 Academia's Contribution to Cyber-security Research and Education

Academic institutions are fundamental to advancing cyber-security through research, education, and the cultivation of technical expertise. Universities and research centers conduct pioneering studies on cyber-threats, cryptographic innovations, and digital forensics, often in collaboration with government agencies and private sector partners. Institutions such as MIT's Computer Science and Artificial Intelligence Laboratory (CSAIL), Stanford's Center for International Security and Cooperation (CISAC), and the University of Cambridge's Cybercrime Centre produce groundbreaking work that informs both policy and technological development.

Additionally, academic programs in cyber-security, computer science, and international relations prepare the next generation of professionals equipped to address digital threats. These educational initiatives are essential for building a skilled workforce capable of defending against sophisticated cyber attacks and developing secure digital infrastructures. The interdisciplinary nature of academic research further enriches cyber-security governance by integrating perspectives from law, political science, and engineering, ensuring that policies are both technically sound and socially responsible.

10.3.3 International NGOs and the Advocacy for Digital Rights and Security

International NGOs play a critical role in cyber-security governance by advocating for digital rights, transparency, and equitable access to technology. Organizations such as Access Now, the Electronic Frontier Foundation (EFF), and the Internet Society work to ensure that cyber-security policies respect human rights, privacy, and democratic values. These NGOs often highlight the potential for cyber-security measures to be misused for surveillance, censorship, or repression, pushing for safeguards that protect civil liberties in the digital age.

They also engage in capacity-building initiatives, providing technical assistance and training to civil society organizations, journalists, and activists operating in high-risk environments. By amplifying the voices of marginalized communities and advocating for inclusive governance models, international NGOs contribute to a more balanced and rights-respecting approach to cyber-security. Their efforts are particularly vital in regions where digital infrastructure is underdeveloped, ensuring that cyber-security policies do not exacerbate existing inequalities.

10.3.4 Collaboration between Think Tanks, Academia, and NGOs

The synergy between think tanks, academic institutions, and international NGOs enhances the effectiveness of cyber-security governance by combining policy expertise, technical research, and advocacy. Joint initiatives often take the form of collaborative research projects, policy briefings, and international conferences that bring together diverse perspectives. For example, think tanks may partner with academic researchers to produce evidence-based policy recommendations, while NGOs ensure that these proposals incorporate human rights considerations and civil society input. This interdisciplinary collaboration is essential for addressing complex cyber-security challenges that require both technical solutions and policy innovation. By fostering these partnerships, non-state actors contribute to a more holistic and adaptive approach to cyber-security governance, where strategies are informed by rigorous analysis, grounded in technical expertise, and aligned with democratic values.

10.3.5 Role of Non-State Actors in International Cyber-security Norms

Non-state actors have become instrumental in shaping international cyber-security norms, influencing the development of treaties, agreements, and best practices. Think tanks often provide the intellectual foundation for international negotiations, offering policy frameworks that guide diplomatic efforts. Academic institutions contribute by developing technical standards and protocols that underpin global cyber-security architectures. NGOs, meanwhile, advocate for norms that prioritize human rights, transparency, and accountability in cyber-security governance. Their collective efforts have been particularly evident in forums such as the United Nations Open-Ended Working Group (OEWG) on cyber-security, where non-state actors provide expert input, facilitate stakeholder engagement, and push for inclusive policy outcomes. By participating in these international processes, think tanks, academia, and NGOs ensure that cyber-security norms are not only technically robust but also socially responsible and globally applicable.

10.3.6 Challenges and Limitations of Non-State Actor Involvement

Despite their significant contributions, non-state actors face challenges in influencing cyber-security governance, particularly in environments where state sovereignty and national security concerns dominate. Governments may be reluctant to incorporate non-state perspectives, especially when policy decisions involve sensitive intelligence or military considerations. Additionally, the diversity of non-state actors can lead to fragmented or competing recommendations, complicating efforts to achieve consensus. Resource constraints further limit the ability of some NGOs and academic institutions to participate fully in international cyber-security dialogues. These challenges underscore the need for structured mechanisms that integrate non-state expertise into policy processes while respecting the prerogatives of sovereign states. Achieving this balance will be essential for ensuring that cyber-security governance benefits from the full spectrum of stakeholder insights.

10.3.7 Case Studies: Non-State Actors in Action

Several case studies illustrate the impact of non-state actors on cyber-security policy and practice. The Carnegie Endowment for International Peace, for instance, has been influential in shaping discussions on cyber norms and international law, providing policy recommendations that have informed diplomatic negotiations. Academic institutions such as the Georgia Institute of Technology have contributed to the development of cyber-security standards through their research on secure software and network architectures. NGOs like the Citizen Lab have exposed cyber espionage campaigns and advocated for stronger protections against digital surveillance, influencing both public opinion and policy responses. These examples demonstrate how non-state actors drive innovation, accountability, and inclusivity in cyber-security governance, ensuring that policies are responsive to both technical realities and societal needs.

10.4 TECHNICAL ASSISTANCE AND DEVELOPMENTAL CYBER-DIPLOMACY

Technical assistance and developmental cyber-diplomacy are central to building an inclusive and resilient digital future. They address the multifaceted challenges of infrastructure gaps, skills shortages, policy deficits, and cyber-security vulnerabilities that hinder many developing nations. At the same time, they create opportunities for inclusive growth, enabling societies to harness digital technologies for economic development and social progress.

The effectiveness of these efforts depends on genuine cooperation, local ownership, and alignment with broader goals of human rights and sustainable development. As cyberspace continues to expand and evolve, bridging capacity gaps through assistance and diplomacy will remain not only a developmental imperative but also a global necessity, ensuring that the benefits of the digital age are shared by all.

Looking ahead, technical assistance and developmental cyber-diplomacy will become even more critical as new technologies reshape the digital landscape. Artificial intelligence, quantum computing, and blockchain introduce new opportunities but also new risks that require advanced expertise and governance frameworks. Developing nations will need continued support to adapt to these changes, and international cooperation will be vital in ensuring that technological innovations do not exacerbate global inequalities. Future cyber-diplomacy must also adapt to the growing multipolarity of global politics, where multiple powers and regions assert competing visions of digital governance. By fostering inclusive, transparent, and sustainable partnerships, developmental cyber-diplomacy can help bridge divides and ensure that cyberspace remains a space of shared opportunity rather than deepening fragmentation.

10.5 WOMEN AND UNDERREPRESENTED GROUPS IN CYBER-DIPLOMACY

The pursuit of a more inclusive cyber-diplomacy is not a box-ticking exercise in political correctness. It is a strategic necessity for enhancing national and international security in the digital age. The challenges posed by a malicious and evolving cyber threat landscape are too complex to be addressed by a small and homogenous group of individuals.

By actively breaking down barriers and embracing the full spectrum of human talent, the field of cyber-diplomacy can become more innovative, more representative, and more effective. Empowering women and individuals from all backgrounds to become shapers of our digital future will lead to policies that are more comprehensive, equitable, and resilient. Ultimately, the security of our interconnected world depends on harnessing every available ounce of wisdom, creativity, and perspective. Failing to do so is a risk we cannot afford to take.

Addressing the current imbalance requires a concerted and multi-faceted effort from governments, academic institutions, and the private sector. It begins with intentional pipeline development. This involves creating and funding educational pathways, such as scholarships, internships, and mentorship programs, specifically targeted at encouraging women and students from underrepresented backgrounds to pursue studies in cyber-security, international relations, and international law.

Outreach must start at the secondary school level to spark interest and demystify these career paths. Within foreign ministries and relevant agencies, a thorough review of human resources practices is necessary. This includes implementing blind recruitment processes to mitigate unconscious bias, establishing clear and transparent criteria for promotion, and creating sponsorship programs that actively advocate for high-potential individuals from diverse backgrounds.

Critically, organizational culture must evolve to become genuinely inclusive and supportive. This entails a zero-tolerance policy for discrimination and harassment, the provision of flexible work arrangements to support caregivers (a burden that still falls disproportionately on women), and the active promotion of diverse voices into leadership and visible speaking roles. Senior leadership must champion this agenda, setting concrete diversity goals and being held accountable for progress. Finally, the international community itself can play a role by promoting diversity within its own structures. Multilateral organizations like the United Nations and the Organization for Security and Co-operation in Europe (OSCE) can ensure that women and representatives from the Global South are not only participants but also chairs and key influencers in the processes that shape global cyber norms.

CHAPTER 11

Emerging Issues in Cyber-diplomacy

11.1 AI GOVERNANCE AND ALGORITHMIC DIPLOMACY

11.1.1 Rise of AI Governance

AI governance has emerged because the rapid spread of AI technologies has outpaced regulatory and ethical frameworks. Governments and international bodies recognize that AI systems influence critical decisions about individuals and societies, from judicial rulings supported by predictive analytics to automated hiring systems in corporations. AI governance therefore seeks to establish guardrails that ensure transparency, accountability, safety, and fairness.

Governance frameworks include national AI strategies, regulatory proposals such as the European Union's AI Act, and guidelines developed by international organizations. Unlike traditional technologies, AI evolves rapidly and unpredictably, which makes governance particularly challenging. Policymakers must strike a balance between fostering innovation and addressing concerns about bias, discrimination, privacy, and potential misuse. The governance debate is not limited to technical issues but extends to broader societal and geopolitical concerns, making it inherently global in scope.

11.1.2 Global Dimensions of AI Governance

AI governance cannot be confined within national boundaries. Algorithms deployed by multinational corporations, such as search engines or social media platforms, shape public opinion and behavior worldwide. Similarly, autonomous weapons and surveillance technologies raise transnational security implications. Because of this interconnectedness, global cooperation is necessary to harmonize principles and prevent fragmented standards that might undermine trust and fairness.

Organizations like the OECD, UNESCO, and the G20 have put forward frameworks for ethical AI, emphasizing principles such as transparency, inclusivity, and human oversight. However, these frameworks often reflect the values of dominant powers and raise concerns about their universality. The global dimension of AI governance is also marked by competition, as nations such as the United States, China, and members of the European Union promote distinct governance models that reflect their strategic priorities and political ideologies.

11.1.3 Algorithmic Diplomacy

Algorithmic diplomacy refers to the use of diplomatic processes to address challenges and opportunities arising from algorithmic systems. Just as cyber-diplomacy emerged in response to the global governance of the internet, algorithmic diplomacy has become necessary to negotiate the norms, standards, and ethical frameworks surrounding AI. It involves dialogues between states, corporations, and international organizations to ensure that AI serves as a tool for cooperation rather than conflict. Algorithmic diplomacy addresses questions of data flows, cross-border accountability, intellectual property rights, and ethical principles. It also emphasizes trust-building, as nations seek assurances that AI technologies will not be weaponized or used in ways that destabilize international relations. In this sense, algorithmic diplomacy is not simply a technical negotiation but a deeply political process involving issues of power, sovereignty, and values.

11.1.4 Competing Governance Models

A central challenge in AI governance and algorithmic diplomacy lies in the competing visions of how AI should be regulated. The European Union has promoted a rights-based approach, exemplified by its AI Act, which emphasizes transparency, risk classification, and accountability. The United States has tended to favor a market-driven approach, allowing innovation to flourish under minimal regulation while encouraging voluntary ethical guidelines. China, meanwhile, has pursued a state-centric model, using AI both for economic advancement and social governance, often emphasizing control and state authority. These competing models reflect different political cultures and strategic interests, making consensus difficult. Algorithmic diplomacy must navigate these divides, seeking common ground while respecting diversity. Without such engagement, the risk of regulatory fragmentation could undermine trust in AI systems and hinder international cooperation.

11.1.5 Security and Geopolitical Implications

AI governance and algorithmic diplomacy are not only about ethics and fairness but also about security and geopolitics. AI is increasingly integrated into military systems, from autonomous drones to cyber-defense tools, raising fears of an AI-driven arms race. Diplomatic engagement is needed to establish norms that prevent destabilizing uses of AI in warfare and espionage. Moreover, control over AI technologies has become a geopolitical asset, with nations investing heavily in AI research to gain economic and strategic advantages. Algorithmic diplomacy must therefore address issues of technology transfer, intellectual property, and competition while seeking to prevent AI from becoming a source of international conflict. Just as nuclear diplomacy shaped the Cold War era, algorithmic diplomacy may become a defining feature of the twenty-first century, where control over algorithms equates to influence over global power dynamics.

11.1.6 Ethical and Human Rights Dimensions

At the heart of AI governance lies the question of ethics and human rights. Algorithms can replicate or even exacerbate social biases, leading to discriminatory outcomes in hiring, law enforcement, and access to services. AI-driven surveillance raises concerns about privacy and freedom of expression. These challenges underscore the need for governance frameworks that prioritize human rights and dignity. Algorithmic diplomacy plays a vital role in ensuring that ethical principles are incorporated into international agreements and industry standards.

For example, UNESCO's Recommendation on the Ethics of Artificial Intelligence highlights the need for inclusivity, transparency, and accountability. Ensuring that these values are respected globally requires diplomatic negotiations that bridge cultural differences while upholding universal principles. Without such engagement, the risk of AI reinforcing inequality and authoritarian practices remains high.

11.1.7 Role of Multistakeholder Engagement

AI governance and algorithmic diplomacy are inherently multistakeholder in nature. Governments alone cannot regulate or negotiate AI's global impact, as much of its development and deployment is driven by private corporations. Civil society, academia, and technical experts also play crucial roles in shaping ethical guidelines and highlighting risks. Multistakeholder engagement ensures that governance frameworks reflect diverse perspectives and are not dominated by the interests of a few powerful states or corporations. Algorithmic diplomacy must therefore create spaces for inclusive dialogue, where voices from developing nations, marginalized communities, and independent experts are heard. This inclusivity is essential to building legitimacy and trust in global AI governance, ensuring that it serves humanity as a whole rather than narrow interests.

11.2 QUANTUM-SECURE DIPLOMACY AND CRYPTOGRAPHY

11.2.1 Emergence of Quantum-Secure Cryptography

In response to this existential threat, the global scientific and cryptographic community has embarked on a urgent mission to develop and standardize quantum-resistant cryptography, also known as post-quantum cryptography (PQC). Unlike quantum cryptography, which often refers to quantum key distribution (QKD) relying on physics-based principles, PQC involves creating new mathematical algorithms designed to be secure against attacks from both classical and quantum computers. These algorithms are built upon mathematical problems that are believed to be hard for quantum computers to solve, such as lattice-based problems, code-based problems, multivariate equations, and hash-based signatures.

The goal is to create a drop-in replacement for current cryptographic standards, allowing for the protection of digital infrastructure without requiring a complete overhaul of existing systems. Leading national standards bodies, most notably the U.S. National Institute of Standards and Technology (NIST), have been running a rigorous multi-year process to evaluate and select a suite of PQC algorithms for standardization. This effort is critical to establishing a new, trusted global baseline for security in the quantum era.

11.2.2 Diplomatic Imperative for a Coordinated Transition

The transition to a quantum-secure world is not merely a technical challenge; it is a profound diplomatic and geopolitical endeavor. The process of migrating the world's digital infrastructure to new cryptographic standards is unprecedented in its scale and complexity. It requires meticulous planning, massive investment, and, most importantly, international coordination. If nations pursue divergent paths, adopting different standards or timelines, the result could be a fragmented global digital ecosystem fraught with interoperability issues. This fragmentation would create significant vulnerabilities and hinder secure international communication, data exchange, and trade.

Therefore, quantum security has rapidly ascended as a critical agenda item in bilateral and multilateral dialogues. Diplomats and technical experts must engage in sustained cooperation to foster alignment on core standards, share best practices for migration, and establish common protocols for secure communication. This diplomatic effort is essential to prevent a chaotic and insecure transition that could be exploited by malicious actors. Forging international consensus on PQC is as crucial as the algorithms themselves, ensuring that the future digital world remains interconnected and secure.

11.2.3 Quantum Security as a New Domain of Geopolitical Competition

While cooperation is essential, the race for quantum supremacy and the development of quantum-resistant technologies also injects a new dimension of competition into international relations. Nations recognize that leadership in quantum technologies confers significant strategic and economic advantages. A country that develops a powerful quantum computer first could gain a temporary but decisive intelligence advantage by being able to decipher the encrypted communications of others while protecting its own. Consequently, major powers are investing billions in national quantum initiatives, turning quantum technology into a focal point of geopolitical rivalry. This competition extends to the setting of global standards. The algorithms selected to become the world's new cryptographic foundation will have immense long-term influence. There is a diplomatic push to ensure that nationally championed algorithms are represented in international standards, which can boost domestic technology sectors and provide assurance against potential hidden vulnerabilities inserted by foreign rivals. The diplomatic discourse around PQC is thus a delicate balance between the necessity of open, transparent international collaboration and the imperative of protecting national security interests and technological sovereignty.

11.2.4 Building a Diplomatic Framework for Quantum Stability

The potential for quantum technologies to destabilize international security necessitates the development of new diplomatic frameworks and confidence-building measures. The concept of "quantum stability" is emerging, akin to nuclear stability during the Cold War, where mutual vulnerability encouraged restraint. Diplomats and policymakers must begin discussions on norms of responsible behavior concerning quantum capabilities.

This could include bilateral or multilateral agreements on transparency measures regarding quantum computing progress, commitments against the theft of encrypted data for future decryption, and even discussions around the verification of quantum capabilities. Furthermore, international aid and capacity building will be vital components of a secure global transition. A digital security divide could emerge if developed nations successfully migrate to PQC while less-resourced countries are left behind with vulnerable systems. This would create soft targets for state and non-state actors, threatening the security of the entire international system. Therefore, diplomatic efforts must include programs to share knowledge, provide technical assistance, and support the quantum readiness of all nations, ensuring that the global digital commons is strengthened, not weakened, by the quantum transition.

11.3 SPACE-CYBER INTERFACE: SATELLITE SECURITY AND DATA

11.3.1 Growing Importance of Satellite Networks in Global Infrastructure

Satellite networks have evolved from specialized military and scientific tools to foundational elements of global infrastructure, supporting everything from GPS navigation to internet connectivity and disaster response. The proliferation of low Earth orbit (LEO) satellite constellations, such as those deployed by SpaceX's Starlink and OneWeb, has further expanded the role of space-based systems in everyday life. These advancements have also increased the attack surface for cyber-threats, as satellites and their associated ground systems become targets for espionage, disruption, and sabotage. The reliance on satellite data for critical functions—such as financial markets, emergency communications, and military logistics—makes their security a matter of national and economic security. As these networks grow in complexity and scale, the need to protect them from cyber-intrusions has become a priority for governments, private sector operators, and international organizations alike.

11.3.2 Cyber-threats to Satellite Systems and Ground Infrastructure

The cyber-threats facing satellite systems are multifaceted, targeting both the orbital assets and their terrestrial support networks. Adversaries may employ techniques such as signal jamming, spoofing, and cyber-intrusions to disrupt satellite communications or manipulate their data transmissions. Ground stations, which serve as the interface between satellites and terrestrial networks, are particularly vulnerable to cyber-attacks, as they rely on digital systems that can be exploited through malware, phishing, or supply chain compromises.

Additionally, the increasing integration of satellite networks with internet-based systems has introduced new risks, as cybercriminals and state-sponsored actors seek to exploit these connections for espionage or sabotage. The potential consequences of such attacks are severe, ranging from the disruption of military operations to the compromise of financial and civilian communications. Addressing these threats requires a comprehensive approach that encompasses both technical defenses and policy frameworks to mitigate vulnerabilities.

11.3.3 Role of Encryption and Secure Data Transmission in Satellite Security

Encryption and secure data transmission protocols are fundamental to protecting satellite communications from cyber-threats. Modern satellites employ advanced cryptographic techniques to safeguard their signals, ensuring that data remains confidential and tamper-proof as it traverses between space and Earth. These measures are essential for preventing eavesdropping, signal manipulation, and unauthorized access to satellite networks.

However, the implementation of encryption in satellite systems presents unique challenges, as the computational constraints of orbital assets and the need for real-time data processing require specialized solutions. Additionally, the management of cryptographic keys and the integration of secure protocols across diverse satellite architectures demand rigorous standards and interoperability frameworks. The development of quantum-resistant encryption, for example, has become a priority as nations prepare for the potential threats posed by quantum computing to traditional cryptographic methods.

11.3.4 International Cooperation and Norms for Space-Cyber Security

The security of satellite systems and their associated cyber infrastructure necessitates international cooperation, as the global nature of space and digital networks transcends national boundaries. Organizations such as the United Nations Office for Outer Space Affairs (UNOOSA) and the International Telecommunication Union (ITU) play pivotal roles in fostering dialogue and establishing norms for the responsible use of space and cyber technologies.

Initiatives such as the Artemis Accords, which outline principles for sustainable and secure space exploration, reflect efforts to align international practices in satellite security. Additionally, bilateral and multilateral agreements on cyber-security and space operations provide frameworks for collaboration in threat detection, incident response, and information sharing. These cooperative efforts are essential for addressing the collective risks posed by cyber-threats to satellite systems, ensuring that nations can respond effectively to attacks that may originate from or target assets beyond their jurisdictions.

11.3.5 Intersection of Military and Civilian Satellite Security

The dual-use nature of satellite technology, where systems serve both military and civilian purposes, complicates the security landscape and demands integrated approaches to cyber-defense. Military satellites, which support command, control, and intelligence operations, are prime targets for adversarial cyber-activities, as their compromise could have strategic implications for national security. Civilian satellites, meanwhile, underpin critical infrastructure such as telecommunications, weather monitoring, and navigation, making their protection equally vital. The convergence of these systems in shared orbital environments and ground networks introduces risks of collateral damage, where attacks on military assets could inadvertently disrupt civilian services. This interdependence necessitates coordinated security strategies that address the unique vulnerabilities of each domain while ensuring the resilience of the broader satellite ecosystem. The development of joint military-civilian cyber-security frameworks, such as those employed by NATO and its partners, exemplifies efforts to harmonize defenses across these sectors.

11.3.6 Emerging Technologies and Future Challenges in Satellite Security

The rapid advancement of technologies such as artificial intelligence, quantum computing, and advanced satellite constellations introduces both opportunities and challenges for space-cyber security. AI-driven cyber-defenses, for example, offer the potential to enhance threat detection and response capabilities, enabling autonomous protection of satellite networks. However, these same technologies can also be exploited by adversaries to develop more sophisticated attack methodologies, such as AI-powered signal manipulation or quantum decryption techniques. The proliferation of small satellites and mega-constellations further complicates the security landscape, as the sheer volume of orbital assets increases the potential for cyber vulnerabilities.

Addressing these challenges will require continuous innovation in cyber-security measures, as well as adaptive policy frameworks that can evolve alongside technological developments. The integration of space and cyber-security strategies, as seen in initiatives such as the U.S. Space Force's cyber protection teams, reflects the growing recognition of the need for specialized defenses in this domain.

11.3.7 Role of Private Sector and Public-Private Partnerships in Satellite Security

The private sector has become a critical partner in securing satellite systems, as commercial operators increasingly dominate the space industry and possess advanced technical capabilities. Companies such as SpaceX, Lockheed Martin, and Thales play essential roles in developing secure satellite architectures, implementing cyber-defenses, and responding to threats. Public-private partnerships have emerged as a key mechanism for enhancing space-cyber security, enabling governments to leverage industry expertise while ensuring that national security priorities are met. These collaborations often involve joint research and development initiatives, threat intelligence sharing, and coordinated incident response efforts. The involvement of private sector entities is particularly vital for addressing the cyber-security challenges of commercial satellite networks, which may lack the resources or regulatory oversight of government-operated systems. By fostering these partnerships, nations can enhance the resilience of their space assets while promoting innovation and efficiency in satellite security.

11.3.8 Policy and Regulatory Frameworks for Space-Cyber Security

Effective space-cyber security requires robust policy and regulatory frameworks that address the unique challenges of this domain. Governments have increasingly recognized the need for specialized legislation and guidelines that govern the cyber-security of satellite systems, from their design and deployment to their operational management. Initiatives such as the U.S. National Cyber Strategy and the European Union's Cyber-security Act provide structures for protecting critical infrastructure, including space-based assets.

Additionally, international agreements such as the Wassenaar Arrangement, which regulates the export of dual-use technologies, play a role in preventing the proliferation of cyber capabilities that could be used to target satellite networks. The development of these frameworks must balance the imperatives of security with the need for innovation and commercial viability, ensuring that regulations do not stifle the growth of the space industry while addressing its vulnerabilities. The harmonization of these policies across jurisdictions will be essential for fostering a secure and resilient global satellite ecosystem.

11.4 CYBER-DIPLOMACY IN CLIMATE CHANGE, HEALTH, AND DEVELOPMENT

11.4.1 Cyber-diplomacy and Climate Change

Climate change represents one of the greatest collective challenges of our time, requiring cooperation across borders, sectors, and generations. Cyber-diplomacy plays a vital role in supporting climate governance through the integration of digital technologies and diplomatic efforts. Data-driven insights are essential for understanding climate patterns, predicting disasters, and designing mitigation strategies. Satellites, sensors, and AI-based models generate vast amounts of data, but this information must be shared across borders to be effective. Cyber-diplomacy enables agreements that promote open access to climate data, ensure interoperability of systems, and protect the integrity of shared information.

Furthermore, cyber-diplomacy facilitates collaboration on green technologies and digital infrastructure that support sustainability. Smart grids, renewable energy platforms, and digital carbon-trading systems depend on secure and reliable cyber connections. International negotiations now include discussions about protecting critical energy and environmental infrastructures from cyber-threats, recognizing that climate action is inseparable from cyber-security. By linking climate goals with cyber-cooperation, nations can create trust-based frameworks that enable shared progress on emission reductions, adaptation strategies, and sustainable development.

11.4.2 Health Diplomacy in the Digital Age

Health crises such as the COVID-19 pandemic have revealed the importance of digital technologies in global health governance. Cyber-diplomacy has become central to health cooperation, as digital systems facilitate the sharing of epidemiological data, the coordination of responses, and the dissemination of scientific knowledge. During the pandemic, digital platforms were used to track infections, model the spread of the virus, and distribute vaccines. However, disparities in digital capacities and concerns over misinformation highlighted the need for stronger international coordination. Cyber-diplomacy in health focuses on promoting secure data exchanges, safeguarding patient privacy, and ensuring that digital health innovations benefit all nations. Agreements on health-related cyber-security are crucial, as hospitals, research institutions, and vaccine supply chains are frequent targets of cyber-attacks. Diplomatic initiatives promote norms that protect health infrastructure and encourage responsible use of health data. Beyond emergencies, cyber-diplomacy also supports broader health initiatives such as telemedicine, digital health records, and cross-border medical research. By embedding digital cooperation into health diplomacy, nations can build resilient systems that not only respond to crises but also improve long-term public health outcomes.

11.4.3 Digital Cooperation for Development

Development has always been a central theme of international diplomacy, but the digital era has redefined what development means. Cyber-diplomacy in development focuses on bridging digital divides and ensuring that all nations can participate in and benefit from the digital economy. Access to the internet, digital literacy, and cyber capacity are now prerequisites for economic growth and social inclusion. Cyber-diplomacy creates frameworks for international assistance, technology transfer, and capacity-building initiatives that empower developing nations.

For example, international organizations and partnerships have promoted programs to expand broadband access, create digital skills training, and build cyber-security resilience in low- and middle-income countries. These efforts are not only about economic growth but also about inclusivity, ensuring that marginalized populations are not left behind in the digital transformation. Cyber-diplomacy also plays a role in aligning digital development with the United Nations Sustainable Development Goals. By linking digital inclusion with poverty reduction, education, gender equality, and environmental sustainability, cyber-diplomacy ensures that digital progress contributes to holistic development outcomes.

11.4.4 Intersections of Climate, Health, and Development

While climate change, health, and development are often treated as separate domains, cyber-diplomacy highlights their interconnectedness. Climate change has direct implications for health, as rising temperatures contribute to the spread of diseases and extreme weather events threaten food security. Development, in turn, is closely tied to both health and environmental sustainability, as poverty reduction and infrastructure growth are essential for resilience. Digital technologies provide the tools to integrate these domains, creating synergies that enhance collective responses.

For example, digital platforms can be used to monitor the health impacts of climate change, track food security in vulnerable regions, and design targeted interventions that support sustainable development. Cyber-diplomacy enables the agreements and partnerships necessary to share this information and coordinate action. By emphasizing the intersections of these issues, cyber-diplomacy promotes a holistic approach to global governance, ensuring that solutions are not fragmented but interconnected and mutually reinforcing.

11.4.5 Role of International Organizations

International organizations are central actors in advancing cyber-diplomacy across climate, health, and development. The United Nations has promoted digital cooperation through initiatives like the UN Secretary-General's Roadmap for Digital Cooperation. Specialized agencies such as the World Health Organization and the International Telecommunication Union facilitate cross-border cooperation in health and digital infrastructure. Similarly, frameworks like the Paris Agreement highlight the importance of data-sharing and technology transfer in climate governance. These organizations serve as platforms where states can negotiate common principles, share expertise, and align efforts. They also involve private sector actors, civil society, and academia in multistakeholder processes that reflect the complexity of global challenges. By leveraging the authority and resources of international organizations, cyber-diplomacy gains legitimacy and capacity to influence global governance in climate, health, and development.

11.5 FUTURE CHALLENGES: AUTONOMY, SURVEILLANCE, AND DIGITAL ETHICS

Unprecedented Convergence of Technology and Human Agency

The trajectory of digital innovation is propelling humanity toward a future fraught with both extraordinary potential and profound ethical dilemmas. The convergence of artificial intelligence, ubiquitous connectivity, and vast data collection capabilities is creating a new paradigm for human existence, reshaping everything from individual autonomy to the structure of global power. This technological shift is not merely an evolution of tools; it is a fundamental transformation of the social contract, challenging long-held notions of privacy, freedom, and human dignity.

The central challenges of this coming era will revolve around three interconnected pillars: the delegation of decision-making to autonomous systems, the normalization of pervasive surveillance, and the urgent need to establish a robust framework of digital ethics. Navigating this complex landscape requires a proactive and multidisciplinary approach, moving beyond technical specifications to address the core philosophical and political questions about the kind of future we wish to build. The decisions made today regarding the governance and application of these technologies will irrevocably shape the contours of society for generations to come, making this one of the most defining issues of our time.

Erosion of Autonomy in an Algorithmic Age

Human autonomy, the capacity for self-governance and independent decision-making, faces unprecedented challenges from the rise of automated systems.

Algorithms now curate our news feeds, recommend our consumer choices, and even influence major life decisions such as career paths or romantic partnerships through predictive analytics. While often framed as convenience or personalization, this algorithmic influence can subtly and insidiously shape human behavior, preferences, and worldviews.

The architecture of these systems is designed to capture and hold attention, often prioritizing engagement over well-being, which can lead to the creation of filter bubbles and the amplification of extreme content. A more acute threat emerges from the use of automated systems in high-stakes domains such as criminal justice, where risk assessment algorithms may perpetuate existing biases, or in healthcare, where diagnostic tools could override clinical judgment.

The delegation of consequential decisions to opaque algorithms raises fundamental questions about accountability, transparency, and the very right to a human appeal. When a system makes a mistake, who is responsible? How can a citizen challenge a decision they do not understand? Preserving meaningful human autonomy in the face of such pervasive automation requires legal and regulatory frameworks that ensure human oversight, algorithmic transparency, and the right to explanation for any decision that significantly impacts an individual's life.

Normalization of Pervasive Surveillance

The digital age has ushered in a new era of surveillance that is fundamentally different from historical precedents in its scale, scope, and subtlety. The traditional model of state-led monitoring has been exponentially augmented by corporate data collection, creating a pervasive ecosystem of observation often termed "surveillance capitalism."

Through the devices we carry, the platforms we use, and the smart environments we inhabit, vast quantities of personal data are continuously harvested, analyzed, and monetized. This data can be used to infer intimate details about our personalities, habits, political affiliations, and mental states. The danger lies not only in the violation of privacy but in the potential for social control and manipulation.

The knowledge that one is being watched can lead to self-censorship and conformity, chilling free expression and stifling dissent. Furthermore, the integration of facial recognition, predictive policing, and social scoring systems in various parts of the world points toward a future where surveillance is used for pre-emptive social sorting, rewarding compliance and punishing deviation. This creates a power imbalance of historic proportions between those who control the data and those who are subjected to its collection. Resisting the normalization of this panopticon requires strong data protection laws, limits on the use of biometric identification in public spaces, and a cultural shift that revalues privacy not as a right to hide, but as a essential foundation for a free and democratic society.

Imperative for a New Digital Ethics

The scale and speed of technological change have far outstripped the development of the ethical frameworks needed to govern it. Existing laws and social norms are inadequate to address challenges such as deepfakes, autonomous weapons, algorithmic bias, and the mental health impacts of social media. A new digital ethics must therefore be developed through inclusive and global dialogue, involving not just engineers and corporations, but also philosophers, sociologists, legal scholars, and the broader public.

This ethics must be action-oriented, translating abstract principles into concrete design requirements and regulatory standards. Core to this framework must be a commitment to human dignity, ensuring that technology serves to enhance rather than diminish human capabilities and rights. It must prioritize fairness and justice, actively working to identify and mitigate biases embedded in datasets and algorithms to prevent the automation of discrimination. It must demand transparency and explainability, particularly for systems that make significant decisions, so that their logic is open to scrutiny and challenge. Finally, it must embrace a principle of proportionality, ensuring that the use of powerful technologies like mass surveillance or autonomous systems is strictly necessary and proportionate to a legitimate aim. Embedding these ethical considerations into the lifecycle of technology development—from research and design to deployment and regulation—is the only way to ensure innovation progresses responsibly.

Forging a Human-Centric Digital Future

The challenges posed by autonomy, surveillance, and digital ethics are immense, but they are not insurmountable. Addressing them requires a concerted effort across all sectors of society. Governments must move beyond their current reactive posture to enact forward-looking legislation that protects citizens' rights without stifling innovation. This includes creating agile regulatory bodies equipped with the technical expertise to oversee rapidly evolving industries. Corporations, particularly technology giants, must accept a greater degree of social responsibility, moving from a culture of "move fast and break things" to one of "measure twice, cut once," where ethical impact assessments are a mandatory part of the development process.

The academic and research communities have a vital role to play in critically analyzing the societal implications of technology and developing the tools for accountability, such as algorithmic auditing. Most importantly, the public must be engaged in these conversations through education and transparent discourse, empowering individuals to understand and shape the technological forces that affect their lives. The goal is not to halt progress but to steer it deliberately toward a future that is equitable, democratic, and fundamentally human-centric. By confronting these challenges with wisdom, foresight, and a collective commitment to the public good, we can harness the power of technology to create a better world, rather than allowing it to become a force of oppression and control.

CHAPTER 12

Case Studies

12.1 US-CHINA CYBER RELATIONS AND CYBER-SECURITY AGREEMENTS

12.1.1 Historical Background of Cyber Tensions

The roots of US-China cyber tensions can be traced to the early 2000s, when reports of Chinese cyber-intrusions into US government and corporate networks began to surface. Allegations of intellectual property theft became a recurring theme, with American companies claiming that Chinese actors, often linked to state entities, had stolen trade secrets worth billions of dollars. The US government publicly accused China of sponsoring cyber espionage, framing it as an unfair practice that threatened both economic competitiveness and national security. For China, these accusations were often rejected as politically motivated, and Beijing countered by highlighting US surveillance programs revealed by Edward Snowden, which showed extensive American monitoring of global communications. This mutual suspicion laid the foundation for a complex relationship defined by both confrontation and reluctant dialogue.

12.1.2 Cyber Espionage and Intellectual Property Theft

One of the most persistent sources of friction in US-China cyber relations is the issue of cyber-enabled theft of intellectual property. American companies in industries such as aerospace, energy, and technology reported systematic intrusions by Chinese hackers aimed at stealing proprietary data. The US claimed that this practice not only undermined its businesses but also gave Chinese firms unfair advantages in global markets. In 2014, the US Department of Justice indicted five Chinese military officers on charges of cyber espionage, an unprecedented move that underscored the seriousness of the issue. China dismissed the charges as baseless and politically motivated, but the indictments marked a turning point, signaling that cyber-operations could become a source of direct diplomatic confrontation. For Washington, distinguishing between legitimate state espionage and commercial theft became a key principle of its cyber-diplomacy.

12.1.3 2015 US-China Cyber-security Agreement

Despite ongoing tensions, the US and China achieved a significant milestone in 2015, when President Barack Obama and President Xi Jinping announced a cyber-security agreement. The accord included a commitment that neither government would conduct or knowingly support cyber-enabled theft of intellectual property for commercial gain.

It also established a high-level dialogue mechanism, enabling the two sides to share information and cooperate on cybercrime investigations. Initially, the agreement was hailed as a breakthrough, as reports suggested a temporary decline in Chinese intrusions targeting American companies. However, questions soon emerged about the durability of the commitment. While the agreement represented progress in establishing norms, the absence of enforcement mechanisms and mutual distrust limited its long-term effectiveness. Still, it provided a valuable precedent for how cyber-diplomacy could reduce tensions even amid broader rivalry.

12.1.4 Renewed Tensions under the Trump Administration

The fragile progress of the 2015 agreement unraveled in subsequent years as broader US-China relations deteriorated. The Trump administration adopted a more confrontational stance toward China, labeling it a strategic competitor and escalating trade disputes. Cyber-security once again became a point of contention, with US officials accusing China of resuming large-scale hacking operations. High-profile incidents, such as the Equifax breach in 2017, which was later attributed to Chinese actors, reinforced American concerns.

Washington also took aggressive measures against Chinese technology companies, most notably Huawei, citing fears that Chinese firms could be used for espionage or sabotage. These actions highlighted how cyber-issues were increasingly intertwined with economic and geopolitical competition, reducing the space for cooperative agreements.

12.1.5 Strategic Competition in Emerging Technologies

Beyond espionage, US-China cyber relations are shaped by competition in emerging technologies such as artificial intelligence, quantum computing, and 5G networks. Both nations view leadership in these domains as critical to future power. For the US, maintaining technological superiority is seen as essential for national security and global influence.

For China, technological self-reliance and global leadership in digital infrastructure are core elements of its long-term strategy. This competition has led to cyber-related diplomatic disputes, with Washington pressing allies to exclude Huawei from 5G networks and Beijing framing such actions as attempts to contain its rise. The rivalry in emerging technologies thus reinforces mistrust in cyberspace, making agreements harder to sustain.

12.2 EU CYBER SANCTIONS FRAMEWORK IN ACTION

12.2.1 Legal and Procedural Architecture of the Framework

The operationalization of the EU Cyber Sanctions Framework is a complex process built upon a meticulous legal architecture designed to uphold due process and ensure unanimity among member states. The framework specifically targets actions constituting cyber attacks with a significant external effect that threaten the Union or its member states. These include attacks against critical infrastructure, disruptions of state functions by disabling essential services, and attacks stealing sensitive business or governmental data.

The legal basis requires that a link to a third country or a supported non-state actor be established, ensuring the sanctions are a tool of foreign policy. The process for listing individuals or entities is rigorous and multi-layered. It typically begins with a proposal from a member state or the High Representative of the Union for Foreign Affairs and Security Policy. This proposal is then examined by the relevant Council working groups, involving cyber and sanctions experts, before proceeding to the Committee of Permanent Representatives (COREPER) and finally requiring unanimous approval from the Council of the European Union itself. This high bar for action is both a strength and a weakness, ensuring broad buy-in but potentially slowing response times to rapidly evolving cyber-threats.

12.2.2 Framework in Action: Case Studies of Deployment

The practical application of the EU Cyber Sanctions Framework has provided valuable insights into its utility and limitations. Its first activation in July 2020 was a landmark moment, imposing asset freezes and travel bans on individuals and entities from Russia, China, and North Korea. This initial wave targeted units of the Russian military intelligence (GRU) for the NotPetya attack and attempted cyber espionage against the Organisation for the Prohibition of Chemical Weapons (OPCW), as well as Chinese entities for the campaign known as Cloud Hopper, which targeted managed service providers.

A second significant round of sanctions occurred in October 2020, focusing on the Russian GRU officers responsible for the hacking of the German Bundestag in 2015. These actions demonstrated the framework's primary function: to publicly attribute and impose tangible costs for specific malicious cyber-activities. The sanctions serve as a powerful symbol of the EU's collective resolve, naming and shaming perpetrators while seeking to disrupt their operational capabilities by limiting their access to the European financial system and freedom of movement. The very public nature of these designations also serves a deterrent function, signaling to other malicious actors that certain lines, when crossed, will trigger a coordinated response.

12.2.3 Navigating Challenges and Strategic Considerations

Despite its strategic value, the deployment of the Cyber Sanctions Framework is fraught with political and practical challenges. The requirement for unanimity among all 27 member states is the most significant hurdle. Divergent national threat perceptions, economic relationships, and political sensitivities can complicate and delay consensus-building. A member state with strong economic ties to a country accused of a cyber attack may be reluctant to support sanctions, potentially watering down a proposed response or blocking it entirely. Furthermore, the measurable impact of the sanctions themselves is a subject of ongoing debate. While asset freezes and travel bans impose a cost, sophisticated state-sponsored actors often operate through complex networks of front companies and individuals who may not hold assets within EU jurisdiction. This raises questions about the direct financial pain inflicted. Moreover, the framework is inherently reactive; it is a tool for imposing consequences after an attack has occurred rather than preventing it from happening in the first place. This necessitates its use as part of a broader strategy that includes resilience-building, capacity sharing, and proactive cyber-defense. The EU must also continuously navigate the risk of escalation, as targeted states may respond with counter-sanctions or increased cyber aggression, creating a cycle of retaliation that undermines stability.

12.3 THE SOLARWINDS BREACH AND DIPLOMATIC RAMIFICATIONS

12.3.1 Technical Mechanics of the SolarWinds Attack

The SolarWinds breach demonstrated an unprecedented level of operational sophistication, where attackers compromised the software development environment of a trusted vendor to distribute malicious updates to its customers. The hackers inserted a backdoor into SolarWinds' Orion platform, allowing them to move laterally across networks, escalate privileges, and exfiltrate sensitive data. The attack's stealth and persistence were particularly notable, as the malicious code remained undetected for months, evading traditional cyber-security defenses. The exploitation of a supply chain vector—a method that targets software providers rather than end-users—highlighted a critical vulnerability in modern digital ecosystems, where trust in third-party vendors can be weaponized by adversaries. This technique has since become a model for other state-sponsored cyber-operations, prompting governments and corporations to reassess their cyber-security postures and supply chain risk management strategies.

12.3.2 Attribution and the Geopolitical Context of the Breach

The U.S. government, along with its allies, attributed the SolarWinds attack to Russia's Foreign Intelligence Service (SVR), marking a rare instance of public attribution in cyber espionage cases. This accusation was part of a broader pattern of Russian cyber-operations targeting Western governments and corporations, reflecting Moscow's strategic use of digital intrusions for intelligence gathering and geopolitical leverage.

The attribution process itself was complex, relying on forensic analysis, intelligence sharing, and diplomatic coordination among affected nations. The public naming of Russia as the perpetrator carried significant diplomatic weight, as it set a precedent for how nations respond to state-sponsored cyber-intrusions. However, the attribution also raised questions about the effectiveness of such measures in deterring future attacks, as Russia denied involvement and continued its cyber-operations despite international condemnation. This dynamic underscored the challenges of enforcing accountability in cyberspace, where attribution alone may not suffice to alter adversarial behavior.

12.3.3 Diplomatic Responses and International Repercussions

The diplomatic fallout from the SolarWinds breach was substantial, as it occurred against the backdrop of already strained U.S.-Russia relations. The Biden administration, which took office shortly after the attack's discovery, imposed sanctions on Russian entities and expelled diplomats in response to the breach and other malign activities. These measures were part of a broader strategy to impose costs on Moscow for its cyber-operations, though their effectiveness in altering Russian behavior remained debated.

The breach also prompted discussions among Western allies about collective responses to cyber-threats, including the potential for coordinated sanctions, cyber countermeasures, and enhanced intelligence sharing. The European Union, NATO, and other partners engaged in dialogues about strengthening cyber-security cooperation and developing norms for responsible state behavior in cyberspace. These diplomatic efforts reflected a growing recognition that cyber-threats require multinational solutions, as unilateral actions may prove insufficient against sophisticated, state-sponsored adversaries.

12.3.4 Impact on Cyber-security Policy and Supply Chain Resilience

The SolarWinds attack had a transformative effect on cyber-security policy, particularly in the realm of supply chain security. Governments and corporations alike accelerated efforts to identify and mitigate vulnerabilities in their digital supply chains, recognizing that third-party software and services could serve as vectors for large-scale intrusions. In the United States, the breach prompted executive actions and legislative proposals aimed at enhancing federal cyber-security, including mandates for zero-trust architectures, improved threat detection, and stricter vendor risk assessments. The attack also spurred international discussions about supply chain transparency, software integrity, and the need for global standards in cyber-security. These policy shifts reflected a broader reevaluation of digital trust, where the assumption that commercial software is inherently secure was challenged by the realities of state-sponsored exploitation. The SolarWinds incident thus became a catalyst for rethinking how nations and corporations approach cyber-security in an interconnected world.

12.3.5 Broader Implications for International Cyber Norms

The SolarWinds breach raised fundamental questions about the adequacy of existing international norms and legal frameworks in addressing state-sponsored cyber-operations. The attack occurred in a context where discussions about cyber norms had been ongoing for years, with forums such as the United Nations Group of Governmental Experts (UNGGE) and the Open-Ended Working Group (OEWG) seeking to establish rules for responsible state behavior in cyberspace.

However, the SolarWinds incident demonstrated the limitations of these normative efforts, as Russia's actions violated principles such as the protection of critical infrastructure and the prohibition of cyber espionage against civilian targets.

The breach thus underscored the need for more robust enforcement mechanisms, clearer definitions of prohibited cyber-activities, and consequences for violations. The diplomatic ramifications of the attack highlighted the urgency of developing a rules-based order in cyberspace, where norms are not only agreed upon but also adhered to and enforced.

12.3.6 Role of Private Sector Collaboration in Cyber-defense

The SolarWinds attack underscored the indispensable role of the private sector in cyber-defense, as the breach targeted a commercial software provider and affected numerous private enterprises.

The incident prompted unprecedented collaboration between government agencies and technology companies, as firms such as Microsoft and FireEye played crucial roles in detecting, analyzing, and mitigating the intrusion. This partnership reflected a growing recognition that cyber-security is a shared responsibility, where public and private entities must work together to address threats that transcend traditional boundaries.

The attack also spurred discussions about information sharing, threat intelligence collaboration, and the need for standardized cyber-security practices across industries. These developments highlighted how the private sector's technical expertise and operational capabilities are essential for enhancing national and global cyber resilience, particularly in an era where supply chain vulnerabilities are a primary vector for cyber-intrusions.

12.4 CYBER DIALOGUE IN THE INDIA–EU–US TRIAD

12.4.1 Strategic Context of Cyber Engagement

The strategic context for cyber dialogue in the India–EU–US triad is shaped by rising cyber-threats, technological rivalry, and the fragmentation of the global internet. States, non-state actors, and criminal groups increasingly exploit digital vulnerabilities, while major powers compete to set standards for the digital economy and cyberspace governance. In this environment, partnerships among democracies are seen as crucial to maintaining openness, interoperability, and resilience in cyberspace. The United States has long positioned itself as a global leader in cyber capabilities and norm-setting. The European Union has emerged as a regulatory power, particularly through frameworks like the General Data Protection Regulation (GDPR), which has influenced global data governance. India, with its rapidly expanding digital economy and large internet user base, is both a key stakeholder and a bridge between advanced economies and developing nations. This convergence of interests makes the triad a natural platform for sustained dialogue.

12.4.2 India's Role in the Triad

India's role in cyber dialogue is underpinned by its status as the world's largest democracy and one of the fastest-growing digital societies. With hundreds of millions of internet users, India represents both an opportunity and a challenge for global cyber-security. On one hand, its technological innovation, digital public infrastructure, and skilled workforce contribute to shaping the future of cyberspace. On the other hand, India faces vulnerabilities in the form of cybercrime, infrastructure gaps, and concerns over data protection. India has increasingly sought to position itself as a rule-shaper in cyber-governance, advocating for sovereignty in digital matters while also aligning with like-minded democracies on issues such as cybercrime and countering disinformation. By engaging with the EU and the US, India strengthens its capacity to protect its networks, while also amplifying its voice in global forums on digital governance.

12.4.3 European Union's Cyber-governance Model

The European Union approaches cyber-diplomacy through its regulatory and normative power. Its most notable contribution to the global debate is the GDPR, which has set a benchmark for data protection worldwide. The EU also emphasizes a multi-stakeholder model of internet governance, balancing state interests with those of private actors and civil society. Its cyber dialogues often focus on promoting trust, accountability, and human rights in the digital domain. In the India–EU–US triad, the EU plays the role of norm entrepreneur, advocating for responsible state behavior in cyberspace and the development of binding international frameworks.

It also brings technical expertise and resources for capacity building, particularly in assisting countries to strengthen cyber resilience. For the EU, collaboration with India and the US is not only about security but also about ensuring that democratic principles remain central to global cyber-governance.

12.4.4 United States as a Cyber Power

The United States remains the most advanced cyber power, with unmatched offensive and defensive capabilities, as well as technological innovation driven by its private sector. US cyber-diplomacy has historically focused on deterring malicious state behavior, countering cyber espionage, and promoting a free and open internet. In recent years, Washington has also emphasized collaboration with allies and partners to counter cyber-threats emanating from authoritarian powers such as Russia and China. In the context of the India–EU–US triad, the US brings military strength, intelligence-sharing networks, and private sector leadership in emerging technologies like artificial intelligence and quantum computing. Its engagement with India and the EU is motivated not only by security concerns but also by the need to build coalitions that can set global standards and resist digital authoritarianism.

12.4.5 Areas of Convergence in the Triad

There are significant areas of convergence that make the cyber dialogue among India, the EU, and the US both feasible and promising. All three actors share an interest in ensuring an open, secure, and interoperable internet. They are concerned about cybercrime, ransomware, and state-sponsored attacks that target critical infrastructure. They also share apprehensions about the weaponization of disinformation, which undermines democratic processes. Beyond security, they are aligned on the importance of protecting privacy, ensuring ethical use of artificial intelligence, and promoting transparency in algorithmic decision-making. These shared priorities create fertile ground for a structured dialogue that goes beyond ad hoc cooperation and evolves into a framework of trust and collective action.

12.4.6 Institutionalizing Triangular Cyber Dialogue

One of the key priorities for advancing the India–EU–US cyber dialogue is institutionalization. This involves creating formal platforms for regular consultations, information sharing, and joint initiatives. Trilateral cyber dialogues can build on existing bilateral mechanisms, such as the US-India Cyber Dialogue and the EU-US Cyber Dialogue, by expanding them into a triangular format. Working groups could be established to address specific issues such as critical infrastructure protection, cybercrime investigations, and capacity building. Joint exercises, including cyber incident response simulations, would also strengthen trust and interoperability. Institutionalization ensures that cooperation is not contingent on political cycles or ad hoc responses to crises but becomes a sustained feature of the strategic partnership.

12.4.7 Broader Implications for Global Cyber-governance

The implications of cyber dialogue within the India–EU–US triad extend beyond the three actors themselves. By coordinating their approaches, they can shape global norms on issues such as state behavior in cyberspace, responsible development of artificial intelligence, and cross-border data governance. Their cooperation also offers an alternative model to authoritarian approaches that emphasize surveillance, censorship, and state control over the internet. Furthermore, by engaging India, the EU and US ensure that the perspectives of the Global South are included in cyber-governance debates. This inclusivity enhances the legitimacy of emerging frameworks and prevents the fragmentation of the internet into competing blocs. The triad thus has the potential to serve as a cornerstone of a democratic digital order.

12.5 ESTONIAN CYBER-DIPLOMACY POST-2007 ATTACKS

12.5.1 Building a Model of National Cyber Resilience

Estonia's first and most critical diplomatic lesson from the attacks was that resilience is the foundational element of national security in the digital age. A nation cannot effectively advocate for its interests on the international stage if its own digital society is vulnerable. Consequently, Estonia embarked on an ambitious project to harden its national infrastructure, creating one of the most robust and decentralized digital ecosystems in the world.

This involved the development of redundant data systems, the mandatory implementation of strong cyber-security standards across both public and private sectors, and a massive investment in cyber-security education for its citizenry. Crucially, Estonia pioneered the concept of digital continuity of government, establishing the world's first data embassy in Luxembourg in 2017. This secure server facility housed in an allied country ensures that even in the event of a physical occupation or catastrophic cyber attack, the Estonian state's critical data and registries remain secure and sovereign, allowing the government to continue functioning in exile.

This tangible manifestation of resilience became a central pillar of its diplomatic narrative. Estonia did not just build these systems for itself; it actively exports this model, offering its expertise and technology to other nations seeking to secure their own digital transformation. By demonstrating what a resilient society looks like in practice, Estonia gained immense credibility and moral authority in international cyber discussions, allowing it to speak not from a position of theoretical vulnerability but from one of proven practical experience.

12.5.2 Championing NATO's Cyber-defense and Collective Security

The 2007 attacks forced a fundamental re-evaluation of the role of collective defense alliances in the cyber domain. As a NATO member, Estonia's experience directly tested the boundaries of Article 5, the alliance's collective defense clause. While the attacks did not trigger an Article 5 response, they served as a stark wake-up call, demonstrating that a cyber attack could potentially reach a threshold that threatened a member state's territorial integrity and democratic institutions. Estonia became the primary and most persistent advocate for the formal recognition of cyberspace as a domain of military operations within NATO, a goal that was achieved in 2016.

This diplomatic campaign was relentless, leveraging every platform within the alliance to argue that a cyber attack could have effects just as destructive as a conventional military strike. Furthermore, Estonia took the lead in operationalizing cyber-cooperation within the alliance by championing the creation of the NATO Cooperative Cyber Defence Centre of Excellence (CCDCOE) in Tallinn. Inaugurated in 2008, the CCDCOE is not a military command but an international hub of strategic thought, training, and legal analysis.

It is most famous for authoring the Tallinn Manual, a groundbreaking academic study that explores how existing international law applies to cyber-warfare. By hosting and leading this institution, Estonia positioned itself at the very heart of the global conversation on cyber conflict law and norms, transforming its capital into a de facto cyber-diplomacy capital and ensuring that the lessons of 2007 would inform NATO policy for decades to come.

12.5.3 Advancing a Normative Framework for State Behavior

Beyond its work with NATO, Estonia has pursued a sophisticated and multi-layered diplomatic strategy aimed at shaping a rules-based international order in cyberspace. Its foreign policy is characterized by a clear and consistent messaging campaign across every available multilateral forum, including the United Nations, the Organisation for Security and Co-operation in Europe (OSCE), and the European Union.

The core of Estonia's normative argument is the applicability of existing international law, including the UN Charter, to state behavior in cyberspace. It staunchly opposes efforts by some nations to create an entirely new legal regime for the internet, arguing that this could be used to legitimize greater state control and censorship. Instead, Estonia advocates for the development and adherence to voluntary peacetime norms of responsible state behavior, such as the pledges made in the UN Group of Governmental Experts (UNGGE) reports, which include commitments not to attack critical infrastructure or to hinder emergency response teams during a cyber incident. Estonian diplomats are skilled at building broad coalitions with like-minded states, often acting as a bridge between larger powers and smaller nations that feel particularly vulnerable to digital coercion. This diplomatic agility allows it to punch far above its weight, ensuring that the principles of an open, free, and secure internet are defended against alternative visions that favor sovereignty and state control over human rights and global connectivity.

CHAPTER 13

Appendices

13.1 GLOSSARY OF CYBER-DIPLOMACY TERMS

- **Advanced Persistent Threat (APT):** A prolonged, targeted cyberattack, often state-sponsored, aimed at stealing data or disrupting systems.
- **Attribution:** The process of identifying the source of a cyberattack, often politically sensitive in diplomacy.
- **Budapest Convention (Convention on Cybercrime):** The first international treaty addressing cybercrime, adopted by the Council of Europe in 2001.
- **Cyber Deterrence:** Strategies to discourage cyber-attacks through threats of retaliation or other consequences.
- **Cyber-diplomacy:** The use of diplomatic efforts to manage cyber-security issues, norms, and international cooperation.
- **Cyber Norms:** Informal or formal rules governing state behavior in cyberspace (e.g., UN Group of Governmental Experts (GGE) norms).
- **Cyber-warfare:** The use of digital attacks to disrupt, damage, or gain military or strategic advantage.
- **Cyberspace:** The global domain of interconnected digital networks, infrastructure, and data.
- **Digital Sovereignty:** A country's assertion of control over its digital infrastructure and data flows.
- **Disinformation:** Deliberately false or misleading information spread to influence public opinion or political outcomes.
- **Espionage (Cyber Espionage):** The use of cyber means to steal sensitive information, often conducted by state actors.
- **GGE (UN Group of Governmental Experts on Cyber-security):** A UN-led forum that develops norms for responsible state behavior in cyberspace.
- **Global Commission on the Stability of Cyberspace (GCSC):** A multistakeholder initiative proposing norms to enhance cyber stability.

- **Hacktivism:** Cyber-attacks carried out by activists to promote political or social causes.
- **International Telecommunication Union (ITU):** A UN agency that sets global standards for telecommunications and cyber-security.
- **Internet Governance:** The development and application of shared principles, norms, and policies for the internet.
- **Malware:** Malicious software designed to harm or exploit systems.
- **Multistakeholder Model:** A governance approach involving governments, private sector, civil society, and technical communities in cyber policy.
- **Nation-State Actors:** Governments or state-affiliated groups conducting cyber-operations.
- **Norms of Responsible State Behavior in Cyberspace:** Agreed-upon principles to reduce conflict in cyberspace (e.g., non-interference in critical infrastructure).
- **Open-Ended Working Group (OEWG):** A UN forum discussing cyber-security norms and international cooperation.
- **Phishing:** A cyber-attack method using deceptive emails or messages to trick users into revealing sensitive information.
- **Public-Private Partnership (PPP):** Collaboration between governments and private companies to enhance cyber-security.
- **Ransomware:** Malware that encrypts data and demands payment for its release.
- **Responsible State Behavior:** The expectation that nations act in accordance with agreed cyber norms to prevent conflict.
- **Sovereignty in Cyberspace:** The principle that states have authority over cyber-activities within their borders.
- **Supply Chain Attack:** A cyber-attack targeting vulnerabilities in third-party vendors or software suppliers.
- **Tallinn Manual:** A NATO-sponsored guide on how international law applies to cyber-warfare.
- **Threat Intelligence:** Information used to understand and mitigate cyber-threats.
- **UN Programme of Action (PoA) on Cyber-security:** A proposed framework for global cyber-security cooperation under the UN.
- **Zero-Day Exploit:** An attack targeting a previously unknown software vulnerability.

13.2 MAJOR TREATIES AND AGREEMENTS

13.2.1 Budapest Convention on Cybercrime (2001)

- **Full Name:** *Council of Europe Convention on Cybercrime*
- **Adopted:** 2001 (Entered into force in 2004)
- **Key Provisions:**
  - First international treaty addressing cybercrime.
  - Criminalizes hacking, fraud, child exploitation, and copyright infringement.
  - Establishes procedures for international cooperation in cybercrime investigations.
- **Signatories:** Over 60 countries (including the U.S., EU members, Japan, and others).
- **Criticism:** Russia and China oppose it, favoring alternative frameworks.

13.2. 2 UN Group of Governmental Experts (GGE) Reports (2010–2021)

- **Purpose:** Develops norms for responsible state behavior in cyberspace.
- **Key Reports:**
  - **2013 GGE Report:** First consensus on cyber norms, including the applicability of international law to cyberspace.
  - **2015 GGE Report:** Established 11 voluntary norms (e.g., protecting critical infrastructure, not targeting emergency response teams).
  - **2021 GGE Report:** Reaffirmed norms but failed to reach full consensus due to geopolitical tensions.
- **Status:** Non-binding but influential in shaping state behavior.

13.2.3 Tallinn Manual (2013 & 2017)

- **Developed by:** NATO Cooperative Cyber Defence Centre of Excellence (CCDCOE).
- **Purpose:** Clarifies how international law applies to cyber-warfare.
- **Key Points:**
  - **Tallinn Manual 1.0 (2013):** Focuses on jus ad bellum (laws of war) in cyber-conflicts.
  - **Tallinn Manual 2.0 (2017):** Expands to peacetime cyber-operations and international law.
- **Status:** Non-binding but widely referenced by legal and military experts.

13.2.4 Paris Call for Trust and Security in Cyberspace (2018)

- **Launched by:** France (President Macron) at the UNESCO Internet Governance Forum.
- **Key Principles:**
  - Protect critical infrastructure.
  - Prevent interference in electoral processes.
  - Strengthen cyber hygiene and cooperation.
- **Signatories:** Over 1,000 entities, including governments (EU, Canada, Japan), tech companies (Microsoft, Google), and civil society.
- **Status:** Voluntary, non-binding but promotes multistakeholder cooperation.

13.2.5 UN Open-Ended Working Group (OEWG) on Cyber-security (2019–Present)

- **Established by:** UN General Assembly (Resolution 73/27).
- **Purpose:** A more inclusive forum (compared to GGE) for discussing cyber norms and threats.
- **Key Outcomes:**
  - **2021 OEWG Report:** First consensus-based UN document on cyber-security, emphasizing capacity-building and confidence-building measures (CBMs).
  - **2025 Programme of Action (PoA):** Proposed framework for long-term cyber-security cooperation.
- **Status:** Ongoing negotiations, with participation from all UN member states.

13.2.6 China's Global Initiative on Data Security (2020)

- **Proposed by:** China (as an alternative to Western-led frameworks).
- **Key Principles:**
  - Opposes mass surveillance and cyber espionage.
  - Calls for supply chain security and data localization.
  - Rejects unilateral sanctions in cyber disputes.
- **Status:** Non-binding, seen as a counter to U.S.-led cyber norms.

13.2.7 U.S.-China Cyber-security Agreement (2015)

- **Signed by:** Presidents Obama and Xi Jinping.
- **Key Provisions:**
  - Commitment not to conduct cyber-enabled theft of intellectual property for commercial gain.

- Established a high-level dialogue on cyber-issues.
- **Status:** Informal, but reduced tensions temporarily before later strains.

13.2.8 EU Cyber-security Strategy (2020) & Cyber-diplomacy Toolbox

- **Adopted by:** European Union.
- **Key Elements:**
  - **Cyber-diplomacy Toolbox (2017, updated 2022):** Allows sanctions against state-sponsored cyber-attacks.
  - **NIS2 Directive (2022):** Strengthens cyber-security requirements for critical infrastructure.
- **Status:** Binding for EU members, influences global cyber norms.

13.2.9 ASEAN Cyber-security Cooperation Framework (2017)

- **Adopted by:** Association of Southeast Asian Nations (ASEAN).
- **Key Goals:**
  - Enhance regional cyber-security cooperation.
  - Promote capacity-building and information-sharing.
- **Status:** Non-binding but guides regional cyber-diplomacy.

13.2.10 African Union Convention on Cyber-security (2014)

- **Adopted by:** African Union (AU).
- **Key Provisions:**
  - Addresses cybercrime, data protection, and e-commerce.
  - Encourages regional cooperation in cyber-security.
- **Status:** Ratified by some AU members but not universally adopted.

13.2.11 Emerging Developments

- **UN Programme of Action (PoA) on Cyber-security (Proposed):** A potential long-term framework for global cyber-security cooperation.
- **Bilateral Cyber Agreements:** Increasingly common (e.g., U.S.-UK, U.S.-India cyber partnerships).

13.3 CYBER-DIPLOMACY ORGANIZATIONAL DIRECTORY

13.3.1 International & Multilateral Organizations

United Nations System

- **UN Office for Disarmament Affairs (UNODA):** Focus: Cyber-security in the context of international peace and security.
- **UN Open-Ended Working Group (OEWG) on Cyber-security:** Mandate: Inclusive UN forum for all member states to discuss cyber norms and threats.

- **UN Group of Governmental Experts (GGE) on Cyber-security:** Role: Develops norms for responsible state behavior in cyberspace.
- **International Telecommunication Union (ITU):** Focus: Global telecom standards, cyber-security frameworks, and digital development.
- **UN Institute for Disarmament Research (UNIDIR):** Research: Cyber-security, disarmament, and emerging threats.

Regional Organizations

- **Cyber-Diplomacy Team**: Leads EU cyber-diplomacy.
- **European Union Agency for Cyber-security (ENISA)**: Supports EU cyber-security policy.
- **EU Cyber-diplomacy Toolbox**: Framework for sanctions and responses to cyber-threats.
- **NATO Cooperative Cyber Defence Centre of Excellence (CCDCOE)**: Research, training, and doctrine development (home of the *Tallinn Manual*).
- **Inter-American Committee against Terrorism (CICTE)**: Cyber-security cooperation in the Americas.
- **ASEAN Ministerial Conference on Cyber-security**: Regional cyber-security policy coordination.
- **African Union Convention on Cyber-security**: Framework for cyber-security and data protection in Africa.

Multistakeholder Initiatives

- **Global Commission on the Stability of Cyberspace (GCSC):** Proposes norms like the "Call to Protect the Public Core of the Internet."
- **Paris Call for Trust and Security in Cyberspace:** Multistakeholder initiative (led by France) promoting cyber norms.
- **CyberPeace Institute:** Focus: Reducing cyber-threats and protecting civilians in cyberspace.
- **Internet Governance Forum (IGF):** UN-backed platform for internet governance and cyber policy discussions.
- **Internet Corporation for Assigned Names and Numbers (ICANN):** Manages domain names and internet infrastructure governance.

13.3.2 National Cyber-diplomacy & Policy Agencies

United States

- **U.S. Department of State – Bureau of Cyberspace and Digital Policy (CDP):** Leads U.S., cyber-diplomacy.

- **Cyber-security and Infrastructure Security Agency (CISA):** Protects U.S. critical infrastructure.
- **National Security Agency (NSA) – Cyber-security Directorate:** National security and cyber-defense.
- **Federal Bureau of Investigation (FBI) – Cyber Division:** Investigates cybercrime and espionage.

European Union & Member States

- **Germany – Federal Foreign Office (AA) Cyber-diplomacy Unit:** Leads Germany's cyber-foreign policy.
- **France – National Cyber-security Agency (ANSSI):** Cyber-security and diplomacy.
- **United Kingdom – National Cyber Security Centre (NCSC):** Part of GCHQ, responsible for UK cyber-defense.

Asia-Pacific

- **China – Ministry of State Security (MSS) & Cyberspace Administration of China (CAC):** Cyber policy and censorship.
- **Japan – National Center of Incident Readiness and Strategy for Cyber-security (NISC):** Coordinates Japan's cyber-security.
- **India – National Cyber Security Coordinator (NCSC) & CERT-In:** Cyber-security and policy.
- **Australia – Australian Signals Directorate (ASD) & Australian Cyber Security Centre (ACSC):** Cyber-defense and policy.

Russia & Post-Soviet States

- **Russia – Federal Security Service (FSB) & Ministry of Digital Development:** Cyber-security and censorship.
- **Collective Security Treaty Organization (CSTO):** Cyber-security cooperation among member states.

Middle East & Africa

- **Israel – National Cyber Directorate (INCD):** Cyber-security and innovation.
- **UAE – National Cyber-security Council:** Coordinates UAE's cyber policies.
- **South Africa – Department of Communications and Digital Technologies:** Cyber-security policy.

13.3.3 Private Sector & Civil Society

- **Microsoft Digital Diplomacy Team:** Engages in cyber norms and policy.
- **Google's Jigsaw & Cyber-security Initiatives:** Counters disinformation and cyber-threats.
- **Cyber-security Tech Accord:** Coalition of tech companies pledging cyber-security improvements.
- **Electronic Frontier Foundation (EFF):** Advocates for digital rights and cyber-security.
- **Citizen Lab (University of Toronto):** Researches cyber espionage and human rights.

13.3.4 Academic & Research Institutions

- **Harvard Belfer Center – Cyber Project:** Research on cyber-security policy.
- **Stanford University – Center for International Security and Cooperation (CISAC):** Cyber-security and governance.
- **Oxford University – Cyber Studies Programme:** Focus on cyber norms and conflict.
- **Carnegie Endowment for International Peace – Cyber Policy Initiative:** Global cyber-governance research.

13.3.5 Key Functions of These Organizations

Category	Primary Roles
International Organizations	Norm-setting, treaty negotiations, global cyber-security standards.
Regional Bodies	Regional cyber-security cooperation, policy alignment.
National Agencies	National cyber-defense, diplomacy, and incident response.
Private Sector	Cyber-security innovation, threat intelligence, policy advocacy.
Civil Society	Digital rights advocacy, research, and public awareness.

13.4 KEY DECLARATIONS, NORMS, AND FRAMEWORKS

13.4.1 Foundational Declarations & Norms

UN Group of Governmental Experts (GGE) Reports

- **2013 GGE Report:**
  - First consensus that **International Law Applies to Cyberspace.**

  - Affirmed the applicability of the **UN Charter** (e.g., sovereignty, non-intervention).
- **2015 GGE Report:**
  - Established **11 voluntary norms** for state behavior, including:
    - States should not damage critical infrastructure.
    - States should not allow their territory to be used for cyber-attacks.
    - States should assist in mitigating malicious cyber activity.
- **2021 GGE Report:** Reaffirmed norms but failed to reach full consensus due to geopolitical tensions.

UN Open-Ended Working Group (OEWG) Reports

- **2021 OEWG Report:**
  - First **consensus-based UN document** on cyber-security, emphasizing:
    - Capacity-building for developing nations.
    - Confidence-building measures (CBMs) to reduce tensions.
- **2025 Programme of Action (PoA) Proposal:** Aims to create a **permanent UN mechanism** for cyber-security dialogue.

13.4.2 Key Frameworks & Agreements

Budapest Convention on Cybercrime (2001):

- **First international treaty** addressing cybercrime.
- Criminalizes hacking, fraud, child exploitation, and copyright infringement.
- **Signatories:** 68+ countries (U.S., EU, Japan, etc.), but **not ratified by Russia or China.**

Tallinn Manual (1.0 & 2.0):

- **Developed by:** NATO CCDCOE.
- **Purpose:** Clarifies how **international law** applies to cyber-warfare:
  - **Tallinn Manual 1.0 (2013):** Focuses on **jus ad bellum** (laws of war) in cyber-conflicts.
  - **Tallinn Manual 2.0 (2017):** Expands to peacetime cyber-operations.

Paris Call for Trust and Security in Cyberspace (2018):

- **Launched by:** France (President Macron).
- **Key Principles:**
  - Protect critical infrastructure.
  - Prevent election interference.
  - Strengthen cyber hygiene.

- **Signatories**: 1,000+ entities (governments, tech firms, NGOs).

Global Commission on the Stability of Cyberspace (GCSC) Norms:

- **"Call to Protect the Public Core of the Internet"** (2017).
- **"Norm to Avoid Tampering with Products"** (2019).

13.4.3 Regional & Bilateral Frameworks

- **Cyber-diplomacy Toolbox (2017, updated 2022)**: Allows **sanctions** against state-sponsored cyber-attacks.
- **NIS2 Directive (2022)**: Strengthens cyber-security for critical infrastructure.
- **ASEAN Cyber-security Cooperation Framework (2017):** Promotes **information-sharing** and **capacity-building** in Southeast Asia.
- **African Union Convention on Cyber-security (2014):** Focuses on **cybercrime, data protection, and e-commerce** in Africa.
- **U.S.-China Cyber-security Agreement (2015): Key Commitment**: Neither country will conduct **cyber-enabled theft of intellectual property** for commercial gain.

13.4.4 Private Sector & Multistakeholder Initiatives

Cyber-security Tech Accord (2018):

- **Signatories**: Microsoft, Google, Facebook, and others.
- **Pledge**: Protect customers from cyber-attacks and not assist governments in offensive cyber-operations.

Microsoft's Digital Geneva Convention Proposal (2017):

- Calls for a **binding international treaty** to protect civilians in cyberspace.

Christchurch Call to Action (2019):

- **Focus:** Eliminating **terrorist and extremist content** online.
- **Signatories:** Governments and tech companies (e.g., New Zealand, France, Google, Facebook).

13.4.5 Emerging & Proposed Frameworks

UN Programme of Action (PoA) on Cyber-security:

- **Proposed**: A **permanent UN mechanism** for cyber-security dialogue.
- **Goal:** Institutionalize cyber norms and cooperation.

EU-U.S. Trade and Technology Council (TTC) Cyber-security Working Group:

- Focuses on **supply chain security, AI, and cyber threat intelligence-sharing.**

China's Global Initiative on Data Security (2020):

- **Key Principles:**
  - Opposes **mass surveillance** and **cyber espionage**.
  - Calls for **data localization** and **supply chain security**.

13.4.6 Comparison of Key Norms & Frameworks

Framework	Scope	Binding	Key Focus
Budapest Convention	Cybercrime	Legally binding	Criminalization of hacking, fraud
Tallinn Manual	Cyber-warfare	Non-binding	International law in cyber-conflicts
Paris Call	Cyber norms	Voluntary	Protecting critical infrastructure
GGE Norms	State behavior	Voluntary	Non-interference, no attacks on CIs
Christchurch Call	Online extremism	Voluntary	Removing terrorist content

13.5 RECOMMENDED TOOLS, PLATFORMS, AND RESOURCES

13.5.1 Policy & Norms Analysis

Official Documents & Databases

- **UN Digital Library** (library.un.org): Access UN reports (GGE, OEWG, PoA) and resolutions on cyber-security.
- **NATO CCDCOE Publications** (ccdcoe.org): *Tallinn Manuals*, legal analyses, and cyber-defense research.
- **EU Cyber-diplomacy Toolbox** (eeas.europa.eu): Framework for EU responses to malicious cyber-activities.

Norms & Frameworks Trackers

- **Cyber Norms Index** (Council on Foreign Relations): Tracks state compliance with cyber norms (e.g., GGE, Paris Call).
- **Digital Watch Observatory** (dig.watch): Monitors global cyber policy developments and treaties.

13.5.2 Threat Intelligence & Incident Tracking

Government & NGO Platforms

- **CISA's Known Exploited Vulnerabilities Catalog** (cisa.gov/kev): Tracks critical vulnerabilities exploited in cyber-attacks.

- **MITRE ATT&CK Framework** (attack.mitre.org): Classifies adversary tactics and techniques for threat analysis.
- **FireEye/Mandiant Threat Intelligence** (mandiant.com): Reports on state-sponsored cyber campaigns (e.g., APT groups).

Real-Time Threat Maps

- **Kaspersky Cyberthreat Real-Time Map** (cybermap.kaspersky.com): Visualizes global cyber-attack trends.
- **Check Point Threat Map** (threatmap.checkpoint.com): Tracks live cyber-threats by region and sector.

13.5.3 Multistakeholder Engagement Platforms

Diplomatic & Policy Networks

- **Global Forum on Cyber Expertise (GFCE)** (thegfce.org): Connects governments, NGOs, and industry for capacity-building.
- **CyberPeace Institute** (cyberpeaceinstitute.org): Focuses on protecting civilians in cyberspace.
- **Internet Governance Forum (IGF)** (intgovforum.org): Annual forum for multistakeholder cyber policy discussions.

Private Sector Initiatives

- **Cyber-security Tech Accord** (cyber-securitytechaccord.org): Coalition of tech companies pledging to improve cyber-security.
- **Microsoft Digital Diplomacy Team** (microsoft.com/digital-diplomacy): Engages in cyber norms and policy advocacy.

13.5.4 Capacity-Building & Training Resources

Government & Academic Programs

- **EU CyberNet** (eucybernet.eu): Supports cyber-security capacity-building in partner countries.
- **NATO CCDCOE Courses** (ccdcoe.org/training): Offers cyber-defense training for diplomats and military personnel.
- **Harvard Belfer Center Cyber Project** (belfercenter.org/cyber): Research and policy recommendations on cyber-security.

Online Learning Platforms

- **Coursera: Cyber-security Specializations** (coursera.org): Courses on cyber policy, threat intelligence, and diplomacy.

- **edX: Cyber-diplomacy & International Law** (edx.org): Includes modules on the *Tallinn Manual* and UN cyber norms.

13.5.5 Research & Analysis Tools

Data & Visualization Tools

- **Google's Chronicle** (chronicle.security): Analyzes cyber-threats using big data.
- **Recorded Future** (recordedfuture.com): Provides real-time threat intelligence and geopolitical risk analysis.

Academic & Think Tank Resources

- **RAND Corporation Cyber-security Research** (rand.org): Reports on cyber conflict, deterrence, and policy.
- **Chatham House Cyber Programme** (chathamhouse.org): Focuses on cyber-governance and international law.

13.5.6 Communication & Collaboration Platforms

Secure Diplomatic Channels

- **Diplomacy.gov Platforms** (e.g., U.S. State Department's cyber-diplomacy hubs)
- **EU's Secure Information Sharing Platform (SISP)** (europa.eu)

Multistakeholder Forums

- **Slack/Discord Communities** (e.g., Cyber-diplomacy Network)
- **LinkedIn Groups** (e.g., "Cyber-diplomacy Professionals")

13.5.7 Legal & Compliance Resources

- **ICANN's Policy Development** (icann.org): Governance of domain names and internet infrastructure.
- **IEEE Cyber-security Standards** (ieee.org): Technical standards for secure systems.

References

After the Digital Tornado: Networks, Algorithms, Humanity, Kevin Werbach, Cambridge University Press, 2020

Algorithms of Oppression: How Search Engines Reinforce Racism, Safiya Umoja Noble, NYU Press, 2018

America's Cyber Future: Security and Prosperity in the Information Age, Kristin M. Lord, CNAS, 2011

Bytes, Bombs, and Spies: The Strategic Dimensions of Offensive Cyber-operations, Abraham M. Denmark, Brookings Institution Press, 2018

Conflicting Codes and Clashing Goals: The Challenge of Cyber-security in the International System, Nicolò Miotto, Routledge, 2021

Cyber Insecurity: Navigating the Perils of the Next Information Age, Richard M. Harrison, Security Studies Group, 2016

Cyber-operations and International Law: François Delerue, Cambridge University Press, 2020

Cyber Persistence Theory: Redefining National Security in Cyberspace, Michael P. Fischerkeller, Emily O. Goldman, Richard J. Harknett, Oxford University Press, 2022

Cyber Security: Law and Guidance, Mark Sutton, Bloomsbury Professional, 2012

Cyber War Will Not Take Place: Thomas Rid, Oxford University Press, 2013

Cyberdiplomacy: Managing Security and Governance Online, Shaun Riordan, Polity Press, 2019

Cyber-security and Cyberwar: What Everyone Needs to Know, P.W. Singer, Allan Friedman, Oxford University Press, 2014

Dark Territory: The Secret History of Cyber War, Fred Kaplan, Simon & Schuster, 2016

Data and Goliath: The Hidden Battles to Collect Your Data and Control Your World, Bruce Schneier, W. W. Norton & Company, 2015

Diplomatic Law in the Digital Age: Paul Behrens, Hart Publishing, 2021

How Everything Became War and the Military Became Everything: Tales from the Pentagon, Rosa Brooks, Simon & Schuster, 2016

Inside Cyber-Warfare: Mapping the Cyber Underworld, Jeffrey Carr, O'Reilly Media, 2011

International Cyber Norms: Legal, Policy & Industry Perspectives, Anna-Maria Osula, Tallinn Paper No. 10, NATO CCDCOE, 2016

International Relations in the Cyber Age: The Co-evolution Dilemma, Nazli Choucri, David D. Clark, The MIT Press, 2018

LikeWar: The Weaponization of Social Media, P.W. Singer, Emerson T. Brooking, Eamon Dolan Books, 2018

No Place to Hide: Edward Snowden, the NSA, and the U.S. Surveillance State, Glenn Greenwald, Metropolitan Books, 2014

Norms of State Behavior in Cyberspace: Joseph S. Nye Jr., Council on Foreign Relations, 2020

Power and Authority in Internet Governance: Return of the State?, Blayne Haggart, Natasha Tusikov, Jan Aart Scholte, Routledge, 2021

Protocol Politics: The Globalization of Internet Governance, Laura DeNardis, The MIT Press, 2009

Sovereignty, Jurisdiction and the Future of Cyberspace: Mark Raymond, Oxford University Press, 2021

Tallinn Manual 2.0 on the International Law Applicable to Cyber-Operations: Michael N. Schmitt, NATO CCDCOE, Cambridge University Press, 2017

Technology and International Relations: The New Frontier in Global Power, Giampiero Giacomello, Edward Elgar Publishing, 2021

The Age of Surveillance Capitalism: The Fight for a Human Future at the New Frontier of Power, Shoshana Zuboff, PublicAffairs, 2019

The Black Box Society: The Secret Algorithms That Control Money and Information, Frank Pasquale, Harvard University Press, 2015

The Code of Capital: How the Law Creates Wealth and Inequality, Katharina Pistor, Princeton University Press, 2019

The Cyber-security Dilemma: Hacking, Trust and Fear Between Nations, Ben Buchanan, Oxford University Press, 2017

The Digital Silk Road: China's Quest to Wire the World and Win the Future, Jonathan E. Hillman, Harper Business, 2021

The Fifth Domain: Defending Our Country, Our Companies, and Ourselves in the Age of Cyber-threats, Richard A. Clarke, Robert K. Knake, Penguin Press, 2019

The Filter Bubble: How the New Personalized Web Is Changing What We Read and How We Think, Eli Pariser, Penguin Press, 2011

The Future of Violence: Robots and Germs, Hackers and Drones, Benjamin Wittes, Gabriella Blum, Basic Books, 2015

The Global War for Internet Governance: Laura DeNardis, Yale University Press, 2014

The Great Firewall of China: How to Build and Control an Alternative Version of the Internet, James Griffiths, Zed Books, 2019

The Hacker and the State: Cyber Attacks and the New Normal of Geopolitics, Ben Buchanan, Harvard University Press, 2020

The Law of Cyber Attack: Sean Watts, Cambridge University Press, 2018

The Master Switch: The Rise and Fall of Information Empires, Tim Wu, Knopf, 2010

The Net Delusion: The Dark Side of Internet Freedom, Evgeny Morozov, PublicAffairs, 2011

The New Digital Age: Reshaping the Future of People, Nations and Business, Eric Schmidt, Jared Cohen, Knopf, 2013

The Perfect Weapon: War, Sabotage, and Fear in the Cyber Age, David E. Sanger, Crown, 2018

The Politics of Privacy in the Digital Age: A Comparative Study, B.-J. Koops, Edward Elgar Publishing, 2013

The Role of International Law in Cyberspace: Katharina Ziolkowski, NATO CCDCOE, 2013

The Virtual Weapon and International Order: Lucas Kello, Yale University Press, 2017

This Is Not Propaganda: Adventures in the War Against Reality, Peter Pomerantsev, PublicAffairs, 2019

Weapons of Math Destruction: How Big Data Increases Inequality and Threatens Democracy, Cathy O'Neil, Crown, 2016

Who Controls the Internet?: Illusions of a Borderless World, Jack Goldsmith, Tim Wu, Oxford University Press, 2006

Index

P

Q

R

S

T

www.ingramcontent.com/pod-product-compliance
Lightning Source LLC
LaVergne TN
LVHW081938200926
848484LV00009B/2459